The
Limits
of
Medicine

The
Limits
of
Medicine

How Science Shapes
Our Hope for the Cure

Edward S. Golub, Ph.D.

TIMES 𝕋 BOOKS

RANDOM HOUSE

Grateful acknowledgment is made to Liveright Publishing Corporation and W. W. Norton & Company Ltd. for permission to reprint four lines from "voices to voices, lip to lip" from *Complete Poems, 1904–1962* by E. E. Cummings, edited by George Firmage. Copyright © 1926, 1954, 1991 by Trustees for the E. E. Cummings Trust. Copyright © 1985 by George Firmage. Rights throughout the British Commonwealth are controlled by W. W. Norton & Company Ltd., London. Reprinted by permission of Liveright Publishing Corporation and W. W. Norton & Company Ltd.

Library of Congress Cataloging-in-Publication Data

Golub, Edward S.
   The limits of medicine : how science shapes our hope for
the cure / Edward S. Golub.
      p.   cm.
   Includes bibliographical references and index.
   ISBN 0-8129-2141-0
   1. Medicine—History. 2. Social medicine. 3. Medicine—
Philosophy. I. Title.
R133.G656 1994
610—dc20   94-10016
                                        CIP

Design by Anistatia R. Miller

Manufactured in the United States of America
9 8 7 6 5 4 3 2
First Edition

To my mother,
Mildred Mazer Golub,
as she enters her
eighty-ninth year

Illness is the night-side of life, a more onerous citizenship. Everyone who is born holds dual citizenship, in the kingdom of the well and in the kingdom of the sick. Although we all prefer to use only the good passport, sooner or later each of us is obliged, at least for a spell, to identify ourselves as citizens of that other place.

—Susan Sontag, *Illness as Metaphor*

Contents

A Few Important Words to the Reader

In writing this book I made what was for me an incredible discovery: that for the vast majority of human history, nothing changed in the way we either conceived of health or treated disease. Like most of us, I had been reared with the heroic version of scientific and medical history, and none of my general education or scientific training prepared me for this finding. For a rather long time I thought that I just must be making a mistake—after all, I am not trained in history—but eventually, historians assured me that my great discovery was no surprise to them. Yet when I lecture or engage in discussions with physicians, scientists, or just plain folks, I rarely find anyone who is not as surprised as I was. So the *first* important word to the reader is a disclaimer: This long period of changelessness will be an important part of the book, but it is not an original discovery. I am indebted to the historians who have worked so hard to make the discovery and all I am doing is trying to get their message out to a wider audience in a different context.

But at this point you are correctly asking, Why is it important to know these facts, startling though they may be? The *second* important word to the reader is that since the message of this book is that nothing changed for such a long time, we have had our present views for a relatively short time. When we realize how amazingly short a time we have had our modern views, it makes the idea of changing the direction we appear to be headed in easier. My main goal is to give the reader the context in which to understand the changes that are going on in the world of science and medicine today, which are usually received in a passive way because we think we are being swept along in the flow of history. We aren't.

The *third* important word to the reader is one of caution. Based on my reading of how we got where we are today, I will point out what I think are some of the choices we can make as individuals and as a society for the future, but there will be no simple solutions. Golub's first rule is that if you can fit the solution to a complex problem on a bumper sticker, it is wrong! (I tried to condense this book to fit onto a bumper sticker and couldn't.) I think that part of our problem is that we have allowed "experts" to make decisions for us because we think the problems are too complex and difficult to solve by ourselves. The details, of course, are complex and difficult, but if we understand the context in which the details are discussed, we can make decisions that lead us where *we* want to go.

The *last* important word to the reader is that the subject matter of this book is serious, but one can be serious without being somber. I tried to eliminate all technical jargon, be it scientific, medical, or cultural. I promised my mother that I would write a book that she and her friends can read and enjoy . . . and I never lie to my mother.

The
Limits
of
Medicine

Introduction

Framing Health and Disease

On October 19, 1970, Dr. Edward H. Kass, professor of medicine at the Harvard Medical School, delivered the presidential address to the Infectious Disease Society of America. The war in Vietnam had already begun to polarize American society, and the economic impact of the war was leading to limitations in funding for biomedical research. Dr. Kass, an honored physician and researcher, told the assembled experts in infectious diseases what they already knew but were glad to hear from a man in his position: "[A]ll that we have asked for is to be able to continue our good works in an atmosphere that will put to effective social use the fruits of our earnest efforts." These efforts, everyone agreed, had been responsible for providing Americans their unsurpassed level of health, so why should the government suddenly cut their funding and interrupt their noble work? But then he dropped a bombshell: "There is nothing basically wrong with this charming scenario of the white-coated medical scientist distributing good works like free beer at a political picnic, although it does seem to have been written by the least sophisticated of writers for the Sunday supplements." There was nothing wrong with the scenario, he told them, except that it was distorted in some of its most basic assumptions!

Just what kind of assumption could these physician-scientists have distorted? After all, everyone knew that it was their predecessors who were responsible for the virtual elimination of infectious diseases and who had extended the life expectancy of the citizens in the industrialized world. To their amazement, Dr. Kass told them it was *not* medical research that had stamped out tuberculosis, diphtheria, pneumonia, and puerperal sepsis; the primary credit for those monumental accomplishments must go to public health, sanitation, and the general improvement in the standard of living brought about by industrialization. What little history the medical scientists in the audience had learned was indeed as accurate and sophisticated as that found in the Sunday supplement. Many had probably been attracted to their profession by reading *Microbe Hunters,* an incredibly popular and stunningly incorrect book by Paul de Kruif, or *Arrowsmith,* Sinclair Lewis's romantic version of the physician-bacteriologist. It is a virtual certainty that the corrected versions of the romantic assumptions Dr. Kass then presented to them were too unbelievable to register properly in their consciousness. He told them that the "data on deaths from tuberculosis [as well as diphtheria, scarlet fever, measles, and whooping cough] show that the mortality rate from this disease has been declining steadily since the middle of the nineteenth century." Furthermore, this steady decline in deaths was not altered measurably by any of the great scientific discoveries of their predecessors. Contrary to all they had been taught, those great scourges of humanity had begun to be brought under control *before* medicine became scientific!

It is extremely important to realize that the president of the Infectious Disease Society of America was *not* telling its members that all of their work was for naught. Far from it. Their work and that of their predecessors was of great value in healing those individual patients who still contracted the diseases. Extending the life and alleviating the pain of the individual patient are the most valued aims of medicine and for this they had every right to be proud of their heritage and of their current work. This part of his message we all can understand, and as one who was cured of tuberculosis because of scientific medicine (and as a result of the experience went on to become a biomedical scientist), I can offer a personal testimony to the power and value of their work. But why were neither I nor that audience nor the vast majority of people with whom I discuss the question aware of the facts of history?

Most of us have been taught that there has been a steady march of progress in medicine, leading inexorably to a high-tech future. I will argue in this book that a realistic understanding of the nature of progress in medicine, and the role that science plays in that progress—a role that is quite different from the romanticized versions we have been taught—is absolutely crucial if we are to see clearly what medicine can give us in the future. Only when we have this realistic understanding can we understand the limits of what science and medicine can give us. This book will show that for most of our history *nothing changed in either our conception of or our treatment of disease.* Change came such a short time ago that it will be clear to even the most romantic reader that our medical future has not been determined by destiny and that we have much more control over what we want from scientific medicine than we have been led to think. But we must realize that medicine has limits; it cannot deliver all the miracles we expect of it.

C onsider these two statements by well-respected historians: "Let me simply put my own view as starkly as possible. . . . I assert, to begin with, that 'disease' does not exist," and "[I]n some ways disease does not exist until we have agreed that it does, by perceiving, naming and responding to it."

How can disease only exist when *we* define it? Isn't disease a scientifically discernible and measurable thing? There probably has never been a time in human history when people did not on occasion perceive themselves to be not well, so were they only deluding themselves? Clearly, the answer is no; disease is as real as anything in our lives, but we all know that some of the most important things in our lives are not scientifically discernible and measurable. When we say we love or hate, have fear or loathing, feel joy or sadness, we are communicating real states of our being and we expect others to understand what we mean. One of my favorite pieces of poetry is a fragment by E. E. Cummings (the poet of the lowercase):

> While you and i have lips and voices which
> are for kissing and to sing with
> who cares if some oneeyed son of a bitch
> invents an instrument to measure Spring with?

Of course we know when spring has arrived and don't need some "oneeyed son of a bitch" to measure it!

The important lesson these historians are teaching us is that our perception of when we are well or ill is defined by time and culture or, to use Susan Sontag's imagery, the use of the "good passport" is not absolute. Through most of the history of the West, death from infectious disease was a regular feature of life and only a small proportion of the population lived to old age. In this setting, the gnarled hands and painful joints associated with arthritis might not have been thought of as disease but rather as the natural condition of those who were lucky (or blessed) enough to have survived the fevers, epidemics, and countless travails of life. But at the end of the twentieth century, when rampant infectious disease has been brought under control and the rate of infant mortality has been reduced, the incapacitation from arthritis has gone from a badge of honor for having survived to being one of the major diseases of our time.

If we need an extreme example from history, a "disease" called *drapetomania*, the insatiable desire of slaves to escape, was identified by a Louisiana physician, Dr. Samuel Cartwright, in 1851. Cartwright was serious; to him and his colleagues in the Louisiana Medical Association, the normal state of life for black people in the American South was involuntary servitude and the normal state of life for white people was to take care of their slaves. Anybody who deviated from this norm was "diseased."

To choose an extreme example from our own time, some have begun to refer to the growing urban violence in the United States as an "epidemic" that should be treated as a medical and scientific problem. In a time when everything seems to be subjected to genetic analysis, serious people have made the suggestion that there is a genetic element in urban violence and have proposed that the "genetics of violence" be studied with the aim of medical treatment. The potential racist implications of this proposal have not escaped the attention of many, and it is very clear that there has long been a tendency to scientificize our social problems.

How we define disease and understanding how we have brought it under control have special implications in this time of AIDS, because if we do not understand the limits of science and medicine, we make unreasonable demands on them that can only lead to disappointment and disillusionment. In June 1993, writer Harold Brodkey wrote an article in *The New Yorker* magazine declaring that he had AIDS. According to *The New York Times*, Mr. Brodkey percolated with annoyance that the federal government had been slow to mobilize an effort to find a cure and declared: "I want Clinton to save my life."

The personal tragedy of this situation tears at the heart because Mr. Brodkey speaks for all who have AIDS, those who love them, and those who live with the fear of contracting this most dreaded disease of our times. Even though in 1992 the United States government spent $4.3 billion on AIDS, more than for any other disease except cancer, the expectations for a cure are so great that Mr. Brodkey was speaking for many in society when he said that the "Federal Government was slow to mobilize an effort to find a cure." Is this really true? Is it really a question of money, and is $4.3 billion not enough? Or is it the scientists who are to blame for not caring enough? Should we also blame them for not caring enough about breast and cervical cancer, Alzheimer's, and heart disease as well? No, the problem is that all of us, medicine, science, public, and the press, still assume what the members of the Infectious Disease Society of America assumed in 1970—that science was responsible for the elimination of infectious diseases in the past, and if we only have the will, science can find the cure for AIDS and *any* disease in the future. Of course, Mr. Brodkey doesn't expect the president to cure his disease, and in his very heart he knows that there are no cures for most cancers and many other diseases. Because AIDS has been associated with gay men, many gay activists who make similar statements are probably reflecting the not unreasonable feeling that the pervasive homophobia in our society has led to a lack of will to marshall the resources necessary to come up with a cure. But that is the very point; the misconception runs deep that with the will to do it, science can cure any disease just as it eliminated tuberculosis, cholera, diphtheria, and measles.

There of course are many diseases that scientific medicine can cure or prevent, and it would be difficult to find many in the industrialized world who would choose to go back to medicine before it became scientific. Penicillin and the Salk polio vaccine have set the standards for what we expect from medicine because of the completeness of their ability to cure or prevent. Insulin and cortisone, on the other hand, neither prevent nor cure diabetes and rheumatoid arthritis, but a world without them is frightening because these drugs have given those who have the diseases the chance of leading reasonably normal lives. Even though neither insulin nor cortisone has had the emotional impact of penicillin and the Salk vaccine, they are good examples of the kind of benefit science brings to medicine.

The problem is that too many people have developed the faith that Science (with a capital *S*) will solve *all* of our health problems and do it as dramatically as penicillin and the Salk vaccine. Consider these words of a Nobel prize-winning biochemist:

[W]e owe science our understanding of the nature of the universe, the origins of life on Earth, and the intimate kinship we have with our earthly neighbors. While we have few or no scientific solutions to economic problems or to living at peace with ourselves and with our neighbors, there is no doubt that in the long term, only a profound grasp of the chemistry of life can offer the hope of solving these difficult problems.

AIDS, cancer, real cures for diabetes and arthritis are not even worth mentioning for this Nobel laureate because he assumes that science will cure them, and he has already turned his vision to a scientific solution to peace and human conflict! When the leaders of science make unreasonable promises about what science will do for humanity in the future, we find a clash in expectations and realities. Science is one of the truly glorious inventions of the human mind, and it has been a dominant force in shaping how we view our world and our place in it. But in the end we must always remember that it is only a mode of problem solving, and one that was introduced quite recently in human history. The Scientific Revolution began in the seventeenth century and only started to affect medicine in the nineteenth, yet by the middle of the twentieth century science has become our secular religion. It is a faith that has become an unquestioned assumption in most of industrialized society, but it is a faith that can be easily lost if its practitioners make claims that are beyond their ability to deliver.

The combination of public health, vaccination, and antibiotics allowed the average life span to increase from around thirty years at the beginning of this century to over seventy as we enter the twenty-first century. We have an aging population; in fact ours has been the first century in which death is associated with old age, and we are finding that the pattern of diseases from which we suffer is changing. The infectious diseases that took the lives of our ancestors at such early ages have been replaced with chronic and degenerative diseases. Even the goals of medicine have changed: When people died young, medicine tried to *extend* life, but now that we die when we are old, its goal is to *improve* remaining life.

My aim in this book is to put the changes that have occurred in medicine and science into a context that allows the reader to see how we have conceived of disease and how we have treated it in the past and what we might reasonably expect to do about our new chronic diseases as we enter the twenty-first century. All of this is crucial for a society trying to make sense of the complexities in the debate about the health-care delivery system, which has focused on who will pay and what services will be covered rather than asking the more difficult questions: What are the reasonable goals of medicine and what are their limits? I hope to show that the *limits of medicine are conceptual, not technical,* and I hope that once this is clear, the reader will be in a better position to think about what the goals of medicine should be.

Part I

Reframing
the External
World

Chapter
1

The Constant Presence of Death

We learn history as a series of epochs: wars, treaties, reigns of terror, synods, schisms, assassinations, intrigues—Great Men causing Great Events. But in the background of all of this, real people led real lives and, in general, it was a life of misery. The Great-Man view of history tells us little of the incredibly high rate of infant death, the even higher rate of sickness, and the appallingly short life expectancy. Great Men and ordinary people lived their lives with the constant presence of death, and the astonishing fact is that this was so until almost the twentieth century. One quarter of children died in the first year of their lives, and life expectancy was only thirty years. How can we even imagine the bleakness of the lot of the average person?

The principal reason for this dreadful state of affairs was the havoc wrought by infectious diseases. We humans have lived with infectious disease—indeed, the limits of our lives have been defined by disease—almost from the beginning of recorded history. Only at the beginning of the twentieth century, when infectious diseases had ceased to carry away the young and epidemics had abated, did the lives of people in the industrial nations change. Disease and the conditions that supported its spread were a tolerated backdrop while Dante was writing *The Divine Comedy*, Rembrandt was painting *Night Watch*, Shakespeare was writing *Hamlet*, Napoleon was conquering Europe, and Jefferson was writing the Declaration of Independence. The suffering caused by disease was so pervasive that until very recently there was little comment on it. Walk through any Renaissance painting collection in a museum and you will see biblical scenes of suffering and salvation but only rarely depictions of contemporary misery. There was no need for artists to show their contemporaries the death that was everywhere around them; the purpose of art was to focus on the deliverance from the everyday suffering that religion could offer.

The Worst of Times and the Best of Times

To understand the magnitude of the changes that have occurred in our relationship to infectious diseases during the twentieth century, which is the best of times in terms of at least this factor, we must try to imagine living in the pre-twentieth-century world, which was the worst of times. It is of course difficult for people living in one period to be able to re-create in their imaginations what it *felt* like to live in another because we live with a romanticized view of the past, seeing the world of our parents and grandparents through the filter of stories and photographs. Literature, art, and films have given us the Renaissance without the plague, the court of the Sun King without the odor, and the American frontier without the hunger and desolation, so to truly understand the magnitude of the changes in what we expect from our world in terms of health and disease, we must try to *feel* what it was like to live in an earlier time. We must try to come as close as we can to being able to smell the smells and feel the fears that made up the world of our grandparents and their grandparents before them.

Fernand Braudel, the great French historian, makes the point very nicely: "It is easy to imagine being transported to, say, Voltaire's house at Ferney, and talking to him for a long time without being too surprised. In the world of ideas, the men of the eighteenth century are our contemporaries: their habits of mind and their feelings are sufficiently close to ours for us not to feel we are in a foreign country. But if the patriarch of Ferney invited us to stay with him for a few days, the details of his everyday life, even the way he looked after himself, would greatly shock us. Between his world and ours, a great gulf would open up: lighting at night, heating, transport, food, illness, medicine. So we have to strip ourselves in imagination of all the surroundings of our own lives if we are to swim against the current of time and look for the rules which for so long locked the world into a stability which is quite hard to explain if one thinks of the fantastic change which was to follow."

14

Voltaire lived from 1649 to 1778; consider the scene that met a contemporary of his, the young Rousseau, when he entered Paris for the first time in 1742: "The strong smell of excrement pervaded the environment, and the stench of public places was both terrible and ceaselessly condemned. The vile-smelling effluvia of the faubourg St.-Marcel assailed [the young Rousseau] when he entered the capital. In the Palais de Justice, in the Louvre, in the Tuileries, at the Museum, even at the Opera . . . the quays revolted the sense of smell." Excrement was everywhere: in alleys; at the foot of milestones; in cabs; in the gutters into which the cesspools were emptied; on the urine-stained walls of houses.

Things were no better at the glorious court at Versailles, where the cesspool was next to the palace. "The unpleasant odors in the park, gardens, even the château, make one's gorge rise. The communicating passages, courtyards, buildings in the wings, corridors, are full of urine and feces; a pork butcher actually sticks and roasts his pigs at the bottom of the ministers' wing every morning; the avenue Saint-Cloud is covered with stagnant water and dead cats." Livestock defecated in the great gallery and the stench even reached the king's chamber.

Statistics help us understand, but in general they affect only the intellect and hardly ever the gut. In any case, how can we use statistics to help us imagine what is unimaginable in our own time? When we are old, we know that we are coming to the end of our life because in our times death is associated with old age, but how many of us are aware that the association of death and old age has come about only during this century? In our great grandparents' time, death was associated with youth. To have lived to old age meant that you had safely traversed a very hazardous course, one that had claimed most of your contemporaries long before you. I often walk through old cemeteries near our summer home on the rugged coast of Maine, noting the ages of death on the eroding tombstones and trying to imagine the silent members of the small, isolated communities huddled at the gravesides as the infants and toddlers were lowered into the inhospitable soil.

Some statistics may help prove the point to the intellect: In seventeenth-century France, while Louis XIV reigned in splendor at Versailles, one person in four died before he reached his first birthday. Another one in four died before his twentieth birthday. Yet another quarter never reached the age of forty-five. Less than 10 percent of the population reached the age of sixty! "The most striking feature which distinguishes the Early Modern family from that of today does not concern either marriage or birth; it was *the constant presence of death* [author's emphasis]. Death was at the center of life, as the cemetery was at the center of the village." A description from France in 1657 shows this juxtaposition of the daily routines of life and death: In the midst of the throng of public writers, seamstresses, booksellers, secondhand-clothes dealers, people had to go about conducting a burial, reopening a tomb, and removing cadavers that were not yet entirely decomposed; "here, even in the dead of winter, the earth of the cemetery gave off mephitic odors."

How then is it possible for us at the end of the twentieth century, when in the industrialized countries our fastest-growing social problems involve the caring for an aging population and we engage in moral debates about assisting the death of old people, to imagine a world in which a person had only a fifty-fifty chance of making it to age forty-five? In 1885, when my own grandparents were alive, the infant death rate in New York City was 273 per 1,000 live births, the same percentage as in the time of Louis XIV. By 1914 the infant death rate had already dropped to 94 per 1,000 (roughly 10 percent) and by 1990 we were scandalized that the mortality rate for black children in New York was as high as 15 per 1,000 live births.

While we almost always focus on the death of children, another consequence of the high mortality rates was that children were left without parents. As recently as 1900, close to a quarter of the children born in the United States had lost one parent by the time they were fifteen years old. It is no accident that the plight of widows and the pity of orphanages filled the literature and thinking of the West until very recent times.

If we cannot feel the "constant presence of *death*" that our great-grandparents felt, perhaps we can come close to feeling the conditions of *life* they lived. The cities teemed with people living in overcrowded, unventilated, often vermin-infested quarters. The gutters and streets were awash with sewage and as often as not acted as conduits carrying human waste to the source of the drinking water. Adults and children alike worked long hours in harsh, cruel conditions. Inadequate nutrition and rotting food were the rule. Some of the descriptions of cities, even in the not-too-distant past, conjure up scenes from Hieronymus Bosch. Consider these descriptions of Philadelphia in 1832 and New York City in 1865.

> Philadelphia was a low, level town, hottest and dampest of all the American seacoast, hotter even than Charleston, Savannah, or the West India cities, people said. Wharves jutted out into the river and cut off the current; high tide deposited rotting stuff on the banks and in the mud. Below the city were swamps, marshes, pools in clay pits, stagnant water. Most of the streets were unpaved. There was no water system, and only one sewer, under the serpentine of Dock Street. Elsewhere holes were dug, as at Market and Fourth streets, to receive water from the gutters. These "sinks" exhaled a noxious effluvia, for dead animals and all kinds of nauseous matters were hurled into them to putrefy. All the wells were shallow; citizens continually pronounced them polluted.

> Domestic garbage and filth of every kind is thrown into the streets [in the sixth ward of New York City in 1865], covering their surface, filling the gutters, obstructing the sewer culverts, and sending forth perennial emanations which must generate pestiferous disease. In winter the filth and garbage, etc, accumulates in the streets to the depth sometimes of two or three feet.
>
> It is estimated that there were 18,000 persons living in cellars in New York in 1865. In a single tenement . . . with a transient population of about 320 persons, there had been 240 cases of fever and 60 deaths in a period of four years.

Under these kinds of conditions, it is hard *not* to imagine death everywhere. Death by malnutrition. Death in childbirth. But mostly, death from infection. In 1894, only six years before the start of the twentieth century, the death rate due to diphtheria in New York City was 785 per 100,000. Only a few years later, in 1900, it had fallen to 300 and by 1940 was 1.1 per 100,000. There are other examples that we are all familiar with, such as tuberculosis, measles, influenza; diseases that had to be coped with by every child in every generation. But there were also great epidemics like the Black Death (plague), cholera, and other scourges that we can only guess at by the descriptions of the symptoms that swept across cities, nations, and even continents.

Indeed, the conditions of life in the not-too-distant past were conducive to the spread of disease in every way. City dwellers were close enough together to cross-contaminate each other; their drinking water and sewage often intermingled. They were physically run down from hard work, long hours, and poor nutrition. Under these conditions, is it any wonder that people were prey to disease-causing agents?

Too many hours spent viewing nature films can be dangerous because we are subjected to a "Bambiization" of nature. The deep voice of the narrator tells us that "in the spring, the young leave their mother and go out into the world," implying that it is a world that is being ruined by humans for these noble animals. No one can seriously argue that humans are not destroying habitats, but the vision of nature "red in tooth and claw" is more apt. An unsentimental viewing of nature reveals living creatures undergoing a continuous struggle between predator and prey. This can be as benign as a cow munching grass (the grass is the prey and the cow is the predator) or as dramatic as a lion attacking a zebra and eating its flesh. But the predator-and-prey relationship is not a matter of the small being the prey of the large. Humans are prey to the bacteria that cause cholera. These kinds of microscopic predators have always been with us, and the course of human affairs has been influenced by them.

Obviously, the fact that we have not only survived as a species but have prospered in so many environments and ecological niches on the earth indicates that for the most part, our relationship with these parasites has not been too harmful to us. As early humans moved into new areas, came in contact with new environments, and ate new foods, they increased the range of parasites with which they had to establish stable relationships. Many of these parasites caused outright disease and even death and may have prevented humans from occupying a particular ecological niche, such as the tropical rain forests. (Of course, modern humans have found a way to solve this problem by cutting down the rain forests, but this has been done at the cost of loosing the parasites that lived in them onto the population living nearby in a kind of cosmic revenge.) The diseases caused by most parasites probably led to low-grade symptoms and debilitation, which in time came to be thought of as part of the human condition.

As humans developed language skills and tools, the ability to communicate and change the environment gave them the power to become dominant over other, much larger, hunters who had preyed upon their recent ancestors. Ultimately, these traits allowed humans to become the dominant predators, giving early humans a freedom that no other living forms had. They could now move into ecological niches that had not been available before and, of course, begin to alter them. But this freedom came with a price. Humans were the masters of the new environments they entered, but they also came into contact with an increasingly wider range of micropredators and now increasingly the subtle debilitation gave way to full-blown disease and death. The human hunters could dominate the mammoth because they could see their prey, outwit it, and kill it with tools, but there was no way to outwit an unseen, untouchable enemy. The price humans paid for the domination over their larger potential predators and the ability to change local environments was gained, with increasing frequency, at the expense of vulnerability to unseen predators.

When early humans lived in small bands, their numbers compared to the space they occupied (a term called *population density*) was probably similar to the population densities of other packs of animals. As their numbers grew, judging by their present-day descendants, they soon took to killing each other. This very human practice probably served to limit numbers and keep the population density low, but eventually, in order to hunt efficiently, protect themselves, and to live with some semblance of order, human societies formed. The benefits of organization resulted in ever larger groupings of people, raising the population density and bringing the members of one group (and their microparasites) into contact with people in other groups. Now those microparasites could be transmitted to other individuals, who had never before come into contact with them. The original conditions for the transmission of infectious diseases had developed. The irony, as one authority has pointed out, is that "we owe the origin of most serious infectious diseases to the conditions which led to our cultural heritage, the city-states made possible by the planting of crops in the flood plains of Mesopotamia, Egypt, and the Indus Valley."

This is not the place to discuss in detail the complex factors that make an individual resistant or susceptible to a particular kind of microparasite. As an example of the evolutionary trade-offs we have made, consider that Africans who had the sickle-cell trait had a survival advantage because they had red blood cells that were not easily infectable by the parasites that cause malaria and as a result were more resistant to that disease. Of course, there was a risk that some of the children born to a woman and man who each had the sickle-cell trait would have the very serious disease called sickle-cell anemia, but it is a fair bet that at some point in prehistory the advantage of resistance to malaria was far greater than the risk of the anemia. Humans gained mastery over large animals quickly, but our interaction with these microparasites has been an ongoing battle. As one authority put it: "If humanity succeeded fairly quickly in gaining mastery over the animals, until the last 100 years it was defenseless against countless living creatures who were so tiny that they escaped notice and so powerful that for millennia they were by far the most significant cause of disease and death." This stunning point is one of the cornerstones of this book.

Societies and Their Diseases

In the Neolithic period, human societies began changing their means of survival from hunting and gathering to farming and the raising of animals. For the first time, people were organizing themselves in a manner that we can recognize: communities of individuals staying in one place, pursuing long-term planned goals for their survival. In the process, they established a balance with the microparasites in the local environments, a kind of ecological balance that is lost when one side is too efficient at predation because the winner soon kills off the source of its maintenance. So while the microparasites gained a new source of nutriment in the newly arrived humans, the humans learned to live with the resident parasites. It is important here not to begin to think of this balance being struck by some kind of reasoning: The microparasites are only able to respond to their environment, not think about it, and the humans didn't even know the parasites were there!

We can only look at the balance from the side of the humans, and it most certainly must not have been a balance maintained without trauma. If debilitation associated with infection became routine, so too did death. There is variation between individual microparasites just as there is variation between individual humans, and some parasites were likely to cause greater degrees of damage than others. Conversely, some humans were likely to be more adversely affected than others, and death was the outcome when the balance was tipped too far in favor of the parasites. This kind of constant interaction between microparasites and the human population results in diseases that we call *endemic*—that is, diseases that are always with a population and are an expected part of life. Being endemic doesn't make them any less dangerous or unwanted, only expected. These endemic diseases, many of them no doubt unique to the locale that the human population settled into, played an important role in the development of human society.

But there is another form of disease that has also played a significant, and very dramatic, role in human history. These are the diseases that we call *epidemic*—diseases that can appear suddenly and spread rapidly through a population, affecting great numbers of people. If a society had learned to live with a certain proportion of people showing behavior that we would now call symptoms (because now we know about disease), imagine the bewilderment of early humans when large numbers of them suddenly began to show behavior or symptoms that were not known before. And imagine the terror when, after the epidemic had subsided, those who had escaped it the first time found that it had returned again months or years later.

I t has been speculated that epidemic disease joined the endemic forms with which the various populations were coming into equilibrium in western Asia about 5000 B.C., the time when farming and husbandry began to replace hunting and gathering and societies began to be organized. This new way of living in communities spread across Europe from its first great manifestation in the Greek world. Greece was at the crossroads of the continents, forming a bridge between Asia, the northern part of Africa, and the western and central parts of Europe, and while it was a good place from which to disseminate civilization, it was also a good place from which diseases could spread. The original Neolithic communities probably consisted of no more than a hundred or so people, although a few very large "cities" have been found, and the groups were generally isolated from each other. But travel by sea developed early and with it came the means for the mingling of endogenous infections of the various communities.

By around 5000 B.C., life had become less brutal and the economy shifted from an agricultural base to one in which artisans and traders flourished, which in turn led to higher concentrations of people in a given place and the importing of labor. The preconditions for epidemic disease were being established. Moreover, during this time the population of all of Europe was growing. By 1000 B.C. it could have been about 10 million people, but they were not evenly distributed; it is estimated that at the time, the population density of Greece was as much as three times that of northern Europe. The numbers of people and the population density continued to increase, and so it comes as no surprise looking back from our vantage point in history that the "plague of Athens," the first catastrophic epidemic in the West whose symptoms and progress are well documented, broke out here.

The only description we have of the great plague of Athens comes from the historian Thucydides, who was not only an observer of the disease but was among the lucky survivors. The Peloponnesian War broke out in 431 B.C. and the plague came a year later, in 430.

That year, as is generally admitted, was particularly free from all other kinds of illness, though those who did have any illness previously all caught the plague in the end. In other cases, however, there seemed to be no reason for the attacks. People in perfect health suddenly began to have burning feelings in the head; their eyes became red and inflamed; inside their mouths there was bleeding from the throat and tongue, and the breath became unnatural and unpleasant. The next symptoms were sneezing and hoarseness of voice, and before long the pain settled on the chest and was accompanied by coughing. Next the stomach was affected with stomachaches and with vomitings of every kind of bile that has been given a name by the medical profession, all this being accompanied by great pain and difficulty. In most cases there were attacks of ineffectual retching, producing violent spasms; this sometimes ended with this stage of the disease, but sometimes continued long afterwards. Externally the body was not very hot to the touch, nor was there any pallor: the skin was rather reddish and livid, breaking out into small pustules and ulcers. But inside there was a feeling of burning, so that people could not bear the touch even of the lightest linen clothing, but wanted to bed completely naked, and indeed most of all would have liked to plunge into cold water. Many of the sick who were uncared for actually did so, plunging into the water-tanks in an effort to relieve a thirst which was unquenchable; for it was just the same with them whether they drank much or little. Then all the time they were afflicted with insomnia and the desperate feeling of not being able to keep still. . . .

Words indeed fail one when one tries to give a general picture of this disease; and for the sufferings of individuals, they seemed almost beyond the capacity of human nature to endure. Here in particular is a point where this plague showed itself to be something quite different from ordinary diseases: though there were many dead bodies lying about unburied, the birds and animals that eat human flesh either did not come near them, or, if they did taste the flesh, died of it afterwards. . . .

T he plague of Athens was the first recorded large-scale disaster due to infectious disease in the West, but we know that centers of population in China were visited by their own "plagues" with disturbing frequency. In modern usage we think of *plague* as the Black Death or bubonic plague, which first arrived in Europe in 1348, but plague was originally used as a generic term for epidemics with disastrous consequences. There can be no doubt that living conditions in Europe and in China, especially population density, played a large role in setting the conditions that allowed plagues to flourish. By the middle of the fourteenth century A.D., chronic overpopulation was, in the words of one scholar, "rendering intolerable the existence of many, if not a majority of Europeans. It is tempting to take a step further and see the Black Death as nature's answer to the problem of over-population, a Malthusian check to the over-exuberance of the preceding centuries."

To understand the conditions in cities at this time it might help to look at the transition that Paris underwent between the twelfth and fourteenth centuries, because it is typical of northern French towns. For years the river that ran through, and the moat around, Paris helped cleanse the city. Dyers worked along canals away from the city, and although they dumped chemicals into the waters, they were too dilute to kill fish. Skinners and tanners of hides worked farther downstream, to take advantage of the chemicals (sulfates of chromium and iron) the dyers dumped into the upstream waters. In town, feces were used as fertilizer for home gardens and pigs consumed the rest of the household garbage. This "golden age of urban ecology" had already become undermined by war and trade disruption by the fourteenth century. People began moving to within the walls of the city for protection, and as the area around the city became deserted, the moats became stagnant marshes. The balance between people and the city changed; each *quartier* created its own dump outside the city walls and Paris became an "enclosed universe, breeding and trapping its own horrific odors." Artisans had to collect urine and the excrement of dogs for industrial purposes, while human and animal feces were gathered by municipal authorities to make saltpeter (potassium and sodium nitrate). With the unavailability of the downstream chemicals, new techniques of dyeing and paper making had to be developed, and not surprisingly, the city stank with the effort. As one sixteenth-century commentator said, "We are packed, pressed, invaded, buckled for all sides, and we take no air but the stinking air between our walls, of our mud, and of our sewers."

The utter enormity of death due to the visitations of disease to cities like these is hard to comprehend. "As a rough and ready rule-of-thumb, therefore, the statement that a third of the population died of the Black Death should not be too misleading. The figure might quite easily be as high as 40% or as low as 30%; it could conceivably be as high as 45%, or as low as 23%." But the Black Death was not the only menace. Between 1485 and 1551, England was visited by a deadly disease called the "sweating sickness," whose first wave killed as much as one third of the population in some areas. Returning again in 1506, it killed as many as half of the population in some communities, only to return in 1516 and then again in 1529. The last epidemic spread through all of northern Europe. Knowing what we know today, we assume that the mysterious "sweating sickness" was caused by a pathogenic microorganism, but we don't know the nature of the agent.

There were also epidemics that caused extremely high levels of illness but little death. In 1410 there was a catastrophic epidemic in Paris of what we now think was influenza. The disease came again in 1510, 1557, and again in 1580. Typhus fever, a disease that had been endemic, reached epidemic proportions in 1490. So by the late medieval and

Renaissance periods in Europe, there was not only the constant background of endemic diseases causing debilitation and high infant mortality but an added horror of widespread epidemics. It is not difficult for us, even at the great distance of time, to grasp, at least intellectually, how the people living with the endemic diseases came to terms with their lot. We are all familiar with the fact that sometimes we are unaware of a pain until it stops and then we wonder that we didn't react before. But can any of us imagine how we would react to the presence of epidemic diseases that could wipe out a quarter or a third of the population in a short time—our family, friends, and neighbors? Those of us who grew up with the terror of polio during the summer months have some faint hint of these kinds of fears. Watching the fear of the AIDS epidemic shows us the juxtaposition of bravery and irrationality in a society during a modern epidemic.

Faith, Reason, and Epidemic Disease

In the twentieth century, when we think of unsanitary conditions we think of infection because we know that these conditions foster the agents that cause disease. But we often forget the fact that the cause of infectious disease was not known until the end of the nineteenth century! That leaves millennia with the constant presence of death from diseases from unknown causes. Is it at all surprising that our distant (and even our recent) ancestors dealt with these sporadic but inevitable visitations with a combination of rational thought and superstition or that they saw epidemic disease as divine punishment?

The idea of disease as corruption or punishment goes back to the earliest of human times and can even be seen in the origin of the word *infection*. Interestingly, the word derives from the Latin *infecto*, which can be traced back to one Theodorus Priscianus, a physician of the fifth century A.D., who devotes a whole chapter to *infecto* in his textbook of medicine. But the chapter is entitled *De infectionibus capillorum*, or "On the dyeing of hair"! So *infecto* means "to stain" or "to dye." Now, it turns out that this is also the principal connotation of the verb *infincere*, which means "to put or dip into something, and the something may be a dye; or to mix with something, especially a poison; or to stain something in the sense that it becomes tainted, spoiled, or corrupted. Indeed, the English word

'to stain' can still be used in the double sense of dyeing as well as pol-
luting. Let us remember, then, that *an infection is basically a pollution*"
(author's emphasis). So there is little question even from the etymology
of the words we use today that infection was equated with impurity and
we know, of course, that one of the major roles of religion is to drive out
the impure. Leviticus 13 tells us how the leper is to be driven out and
isolated because he is unclean:

> And the leper in whom the plague is, his clothes shall be
> rent, and his head bare, and he shall put a covering upon
> his upper lip, and shall cry, Unclean, unclean. All the days
> wherein the plague shall be in him he shall be defiled; he is
> unclean; he shall dwell alone; without the camp shall his habi-
> tation be.

It is tempting to think that this passage and others in the Bible and
classical literature indicate that the ancients had an awareness, perhaps
similar to ours, of the nature of infection and disease, to somehow see
this as the earliest seeds of public health. But when we think about the
balance between faith and reason in the response to epidemic diseases,
we must force ourselves to remember that the people we are talking
about knew nothing of disease-producing microorganisms, a point so
important that it cannot be overstated. It makes sense to isolate the
leper if you suspect that he is the vehicle of the disease, and indeed, as
we will see shortly, quarantines were instituted during times of epidemic disease as a means of preventing the spread. But the anthropologist Mary Douglas has very eloquently argued that there are far more
examples of separation of the "unclean" that do not have any public-
health value than those that do. An important thesis of her book *Purity
and Danger* is that rituals of purity and impurity are the central project of
religion, and of course, religion is the expression of faith.

> A Brahmin should not be in the same part of his cattle shed
> as his Untouchable servant, for fear that they may both step on
> places connected through overlapping straws on the floor.
> Even though a Havik and an Untouchable simultaneously
> bathe in the village pond, the Havik is able to attain a state of
> *Madi* (purity) because the water goes to the ground, and the
> ground does not transmit impurity.

"The more deeply we go into this and similar rules, the more obvious it becomes that we are studying symbolic systems. . . . Are our ideas hygienic where theirs are symbolic? Not a bit of it. . . . our ideas of dirt also express symbolic systems . . . the difference between pollution behaviour in one part of the world and another is only a matter of detail."

The biblical rules that exclude lepers make good sense in modern public-health terms, but the touching of straw does not. The Old Testament rules against eating pork could be seen as having public-health value because of the transmission of Trichinella, but there are other dietary restrictions that do not fill any public-health standard and can only have religious reasons.

> These are the living things which you may eat among all the beasts that are on the earth.
> Whatever parts the hoof and is cloven-footed and chews the cud, among the animals you may eat.
> Nevertheless among those that chew the cud or part the hoof, you shall not eat these: The camel, because it chews the cud but does not part the hoof, is unclean to you.
> And the rock badger, because it chews the cud but does not part the hoof, is unclean to you.
> And the hare, because it chews the cud but does not part the hoof, is unclean to you.
> And the swine, because it parts the hoof and is cloven-footed, but does not chew the cud, is unclean to you. (Leviticus 9)

My grandfather, a man I revered for both his scholarly disposition and politics, shocked me during one of my adolescent bouts of religious fervor by telling me that if I wanted to follow the dietary rules of Orthodox Judaism, I should do it bearing in mind that in his view God could care less. The rules were, he assured me, a vestige of the means used by the priestly caste to control the guilt of the faithful. As I later went through my bouts of socialist and Freudian fervor, his religious and political insights came back to me with new meaning. Assuming that Mary Douglas and Joseph Mazer (my grandfather) are correct, our responses to dirt, pollution, and uncleanliness in many forms have a long-standing basis in faith and not reason, a point we will return to very shortly.

B y the Renaissance, Europe was ravaged by epidemics of infectious diseases, and in their very hearts, the people felt this must be divine punishment. But how to reconcile this with the observations that when people from a town besieged with plague traveled to other towns, they brought the plague with them? Was divine punishment transportable? And as these people, so terrorized by the capriciousness of the attacks of the plague, attempted to modify their actions and environments to prevent or at least control its spread, they hoped they were not interfering with divine will.

Measures we would now call public health were taken in Italy from the earliest outbreak of the plague in 1348. These first steps continued as successive episodes of plague swept across the continent, so that by the middle of the sixteenth century they had become a very complex and sophisticated system of regulations. The basis of the system was the establishment of special *Magistracies,* which combined legislative, judicial, and executive powers in all matters concerning the health of the public. Over time the scope of their actions, while always concerned with control of plague, covered such matters as the recording of deaths and burials, the marketing of food, and overseeing the sewage system, the hospitals, hostelries, and even prostitution. We can get a good sense of what measures were taken in northern Italy by this passage from a treatise by Alessandro Nassarina, who was in charge of sanitary measures at Vicenza in 1577:

> The first death was attributed to garments clandestinely introduced from Padua, where plague prevailed . . . the furniture in the house was burned and every exposed person stripped, given new clothes, and removed outside the city. The house was purified by aromatic fumigations and painted with milk of lime. All infected vestments and bedding received a treatment with strong lye. The disease, however, spread, and in one year the city, with a population of 30,000, suffered 1,908 deaths from plague. As soon as the epidemic established itself the city was divided into thirty-two sections and a daily house-to-house inspection made by sixty-four trustworthy citizens, two to each precinct. All cases of sickness were reported to one of four public physicians. . . . Infected habitations received the same treatment as in the

initial case, except that the furniture was not burned in all instances, but washed instead with lye and left in the sun and open air for thirty days. All garments were put in running water for two days. Persons exposed or under suspicion went to the Campo di Marte, outside the city walls, where wooden houses had been built. A river separated the isolation camp from the lazaretto, where the sick were lodged and where physicians and nurses were in attendance. Suspects developing plague in the isolation camp were taken across the river to the lazaretto, and convalescents from the latter place were transferred to the former. Those who kept well in the Campo di Marti for twenty-two days returned to their disinfected homes in the city, there to remain under observation for an additional twenty-two days. . . . At the height of the epidemic all the houses in the city were closed for forty days, and none but the guards were allowed in the streets.

London was so ravaged by plague at the end of Elizabeth's reign and the beginning of James's (1603), that measures very similar to those instituted by the *Magistracies* were instituted. Here the authorities insisted on the same kinds of measures of burning clothing and isolation. They did allow one person in a household with plague to shop for provisions, but that person had to carry a three-foot red flag so that others would stay away, and they ruled that "no hogs, doges, or cats, or tame pigeons, or conies be suffred to be kept." It has been claimed by one scholar that a London preacher, Henock Clapham, preached too strongly that plague was divine punishment and that there was no need for these strict measures and so was jailed by the authorities to keep him quiet. (There seems to be little question that Clapham was jailed, but it is not clear that it was because of his opposition to the quarantine measures.) The enormity of the plague in London during the period from 1603 to 1613, and the civic response to it, can be seen from the fact that the Globe, Shakespeare's theater, was actually closed more often than it was open. The theater was closed, for example, from March 1603 until September 1604, and then in February and March and October through December of 1605. It was closed for almost thirty of the thirty-six months in the years 1606 and 1608!

These measures were taken when the cause of the plague, if divine punishment as a cause is set aside, was thought to be bad air or dirt or spirits, so the remedies all involve cleansing and purifying and isolating. Much of this seems reasonable even by modern standards, but much of what was done we know now was of no use. It is unfair to those people at risk of their lives to the plague in the fifteenth century to say that they should have behaved as if they lived in the twentieth century: The cause of the plague was beyond the scope of their imagination. How could they even begin to imagine that it was caused by living things invisible to the eye and transported by the fleas of rats? I fully expect that writers four hundred years from now will look back with astonishment at the way we have responded to AIDS.

In Nassarina's description we see the emphasis on reason. In Carlo Cipolla's poignant little book, *Faith, Reason, and the Plague in Seventeenth-Century Tuscany*, we see the conflicts between the representative of the *Magistracies* (reason) and the Church (faith) in the isolated Tuscan village of Monte Lupo in 1630. The local priest planned prayer services, vigils, and processions through the streets that would bring all of the citizens of the village together so that God would have mercy and see that they truly repented for whatever it was that had brought about the divine wrath. At the same time, the representative of the Florentine *Magistracie* came to town and tried to institute measures, such as those described by Nassarina, designed to keep people apart from each other, following the idea that the only way to stop the plague was to rely on methods of isolation and purification. This conflict between faith and reason is understandable and was the rule of the day until the last few decades of the nineteenth century, when science started to become a belief system comparable to religion and faith in the measures of "reason" began to replace faith in the measures of religion.

So we see that since civilization began twelve thousand years ago, death was a constant presence in the lives of ordinary people, until as recent a time as the middle of the nineteenth century. It is necessary to keep the fact of how recent our views of health have been formed as we try to understand why we think as we do about health and disease, the role of science and technology in our lives, and the goals we should expect from our health and science establishments.

Chapter

2

La *Longue durée*

I f sickness, dying, and death were everywhere from the time of the Greeks until the beginning of the twentieth century, what was the response of the people who suffered and those who treated them? How is it that between the fifth century B.C. and the end of the nineteenth century, the whole long period when Western civilization flowered, the general level of health changed so little? A powerful new way of thinking and looking at the world, called *science*, developed in the seventeenth century, and yet for almost three centuries after it began to change dramatically the world and the way we look at our place in it, infant mortality remained at around 25 percent and disease and debilitation were the lot of the average person. How is it that not until the middle of the nineteenth century did medicine begin to use this powerful new way of thinking to bring about the same kinds of changes science was effecting in navigation, manufacturing, mining, and warfare? The answer we will pursue in this book is that so little changed in what we *did* about disease because so little changed about how we *thought* about it. It was not until science developed to the point that health and disease could be reframed that we were able to change what we did about them. But the surprising fact is that this reframing came about after deaths from infectious diseases had already begun to decline. Nevertheless, the reframing of health and disease that science brought about is one of the most significant advances in human history, and an understanding of how it happened is essential if we are to understand what science and medicine can provide for us in the future.

None of us has ever known any way of looking at health and disease other than our modern scientific way, so we find it hard to believe, *really* believe, that the concept of what constitutes health and disease was different from ours from the time of the Greeks until the time when some of our grandparents were still alive. The French historians who called themselves the *Annales* historians, in an attempt to understand what it was like to live in this "world we have lost," began to view the past from the peasants' perspective rather than following the traditional pursuit of studying only wars and treaties. They discovered the amazing fact that through most of history, little changed during the lifetime of one person, and they coined the phrase *la longue durée* to evoke the idea of the relative changelessness of conditions over a long time. And we must admit that for something as important as the idea of what causes us to be healthy or sick, 500 B.C. to A.D. 1850 is a very *longue durée* indeed.

The Long Greek Tradition

Until not too long ago, history texts reflected the general view that to study the past is to study the "correct" path leading to the present—whenever that present happens to be. Modern historians call this way of looking at the past Whig history and have tried to rid themselves of the idea that history has been purposefully marching to where we are today. Another difficult trap historians try to avoid is that of seeing the past through modern eyes, something they call presentism. Modern historians try to see the past from the perspective of the people who lived it, so when we look back at what our ancestors thought about the cause and nature of the diseases that dominated their lives for two millennia, we too must try to imagine in our modern minds what was going on in theirs. We must try to see and feel the world as they did and remember that theirs was a world in which the very idea that human disease could be caused by invisible living creatures was something that a philosopher might think of but had no reality to the overwhelming majority of sick people or those who treated them.

The fact of the matter is that from the earliest times until around 1850, very few people thought about the body as an organized collection of cells, and even though chemistry has a long history, the idea that chemical reactions occurring in our body are responsible for how our body functions was all but inconceivable. And given the constant presence of death, why would anyone have thought that the body had a special defense mechanism to fight disease? In the West, the almost universally held view of how the body functions and what goes wrong in disease came from the Greek physicians through what is called the Hippocratic and Galenic tradition and was passed down with only minor modification until the great revolution of scientific medicine in the mid-nineteenth century. In modern times, we make a clear separation between philosophy and science (the cruelest cut one scientist can make of another when they disagree is to say, "Well, that's only philosophy"), but this was not the case with the early Greeks. Greek philosophers and physicians even before Socrates (who lived from 469 to 399 B.C.) were both asking the same questions: What is man? What is he made of? How does he operate? Both disciplines sought to explain the stability of the body and its capacity to change, and both used the idea that the world was in constant flux to explain and treat. The earliest physicians and philosophers saw health of both body and mind as the proper *balance* of principles.

Given this connection between Greek philosophers and physicians (Aristotle's father was a physician) and the Greek worldview of things in balance, we can see why some of the great Greek healers as early as 500 B.C. developed the idea that health depended on the body's being in balance. Over time the exact nature of just what it was that was in balance would change, but whether it was the humors—yellow bile, phlegm, blood, and black bile—or some other collection of things, the Greek philosopher-physicians could explain the differences among bone, blood, and flesh, or between health and disease, on the basis of their combinations in a healthy person or a sick one.

Considering how difficult it is to put ourselves into that distant world, it is no accident that the Renaissance painters depicted scenes from the Bible or Greek mythology set in Tuscan and Umbrian landscapes. We understand our place in the universe, how our body functions, the nature of health and disease, because of our worldview, and historians a millennium from now will no doubt be trying to reconstruct our worldview to fathom why we held such seemingly bizarre ideas. The philosopher and social critic Michel Foucault talks about modern ideas not as being "correct," but as being ideas of "an era from which we have not yet emerged," a sobering and, I think, realistic way to reduce our Whiggish arrogance. The crucial fact to keep in mind is that while the Western mind bent itself around all kinds of changes, the manner in which the Greeks framed the nature of health and disease, with its emphasis on the maintenance of internal balance, remained largely unchanged for that incredibly *longue durée*.

How did this worldview affect the way Greek physicians looked at their patients? Both external and internal forces could alter the balance of humors, so the roles of climate and place were very important to them. For example, they were convinced that people living in cities exposed to hot winds were susceptible to different kinds of illness than people living in cities facing cold winds. This was because "health is maintained by equal rights of the qualities of the wet, the dry, the cold, the hot, the bitter, the sweet, etc." When one of these opposites dominates, disease occurs; "as to their causes by an excess of heat or cold; as to their occasion by an excess or deficiency of nourishment; as to their locale, blood, marrow, and brain are affected." A whole host of factors can throw the humors into a state of imbalance, because "health is a mixture of the qualities in proper proportion."

Of course, from common sense observation, the Greeks knew that everyone living in a region of hot or cold winds did not come down with the same symptoms, and they certainly knew that in epidemics, even those as calamitous as the plague of Athens, many were spared. The explanation that fit into their worldview was that while changing external conditions could cause an internal imbalance, those who did not come down with disease had somehow managed to maintain the internal balance of their humors in the face of the external force. Heredity too played a role: "One consumptive is born from another," according to Hippocrates. Dropsy, gout, and epilepsy were also thought to be controlled by heredity, or more correctly, heredity was thought to control a predisposition for the humors to become imbalanced in a way that led to the symptoms of diseases that came to be called dropsy, gout, and epilepsy.

The important point is that the observational powers of the Hippocratic physicians were acute. Their explanations of what they saw differs completely from our modern view, but we must remember that their explanations were as consistent with the shared worldview of their patients as our explanations are to us. The detailed descriptions of their patients still serve as models of careful observation of the sick person. Consider this fourth-century B.C. case study, and notice how little it differs from the case of the abbot of Cluny fifteen hundred years later described on page 38:

> In the wife of Polycrates, around the dog days of summer, fever; difficulty breathing, less so in the morning, worse from midday on, when it became a little more rapid; coughing and immediately sputum that was purulent from the start; within, along the throat and windpipe, husky wheezing; good coloring on the face; red cheeks, not dark red but, on the contrary, fairly bright. As time went on, voice becoming hoarse and body wasted, scabs on the loins, and bowel movement on the watery side. The seventieth day: the fever grows very cold externally; on the temples, no throbbing; but the breathing becomes more and more rapid. After this respite, the breathlessness is so heightened that the patient remains seated until the moment of death. In the windpipe, there was a lot of noise; also, terrible sweats; looks full of understanding up to the final moment. Once, her fever lightened for more than five days. After the first few days the patient did not cease spitting up purulent substances.

A modern physician-historian, Mirko Grmek, has analyzed this remarkable case report and cast it into modern terms. "This clinical picture is grippingly real, and except for its silence about blood in the sputum, corresponds completely to the unfolding of pulmonary consumption with a specifically concomitant laryngitis. Nevertheless, one should realize that this retrospective diagnosis is not altogether certain: though the sequence of symptoms corresponds exactly to that which laryngeal and pulmonary tuberculosis can provide, it is also compatible with several other serious diseases of the respiratory organs. One can imagine a diagnosis of cancer of the larynx, trachea, or bronchi, which would produce respiratory wheezing as well as dyspnea turning into orthopnea along with cancerous cachexia. Still, the striking redness of the cheeks tells against malignant consumption and in favor of tuberculosis infection."

The details of Grmek's analysis need not concern us—indeed, they make little sense to anyone not trained in medicine—but two things merit comment. First, between the time of the Greeks and modern scientific medicine, the description of the patient changed from one that is easily understandable by everyone to one that requires a special vocabulary. Anyone can sympathize with the suffering of the wife of Polycrates (whose name was evidently not important to her physician) because everyone understands what she was feeling. But what is the ordinary person, either patient or family, to make of Ms. Polycrates' "dyspnea turning into orthopnea along with cancerous cachexia"? Would the Polycrates family have understood those phrases, even though they were spoken in their language? Most patients and their families today would quite correctly say that "it was Greek to them." In our move to modernity we have relegated the suffering of the patient, which was once understandable to all, to the technical world of the expert, a point to which we will return.

But now comes an even more important, but not unrelated, point. It probably comes as no surprise to the modern reader to learn that the Greek physician could do little that by our modern standards of scientific medicine we would consider adequate to *treat* the symptoms of Ms. Polycrates. He could diagnose, predict the outcome, and comfort the patient and her family. A little-known fact, however, is that the physician even into the early years of the twentieth century could have done very little for her except perform laboratory tests to make the differential diagnosis between consumption or a tumor and then give comfort. This will be quite clear a bit later in this narrative, when we come to the description of what Lewis Thomas and his father before him learned in medical school at the beginning of the twentieth century. Physicians in the early years of the twentieth century could more precisely diagnose an ailment and give a more accurate prediction of its outcome, but still the most valuable thing they could offer to patients and their families was comfort.

So something remarkable happened toward the end of the nineteenth century to create a world in which infectious diseases no longer caused a society of sickness, death was no longer a constant presence, and physicians were able to effectively change the course of disease. And these changes, which we consider the norm of our existence, came about within living memory of a large part of our society.

The Greek Tradition and the Christian West

Hippocrates is thought to have died in 377 B.C. (if in fact he actually lived; the subject is still under debate), but the Hippocratic writings that formed the basis of medicine in the classical world also formed the basis of medicine in the modern world. As the Hellenistic world began to fragment, many sects developed around what were thought to be the Hippocratic teachings, fragmenting the essence of the teaching of the master. This changed when Galen, a Greek who lived and worked in Rome, unified the fragments and reintroduced their original richness. Galen was born around A.D. 130, in Pergamon, in Asia minor, a city famous for its sanctuary of the healing god Asclepius. After his education he went to Alexandria (which was the repository of the Hippocratic writing) and, after a short return home to be physician to the school of gladiators, he went to Rome, where he soon became the dominant force in the medical world. An indefatigable traveler, writer, and talker (he was described by a contemporary as a man who "showed his teeth when laughing, talked much and was rarely silent"), Galen is often considered an early medical scientist. He dissected animals (not humans, it should be noted) and saw that the body was composed of skin, cartilage, muscle, bone, etc., the things we today call the tissues; and since these parts of the body are impaired in disease, he realized that to understand disease, it is important to understand the parts. He even experimented on living animals, showing that the flow of urine was stopped when he tied the tubes leading from the kidney to the bladder, and that when he severed the spinal cord at different levels he could see different kinds of loss of function. The brilliance of Galen was that he was able to unite the teachings of the Hippocratic corpus about the importance of balance with his anatomical and physiological observations.

But let's not confuse this early inquiry with modern views. Agreeing with Aristotle, Galen believed there are four *elements* (fire, air, earth, and water), and four *qualities* (hot, cold, dry, wet). Like everything else, people, animals, and the food they eat were composed of these elements and qualities. He believed that in the process of digestion, food and drink were turned into the juices of the body, which were the humors. While it was obvious that fire, air, earth, and water didn't exist in our bodies, they were represented by the humors (blood, phlegm, yellow bile, and black bile), which formed the solid parts of the body. Once this was accepted, it was obvious to Galen that an imbalance, either an excess or a lack of one or more of these humors, resulted in disease. Galen taught that there could be a wide variation in the humors without disease, so it was important for the person to maintain good health by good habits, but when the balance of humors changed enough to actually result in disease, they could most often be set aright by changes in diet. To Galen, then, good health was the responsibility of the individual and most disease was due to deviation from a good life. Changes in the environment and events that people have no control over often caused the humors to become imbalanced and then the physician's role was to reestablish the proper balance. (Leave out the fire, water, black and yellow bile, and this sounds remarkably "New Age"; *le plus ça change . . .*)

Galen lived and worked at the very beginning of the Christian era, but he never rejected his faith in his "ancestral god" Asclepius, although he knew there were limits to what even such a powerful healing god could do. Some people, he wrote, are so sickly that "they cannot reach the age of sixty, even if you should put Asclepius himself in charge of them." In this worldview, even the gods are bound by matter; they cannot command it—a belief quite different from that which would soon sweep Europe, the Judeo-Christian belief in an omnipotent God who could command matter.

B y the end of the fourth century, Christianity had become the state religion of the Roman empire, and with it came fundamental changes in the worldview. Now sickness, like so many other evils that affect human life, was seen to be a result of the Fall of Man. Disease was sent by God, and the cure of the soul must take precedence over the cure of the body. St. Augustine said that treatment of the body by drugs is so painful that a person only exchanges the pain of his physical disease for the pain of his physical remedy; treatment of the soul, however, results in eternal freedom from pain. Just look at the miracle cures brought about through religious devotion, he told the faithful; can there be any better proof of the superiority of religion over secular healing?

The Church of course was not opposed to secular healing, especially since so many people used it, and monasteries often became places of both religious and secular healing. What had changed was the relationship between the religious and the secular. After all, hadn't St. Augustine also suggested that the founder of the Church himself was a true physician, the healer of souls (primarily) and of bodies (occasionally)? The Muslim East had become the main repository of the Hippocratic and Galenic writings and teachings, but even so, the secular medicine that was practiced in the bleak world of Christian medieval Europe was the medicine of the Greeks.

As the population rose during what is called the Dark Ages, the impoverished, illiterate, primarily rural population became increasingly urbanized as a result of economic growth, and workers increasingly needed to be literate to carry out their tasks. Medicine began to leave the monasteries and by 1100 St. Bernard's was becoming a lone voice when he appealed to his fellow monks living in an area notorious for malaria not to turn to secular physicians. "I fully realize that you live in an unhealthy region and that many of you are sick. . . . It is not at all in keeping with your profession to seek for bodily medicines. . . to seek out doctors and swallow their nostrums, this does not become religious."

The monasteries became very proficient in growing the herbs that were used for healing, and much of our knowledge of the kinds of medicinal plants used during the period come from our understanding of monastic gardens. They also became sanctuaries for the sick and abandoned of society, while bloodletting, emetics, heat, and cold—all things designed to reestablish the balance of the humors—were the stock-in-trade of the secular physician, or *medicus*, and village healers. To physicians in the Hippocratic and Galenic traditions, the individual was primarily responsible for leading a healthy life and maintaining his balance of humors; now the elements of divine will and retribution entered the equation. It is necessary to balance the humors, but the spirit must also be ministered to, and this was the role of the Church.

By the twelfth century, between the end of the Middle Ages and the beginning of the Renaissance, the teachings of the Greek physicians had moved into Christian Europe and secular medicine was practiced widely. We are fortunate to have the written correspondence between Peter the Venerable, the abbot of Cluny, and a *medicus* called Bartholomeus during the winter of 1150–51. Nancy Siraisi, in her book *Medieval and Early Renaissance Medicine*, provides a vivid description of this case that illustrates the therapies that were used and how little the ideas of what constitutes health and disease had changed in the thousand years since Hippocrates. It seems that because of the press of monastery business, the abbot had postponed his regular bimonthly bloodletting for a while. During that time he developed a case of "catarrh," which forced him to further postpone the procedure because his *medicus* told him that bloodletting during an attack of catarrh could lead to a loss of the voice, a drawback to a man who had to celebrate the mass and deliver sermons. But because his catarrh did not improve, Peter concluded that it must be due to an overabundance of blood and phlegm, so finally, after four months, he had two large amounts of blood drawn in a three-week period. The catarrh remained, and as he had been warned, his voice began to be affected. Moreover, his chest felt heavy and he continued to cough up phlegm. The local *medici* told him that his prolonged catarrh was due to the loss of heat from the bloodletting, which left cold and "sluggish phlegm diffused through the veins and vital channels" such as the trachea (hence the loss of voice). They suggested the use of heat and moistening foods and medicines, but Peter, who knew the works of Galen, as did a growing number of educated people, objected on the grounds that a cold, moist disease such as he had should be countered by hot and *dry*, not hot and *moist*, remedies. But the *medici* told him that while this was generally true, the throat ought to be soothed with moist things and not irritated with dry substances. The medicines Peter took during this long, unpleasant illness included hyssop, cumin, licorice, figs steeped in wine, and syrups of tragacanth, butter, or ginger. Since the venerable Peter died in 1156, we must assume that he recovered from his illness.

The story shows dramatically how fifteen hundred years after Hippocrates and 950 years after Galen, the concepts of health and disease, and the medicines of Europe, had not changed. However, science was about to change virtually everything about the way we viewed the world and our place in it; everything except that which mattered the most to real people—how we conceived of disease and how it was treated.

The Beginnings of Modern Science

We live in an era of science, and it is difficult for us not to think about the path to this era as some kind of morality play in which ignorance is abolished and the "correct" way of looking at the world triumphs. We are taught to venerate the Great Men who made the Great Discoveries while vanquishing the small-minded men who stood in their way. It is true that science as we know it emerged from a very different worldview than ours, but we would be wise to remember that it was one that worked for a long time for the people who held it. To appreciate and understand our scientific society it is important that we have some understanding of what science replaced and why people were willing to change.

Surprisingly, we can start this version (and I must emphasize the fact that this is not the last word on the subject, chiseled into stone, but only a possible interpretation of events) of the origins of science with the poet Petrarch. In school we all learned about him as a bizarre figure, the inventor of the sonnet, who spent years composing love poems to a woman called Laura, whom he saw in church one day. This is an unfair and comic caricature of a figure of monumental importance in our intellectual history. Before his time (he lived between 1304 and 1374), scholars, who were primarily Churchmen, divided the history of the world into two periods—the "ancients" and the "modern." Of course, being clerics, they viewed everything in terms of the Church, so "*modern*" meant to them the Christian era. When Petrarch went to Rome to be coronated as poet laureate in 1341, he was awed by the sight of the remnants of the splendors of imperial Rome. The "stone and marble monuments stood as imperishable testimony to both the nobility of man and the majesty of his cultural and political achievements." The effect on him was profound, and he undertook to write a history in which he contrasted the grandeurs of the ancients with the period of darkness (*eta tenebrae*) that followed it. Consider what an amazing thing this was to do; by using the term *dark ages* to refer to the time from the conversion of Constantine (314) to his own day, he had turned around completely the accepted view that what preceded the Christian era was darkness! He was actually calling the early years of the Church the Dark Ages. The true modern period, he claimed, begins with a reawakening of the consciousness of the grandeur of Western civilization and the majesty of the *human* spirit. In a time when man was fallen and the human spirit was seen as base, the duty of man was to glorify God to achieve salvation. Yet here was a devout Christian and revered poet celebrating the nobility of *man* and his cultural achievements.

Following Petrarch's lead, the Renaissance humanists saw their time as a rebirth of human dignity and learning (*la rinàscita*) and distinguished it from the sterility of the preceding dark age. In this rebirth they turned with renewed purpose and enthusiasm to the works and thoughts of the ancients, especially Aristotle, Plato, Virgil, Cicero, and Ovid, not only for their beauty of expression but for their knowledge about statecraft and personal conduct. In these works they found a vision of man as a rational being, one who can put himself into harmony with the world. This view largely contrasted with the teaching of the Church, which held that man had lost rationality when he was cast out of Paradise and, because of his propensity to sin, needed God to live decently. But it is a mistake to see the Church as a monolith opposed to all of this; Thomas Aquinas (1225–74) in his *Summa Theologica* espoused a philosophy that was distinctly Aristotelian and the Thomist tradition was the basis of much of medieval Scholasticism. Nor were the Renaissance humanists carrying out an anti-Church campaign. Their lives, as were the lives of all who lived in the Renaissance, were permeated with religion. "All men's actions from birth to death were permanently controlled by religion; it regulated the smallest details of one's work, one's leisure, what one ate and how one lived; as surely as the church bells rang to signal prayers and offices, religion regulated the rhythms of human life."

It was this very centrality of the Church that began to change during the Renaissance, and without that change it is hard to imagine the Scientific Revolution. Arguably, the most important change brought about by the Renaissance was the idea of progress. By turning their attention to the grandeur of the civilizations humans had brought about, and by beginning to think that they had the ability to change the world, people began to envision the idea of purposeful change. Without this, there could have been no science.

The secularization that was going on in the Renaissance can be seen in the differences between two of the great canonical works of the fourteenth century, Dante's *Divine Comedy* (1307) and Boccaccio's *Decameron* (approx. 1350). Dante centers his poem on the soul's search for salvation and union with God, while Boccaccio's "human comedy" shows a world in which the plan and design of God is no longer clear and man is left to his own resources to find meaning and purpose in the world. Interestingly, it is the plague ravaging Boccaccio's world that provides the reason for his characters to come together, perhaps signifying the disintegration of the old world to make way for the emergence of the new.

Two hundred years later, Machiavelli pursued the same theme of secularization in *The Prince* (1532). All that most of us know about Machiavelli is that he was Machiavellian, a man who urged ruthless and unprincipled actions to achieve personal goals. This is also a caricature. In *The Prince* he argued that the wise ruler must recognize that Fortune and Necessity, not Divine Providence, determine the conditions under which men must live. Only when there are leaders who are not encumbered by the outmoded notions of virtue expounded by the Church will political order be restored and maintained. In other words, *The Prince* is really a plea for the further secularization of human affairs. Machiavelli has little to say about salvation or the role of God in secular affairs; religion is significant only if it inspires people to serve the state and thus helps the prince maintain social order. In two hundred years we see the movement from a gulf between human understanding of God's plan for the world to a view that man must control the world created by God.

The Renaissance humanists were fascinated with the systems and categories of nature they found in the classical texts. But when they turned their attention to nature itself, they slowly realized that much of the classification was incorrect. Aristotle might be fine for defining how people should govern themselves, but he was of little use in understanding nature.

Now it became important to see nature through one's own eyes, not just as it was written about by the ancients. In 1532 in *Gargantua*, Rabelais is instructed by his teacher, Ponocrates, in the natural sciences, geometry, and the full range of the world, but his education was not of the world as written in books but the world as it was . . . "as they walked through the meadows, or other grassy places, they examined the trees and the plants, comparing them with the descriptions in the books of such ancients as Dioscorides, Mariunus, Pliny, Nicander, Macer, and Galen; and they brought back whole handfuls to the house." It is clear that this idea—that what is learned by examining nature can be used to change nature—was the logical extension of the intellectual changes we have been talking about, and it is in this fusion of what was being learned about the world and the means of changing it that we find the beginnings of science as we understand the term.

In our contemporary thought we seldom distinguish between science and technology. The media treat the launching of a rocket and the discovery of the nature of our genetic material as equal triumphs of science, when in fact one is a triumph of technology. The fact is that while many of our technological advances are founded on scientific advances, many of our scientific advances are dependent on technological advances and any social analysis of the proper use of technology in modern society that does not recognize the complex relationship between the two is doomed from the start.

Science is a powerful way of examining the world, one that requires the observer to come to it with an open and inquiring mind. The word *science* derives from the Latin *scientia*, which means "knowledge." What we call science is a mode of thinking that came into practice because the idea that truth was written in Scripture or in the text of the ancients was put aside. Science uses experiment and rigorous logic to explain observed phenomena.

Clearly, science is based on the idea that the world is knowable. Technology is based on the idea that we can bring about purposeful change; it is knowledge that is applied. Even the origin of the word, from the Greek *techne*, for "art," shows the difference.

When science as we know it today began around 1600, as we have just seen, the ground had already been set for this kind of rigorous, systematic way of knowing as a powerful basis from which to achieve application. Science became the way of gaining knowledge and understanding on which to base technology, so the two are linked but distinctly separate endeavors.

Around 1600 "the English intellectual was more than half medieval and around 1660 he was more than half modern." It is against this backdrop of change, starting with Francis Bacon and ending with Newton, that modern science took form. England began its change from an agricultural to an industrial society under the rule of Elizabeth (1558–1603), and by the sixty years after 1575, it had become the leading European country in mining and heavy industries. In the hundred years after 1550, the number of heavy ships the English used for commerce increased ten times, and coal production rose ten thousandfold! English wool had always been sent to Flanders to be turned into cloth, but now weavers were to be found in every town and village, making the cloth that the merchants would sell throughout Europe. The first colonies in America were founded and English pirates, along with the trading fleets, were regularly bringing wealth back to the nation. A society like this needed a religion that favored the power of humans to control their destiny, and as a contemporary religious text stated, "It is for action that God maintaineth us and our activities, work is the moral as well as the natural end of power." The religion of England, reformed under Henry VIII and guided by his daughter Elizabeth, provided the perfect setting for the flourishing of technology and commerce. This was the secularized England in which the thinking of Francis Bacon (1561–1626) was formed, and while he never made any scientific discoveries, he was crucial in establishing an awareness of the importance of scientific research to the economic needs of society and the need for organized scientific collaboration to attain them. Bacon saw the need for the fusion of *scientia* and *techne*, and his writings provided the foundation for attaining that fusion for the greater good of commerce and warfare.

Given this fusion, the view that to be completely educated a person had to study the works of artisans gained increasing popularity in the sixteenth and seventeenth centuries. Work that had been thought to be beneath the dignity of gentlemen and scholars began to be viewed as work that was necessary for the progress of knowledge. With the rise of the merchant class, the ideas that "artisans are considered ignoble persons" and that "that which is base and despicable is commonly called mechanical" became outmoded, associated with "pedants" and bookish learning, which led to nothing practical and was therefore of no value. And pedantic learning which held that *scientia* was knowing only for its own sake, came under double attack from those who were moving to secularize society, as well as those who wanted to put that knowledge to use in the expansion of industry and commerce. It is no accident that there appeared at this time numerous treatises praising the contribution of the mechanical arts to knowledge.

New worlds were literally being discovered and industry was opening new opportunities for ingenuity. The philosophy of progress that replaced Aristotle's was not just a readjustment of classical views. It was genuinely *new*. The titles of Bacon's *New Organon*, Kepler's *New Astronomy*, and Galileo's *Two New Sciences* should be taken at face value: They were consciously new ways of looking at the physical world. Bacon wrote that

Aristotle had "corrupted natural philosophy by his logic...imposing countless other arbitrary restrictions on the nature of things; being always more solicitous to provide an answer to the question and affirm something positive in words, than about the inner truth of things." The "new philosophers" believed that the book of nature was there to be read directly.

Bacon and his contemporaries called this change in ideas the New Philosophy; it is what we call science. In our periodization of history the fulfillment of this change is called the Scientific Revolution, and historian Herbert Butterfield thinks that it is the most important thing to happen since the time of the ancients.

> [It] changed the character of men's habitual mental operations even in the conduct of non-material sciences; while transforming the whole diagram of the physical universe and the very texture of human life itself, it looms so large as the real origin both of the modern world and of the modern mentality that our customary periodisation of European history has become an anachronism and an encumbrance.

Indeed, the "new philosophy" of science changed our view of ourselves and of our world. But as important as this is, it is not why people are so vitally interested in science. If the idea of a fixed world had not begun to disappear, the new mode of thinking would not have been able to convince people that they could now *change* the world because of their new understanding. Science would have remained just another philosophical school that touched the lives of very few people, and there would be no more interest in science by the general public than there is in the philosophy of Aristotle or Michel Foucault. But of course science has not been just another school of philosophy; it has been a major force in the changes we have made in the world through technology, its application.

In 1662, Charles II conferred a charter on a society formed two years earlier by a group of learned men for "the promoting of experimentall [sic] philosophy." The Royal Society, as it would be called, met regularly to put into practice the primary tenet of the new way of thinking: careful examination of the world and the devising of experiments to learn more about it. The physicist Robert Boyle, with his experiments using air pumps, led the way for like-minded intellectuals, but not without opposition. Many English and Continental philosophers were committed to maintaining the traditional "natural philosophy" as a way of looking at the world and were highly critical of the new philosophy and of experiments as a way of producing physical knowledge. The experimentalist's worldview was in many ways counterintuitive to the minds of most people in Restoration England, but the protection and encouragement of the newly reestablished monarch outweighed the opposition.

We know a great deal about the earliest days of modern science because we know a great deal about the early years of the Royal Society. As surprising as it might seem, the great diarist Samuel Pepys was a member, and his journals have given us as much insight into the early days of science as they have of the rest of Restoration London. The time span of Pepys's diaries (which he kept from January 1660 until May 1669) coincides closely with the first decade of the Royal Society. Pepys, of course, was not a scientist but a gentleman and man about town and was also the Clerk of the Acts of the Navy; he knew everyone and everything that happened in London. To understand how our ideas of science have changed from these early days of the Royal Society's founding, realize that Pepys was considered a very well-educated man of his time, having been to St. Paul's and Magdalene College, Cambridge. His education was not much different from that of John Milton, who had graduated from St. Paul's twenty-five years before, an education that placed great emphasis on Grammar, Logic, and Rhetoric (the so-called trivium). But Pepys, like most of his well-educated and influential contemporaries, could not do simple arithmetic because this was still considered a Mechanical study and beneath the dignity of a gentleman. When in his role of clerk of the navy he realized that the king was being cheated out of great sums of money by shipbuilders, he had to hire a tutor so that he could learn to add, subtract, multiply, and divide to save the crown's money.

Like many of the early intellectuals, Pepys was a collector; he collected books, pictures, ballads, and scientific instruments, along with the gossip of London. This was part of the fervor of practitioners of the new philosophy, satirically called *virtuosi*: to organize, categorize, and understand as much as they could about the world. Pepys, along with many of the *virtuosi*, could not grasp the abstractions of the experiments of Boyle or the mathematics of Newton, but he did grasp the underlying idea of organized thinking and framing of the world. And medicine was one of the things that fascinated the *virtuosi* the most.

The question that we are interested in is how all of this "new philosophy" affected medicine and the manner in which physicians and other healers actually dealt with sick people. The general answer is that there was little effect during the *longue durée*, and while, like all generalizations, this answer glosses over all of the complications and subtleties, it has enough resemblance to what most scholars agree upon that we can feel comfortable with it. The complications come from our natural tendency to give modern definitions to terms whose meanings have changed over the years. We use the term *physician* to mean one who practices *medicine* and we all know what both terms mean, but in the period we are discussing, these terms had different meanings. Medicine comes from the Latin verb *medico*, which means "to drug" or "to dye" (recall the origin of the word *infection*!), while *physician* comes from the Greek verb *phusis*, which means "nature," and in the early modern period the terms conformed more closely to the practice. In that time physicians studied natural philosophy because the purpose of "physic" was to preserve health and prolong life; healing was only a small part of what they did. Physicians' education at Oxford or Cambridge involved little if any clinical training; the important thing was to "learne thy philosophy exactlie wherin consist the knowledge of man, the prime subject of medecin." When they received their doctor-of-medicine degree, it signified that they were learned men who knew a great deal of natural philosophy as well as Latin, some Greek, and a great deal of moral philosophy. So it is not surprising that many physicians actually feared that the growth of the "new philosophy" would lead to an emphasis on cures and medicines rather than learned advice. And of course we must remember that the terms *science* and *natural philosophy* were also changing as the relationship between *scientia* and *techne* changed.

A sixteenth-century philosopher, mystic, alchemist, chemist, physician, and general pain in the neck to the establishment named Paracelsus led what can only be thought of as a popular uprising against the medical establishment. Its effects lasted well into the seventeenth century before they began to fade. Born in Switzerland as Theophrastus Bombastus von Hohenheim in the 1490s, Paracelsus strongly opposed the principles of Galenic medicine, arguing that healers should use specific remedies for specific diseases. It is tempting to see the roots of modern medicine, which is based on specificity, here, but while Paracelsus came to many of the same conclusions scientists would come to a few centuries later, his reasons for arriving at them were different. The reasons his ideas did not displace Galenic medicine are complicated, uncertain, and beyond the scope of what we are looking at. Nevertheless, his ideas had a very large popular following for many years, due in no small part to the fact that he wrote and lectured in German rather than Latin, and make us realize that in the early years of modern science medicine was not ignored. One scholar has argued that Shakespeare's *All's Well That Ends Well* is an argument for the medical theory and practice of Paracelsus, and he has been one of the most studied of early physicians, alchemists, philosophers. But his ideas did not last long.

W ith secularization, physicians began to perform dissections on human corpses and saw that the anatomical speculations of Aristotle were often fanciful and that Galen's anatomy (which had been derived from the dissection of animals) was often wrong. The year 1543 was significant not only because Copernicus opened the dialogue that would change our views of our place in the universe, but also because the greatest of early anatomists, Andreas Vesalius, published his magnificent human anatomy book.

But as we will see, the old ideas did not disappear in a flash. The anatomists were still struggling to reconcile a view of biology handed down from Aristotle, which taught them that the differences between men and women were differences of degree but not of kind. It had certainly not escaped anyone's notice that men and women appeared to be different on the outside, so what happened when Vesalius and the other anatomists began to look carefully at their insides? They saw the "proof" of the classical teaching. "The new anatomy displayed, at many levels and with unprecedented vigor the fact that the vagina really is a penis, and the uterus a scrotum." As the historian Thomas Laqueur says, for the anatomists "believing is seeing" and women are only men turned outside in.

A similar reluctance to supplant old theories with new learning is seen with the circulation of the blood as we see from the case of William Harvey, who in 1628 published the results of one of the most elegant and important scientific experiments ever performed in medicine and who is often called one of the founders of modern scientific medicine. Using living sheep, Harvey showed by experimental methods we easily recognize today as "scientific" that the total amount of blood that passed through the heart was almost equal to the total volume of blood in the animal. He concluded that either the animal had to be producing blood at an incredible rate or the existing blood was constantly being circulated through the heart and the blood vessels. This was science at its best, but it also fit nicely with the Galenic view of humors because it provided a mechanism for the humors to be distributed through the body so that even when the new scientists believed what they saw, the framework in which they saw it enabled them to arrive at very different interpretations than we do.

While the Royal Society spent much time and had great interest in things medical, the fascination of these earliest scientists with medicine is a far cry from what we would consider scientific medicine. A quick look at how Robert Boyle, the leading experimentalist of his day, approached health and disease in the early days of modern science will illustrate. During the middle of the seventeenth century, amulets were a valued cure for a broad variety of diseases. A typical amulet, fabricated at the proper phase of the moon, was worn around the neck or from the wrist and might contain "pulverized toads and specified quantities of the first menstrual blood of young maidens, white arsenic, orpiment, dittany roots, pearls, corals, and oriental emeralds." Such amulets were thought to work because they were natural, and natural substances, when prepared under astrologically sympathetic conditions, extract venom from the body and revivify the disturbed spirits.

Robert Boyle, who described himself as being of a frail and weak constitution, claimed that he had been cured of fevers by amulets. This first great experimenter did not question the efficacy of the cures but took the trouble to explain how they worked. The material from the amulets, he was sure, entered the bloodstream via the capillaries close to the skin, and though he thought it to be reasonable for a philosopher living before Harvey's discovery about the circulation of blood to have doubts about amulets, because of Harvey's discoveries he thought it was indefensible for any contemporary to do so.

One of Boyle's contemporaries, who had decided that the elaborate recipe in a popular toad amulet said to cure the plague was too complex, wanted the "Ingenious fellows" of the Royal Society to perform experiments on his simplified version. He had made the remarkable discovery, he told them, that "a toads pisse is so hot yt it will scorche a glove whereon it falls as a live coale would doe," and thought that perhaps toad urine and dung were potent enough to produce by themselves the desired cure and prevention of the plague. In this bizarre case we see that "an Oxford-educated cleric and English provincial gentleman" was being more scientific than the great Robert Boyle.

These examples of how scientists see the world in the terms in which it has been framed are of central importance in understanding the nature of scientific progress even today and we will return to it when we look at what we should reasonably expect from scientific medicine.

J ust as Boyle and the physicists used the "new philosophy" to explore the physical world by experiments, in Holland a rich merchant named Anton van Leeuwenhoek (pronounced *lew*-ven-hook) did the same thing for the invisible biological world by inventing the microscope. When he ground his lenses and examined ordinary objects, he saw small moving particles everywhere. The usual version of events claims that he immediately realized that these otherwise invisible "things" were alive. If this is true, it is quite amazing. Imagine yourself living in Delft in 1670. You know of the philosophical changes going on in the world (you even communicate regularly with the Royal Society in London), but you, like all of the leaders of the new philosophy, are a believing Christian. Your world has been defined for you by Scripture and the accepted secular thinking; you are willing to experiment and to read closely the "book of nature," but you and the rest of the new "scientists" are only doing so to see the workings of the hand of God. What is there to make you for one moment believe that these little things you see are living? But amazingly, after a while Leeuwenhoek began to think that his microscopic discoveries might indeed be alive, and he called them animalcules. Anyone who has ever looked into a microscope without being able to make sense of what he is seeing until he was told what he was look-ing at can appreciate what a creative leap of the mind this represented.

Leeuwenhoek was a true man of the new philosophy. "After various trials made now and then toward the possibility of discovering the strength or hotness which pepper brings to one's tongue . . . I then put anew about ⅓ ounce of whole pepper in water. . . . I saw wherein with great wonder unbelievably very many small animalcules of various sorts; among others, some that were 3 to 4 times long as broad. Their entire thickness was, in my judgement, not much thicker than one of the little hairs that cover the body of a louse . . . there were more animals living in the scum on the teeth in a man's mouth than there are men in the whole kingdom." A physician friend gave him a sample of semen from a syphilitic patient, and what he saw moved him to examine normal semen. He wrote to the Royal Society that he had

> divers times examined the same matter [human semen] from a healthy man, not from a sick man, not spoiled by keeping for a long time and not liquified after the lapse of some time, but immediately after ejaculation before six beats of the pulse had intervened and I have seen so great a number of living animals in it that sometimes more than a thousand were moving about in an amount of material of the size of a grain of sand. . . .
>
> What I investigate is only what, without sinfully defiling myself, remains as a residue after conjugal coitus. And if your Lordships should consider that these observations may dis-gust or scandalize the learned, I earnestly beg your Lordships to regard them as private and to publish or destroy them, as your Lordship thinks fit.

The World as Seen by the Sufferer

But again it must be repeated: these sea changes in the world of government, politics, commerce, art, literature, and now sci-ence had not made any change in the conditions of life. Filth and odor pervaded everyone's life, and death, disease, and misery were still a constant presence. The well born might be adopting a new philosophy and examining the world with a new frame of mind, but most of their children still died young. What was the view of the world from the vantage of the sufferers of all of this disease (the Latin origin of the word *patient* is from "one who suffers")? What effect did knowing that the blood circulated and that there was an invisible, teeming, possibly living world have on the way they viewed their own health and disease and, perhaps even more importantly, on the way they were treated for their illnesses?

Historian Charles Rosenberg has addressed the question of how disease has been framed throughout history, and his colleague Roy Porter asks the question most of us are really interested in when we think of disease and medicine in a bygone era: "When people fell sick in 1660 or 1700, what did they do?" How disease was framed and how it was treated are two sides of the same question, because what is done about the sick person depends on the conception of what is wrong with him or her.

The affluent could consult a physician, a man with a university education and a gentlemanly bearing, who diagnosed, gave advice, and was in regular attendance. These were men of the same social class as their patients; they listened to their complaints, asked them questions and even their opinions about what ailed them and how it should be cured. But if there was a boil to be lanced, a wound to be cleaned, or a bone to be set, this was the job of the surgeon (sometimes called the "poor man's physician"). Surgeons and barbers, both adept at the arts of the knife, were members of the same guild (Barber Surgeons Company of London) from 1540 until they split in 1745 (perhaps because wigs came into fashion, thus reducing the business of barbering). Finally, there was the apothecary, the physician's underling, who dispensed what the physician prescribed. But the physician, it cannot be too strongly emphasized, could only prescribe what had been prescribed for a millennium: herbs, emetics, diuretics, bloodletting, and things perhaps too horrible to contemplate. There is every reason to believe that people were not surprised that the cure should be as harsh as the disease, since life itself could be almost as harsh as both.

In rural areas and among the poor everywhere, if a person trained in the healing arts was to be consulted, it was the surgeon or the apothecary. But most people didn't bother to seek the help of any trained healer, partly because of cost and partly out of conviction. In France, even at the end of the eighteenth century, the population practiced an enormous amount of self-medication. It also consulted quacks, bonesetters, and matrons, listened to ambulant charlatans, and followed the course of treatment prescribed by the sorcerer-healer of the village. Given what we have seen about medical practice by trained healers, one might ask how the average citizen could tell a "quack" from a doctor. *Quack*, according to the *Oxford English Dictionary*, derives from the word *quack-salver*, one who "quacks," or boasts, about the healing power of his salves. Physicians were gentlemen, and of course, a gentleman never boasts! Many people in England supplemented their income through medicine; grocers and peddlers sold drugs, blacksmiths and farriers pulled teeth and set bones, and well-meaning people and less well-meaning charlatans traveled the countryside dispensing "medicines" and brightly colored elixirs (recall Donizetti's *L'Elisir d'Amore*).

Most people practiced this kind of medicine out of neighborliness, good housekeeping, religion, or plain simple self-help. Every village had its wisewoman or nurse who was versed in herbal treatments, and the gentry prided themselves on treating their tenants, often out of sheer necessity, while their wives played "lady bountiful." There was also a fear of physicians and their harsh treatments. In 1464 Margaret Paston warned her husband, "for Goddys sake be war what medysysn ye take of any fysissyans of London," and Samuel Pepys, who was preoccupied with his own and everyone else's illness, didn't share Paston's morbid fear of physicians, but he supplemented physicians' visits with self-medication to be on the safe side. The actor David Garrick (1717–79) used doctors regularly, but it was natural for him to self-medicate and give advice to friends.

> I am sorry that you have been plagu'd with ye cursed Distemper, the Piles . . . live abstemiously for a little time, & take Every night a large tea spoonfull of flower of Brimstone (night & morning) mix'd up with honey or treacle, & you will be ye better for it . . . thank ye Stars for ye Piles—if you had not them, you would have gout, or Stone or both & ye Devil and While I had ye Piles, I had Nothing Else, now I am quit of them, I have Every other disorder.

So it is clear that while people were sick much more often than they are today, they were not "locked into relations with the medical profession" that we have come to think of as normal. The poor could not afford doctors, and the rich used them, but their knowledge of medicine was often on a par with physicians' understanding of it, and so they were apt to treat themselves. Widely read periodicals in the eighteenth century such as *Gentleman's Magazine,* regularly carried articles about medicine and healing, so that the wealthy often knew enough to demystify the knowledge possessed by their doctors.

Medical historians, in their newfound interest in medical practice as seen from the patient's point of view, have called this social setting in which medicine was practiced for so long *bedside medicine.* The physician, because he was dealing with the upper social strata, came to the bedside of the patients, where he talked with them, looked, touched, and smelled them in order to determine how best to reestablish their balance of humors. The poor may not have gotten as much solicitous attention, but even they got personal attention, especially in rural areas, where they were not as desperate as the urban poor. We arrogantly look back at the therapies that were used as benighted and ask how could people have allowed themselves to be subjected to the horrifying treatments of their day? Didn't they know they didn't work? It is all well and good for us to congratulate ourselves and our scientific medicine, but does this give us the right to demean the intelligence of people all the way back to Hippocrates and Galen? For them the medicine of their time worked as well as much of the medicine of our time works for us. We must realize that there were different *expectations* from medicine. Technology and science had not yet intruded into the relationship between healer and sick person, and the human level of interaction left little reason to expect anything but outcomes fraught with very forgivable human failings.

Using the senses, the physician could measure only "intake and outgo." So perspiration, urination, menstruation, defecation, appetite, fever, and pulse rate were the signs that defined both the diseases and treatments. The fact that therapeutics had not changed significantly during almost two millennia prior to 1800 meant that physicians, patients, and the families of the patients were in general agreement about the importance of these signs. Could there be much doubt that raising or lowering the temperature, starting or stopping defecation, the letting of blood, and the application of leeches were treatments that would bring the humors of the body back into their proper alignment? It was often necessary to use harsh treatments because, according to one student of the subject, it was necessary for all concerned—the patient, the physician, and the family—to see the *effect* of the treatment. There could be no mistaking the fact that the blood was being thinned; after all, it was there to see with one's own eyes. It was essential for all to know that the physician was making an earnest, often heroic, attempt to reestablish balance, and therefore health. Treatment was not specific because diseases were not specific. In fact, "the advocacy of a specific drug in treating a specific ill was ordinarily viewed by regular physicians as a symptom of quackery."

If we take a long hard look at most of our science-based modern therapies, it might not be a good idea to bet money on what people five hundred years from now will think of our "advanced" drugs. Anyone who has sat through the last days of a loved one undergoing chemotherapy must have great faith in the philosophical system that calls the failing treatment a "therapy" and congratulates the doctors who administer it and the scientists who discovered it. The same is true for people who were treated before the scientification of medicine.

In the era of bedside medicine "every part of the body was related inevitably and inextricably with every other. A distracted mind could curdle the stomach, a dyspeptic stomach could agitate the mind. Local lesions might reflect imbalances of nutrients in the blood; systemic ills might be caused by fulminating local lesions.... Where empirical observations pointed unavoidably toward the existence of a particular disease state, physicians still sought to preserve their accustomed therapeutic role. The physician's most potent weapon was his ability to regulate the secretions— to extract blood, to promote the perspiration, urination, or defecation, which attested to his having helped the body to regain its customary equilibrium." Anyone could see that the body under normal circumstances was always readjusting its equilibrium "by belching, breaking wind, and ingestion and inhalation." So the efficacy of a therapy was measured by its visible effect. The role of the physician was to decide how best to reestablish equilibrium, and if the purges, emetics, and opium did not work, it showed the ultimate power of God. In the words of a pious mid-nineteenth-century American physician coming to terms with the death of a child:

> The child seemed perfectly well, till it was attacked at the tea table. Remedies, alth' slow in their action, acted well, but were powerless to avert the arm of death. The decrees of Providence . . . cannot be set aside. Man is mortal, & tho' remedies often seem to act promptly and effectually to the saving of life—they often fail in an accountable manner! "So teach me to number my days that I may apply my heart to wisdom."

For all practical purposes, Galen and the gentleman physician of eighteenth century London or Paris treated patients virtually the same way. We would do well to remember that the ideas of science and the doctrinal debates of doctors through *la longue durée* had little (if any) effect on either the amount of disease that real people suffered or the way healers dealt with that disease. This era of bedside medicine did in fact come to an end, but only with the Enlightenment and French Revolution, at the end of the eighteenth century.

Chapter

3

The Seeds of Change

We live in a century that has raised science and technology to the level of a secular religion, and our intuition tells us that the seeds of this belief should be readily seen in history. But as we have just seen, when we do look, what we see is that for over two thousand years little changed in the most fundamental of human concerns—our health and physical well-being—and it was often unexpected things that brought about the changes when they did occur.

It certainly runs counter to the intuition of one trained in the sciences, as I am, to think that the French Revolution may have played a greater role in changing medical practice than any scientific discovery. Like all scientists, I was taught to believe that science is "value-free," and that it drives the changes in society. And yet we have just seen that acceptance of the idea that the blood circulates through the body as scientific truth did not alter the way patients were treated. Indeed, the "scientific truth" only gave more credence to the "intuitive truth" that the humors had to have a way of getting to the solid parts of the body. In the era of the new philosophy of science, if a physician needed a scientific basis for bloodletting, he now had it! Being social equals made physician and patient virtual healing equals, so the subtle fact that the blood circulated did nothing to change their ideas of therapy—because even if the physician did think this new fact might lead to a new therapy, he didn't dare jeopardize his relationship with paying customers and social equals by turning them into guinea pigs. It took more than a new concept of science to change this relationship.

Enlightenment, Revolution, and "Hospital Medicine"

The French called the eighteenth century the *siècle de lumière,* "the century of light," because of the flowering of the idea that human reason and intelligence would illuminate the path to knowledge and progress. When Immanuel Kant, the German metaphysician, was asked in 1785 if he believed he lived in an "enlightened age," he answered: "No, we are living in an age of enlightenment," the term by which the age has become known. The thinkers who formed the Enlightenment (note the capital letter!) were in fact only a loose coalition of privileged men whose sole area of agreement was secularism and the insistence on the freedom to question even the most ingrained assumptions of their time. The advent of the new philosophy of science a century earlier opened a new way of looking at the world, one that insisted on testing ideas, not relying on accepted wisdom handed down from the past; and although only a few of the men of the Enlightenment were scientists, they were all moved by the desire to question and test everything, from the purely scientific to the social. To them, the social order was as proper to examine with the new philosophy as was the physical order. They called themselves *philosophes,* a term that has no English equivalent and can only be rendered as "philosophers," but they really saw themselves as "enlighteners."

The *philosophes* trampled on the accepted prejudices, traditions, and authority. "Everything must be shaken up, without exception and without circumspection," said Diderot, the creator of the great *Encyclopédie des Arts, Sciences et Métiers,* published between 1751 and 1772. Establishing the conditions for questioning, recording the information to be used to draw conclusions rather than accepting the received wisdom of either church or state, was to be the great legacy of the Enlightenment. Building on the new philosophy of science from the seventeenth century, the eighteenth-century *philosophes* posited experience and experiment as the bases for true knowledge and human advancement.

The social program of the Enlightenment was based on the belief that since there were no fixed ideas, people could change their environment by *understanding* everything, a belief that reached its zenith in the monumental *Encyclopédie.* The purpose of collecting and explaining knowledge was to "hand it down to those who follow us, so that the labor of centuries past may not become lost for the centuries to follow." For the first time, an idea of social progress separate from the Christian apocalyptic view of man's pilgrimage on earth, as an education from sin to purity and rewards in the life to follow, had a hold on an influential segment of a population in the West. Granted, the pilgrim's progress was more direct than the *philosophes'*, but they meant to show that the difficult secular road was possible. As they constantly questioned everything except the ability of the human mind, they did not hope for utopian progress—there would be balances and trade-offs, a law of compensation that d'Alembert, the co-editor of the *Encyclopédie*, called "the misery of the human condition." Voltaire called life a "shipwreck," the world "a miserable pile of mud," and history a "depressing tale," while predicting a profound and beneficial triumph from the inevitable victory of philosophy!

We tend to think of the Enlightenment as a French phenomenon because of the association of the *philosophes* with the French Revolution of 1789, but the movement was truly a European one. For the purposes of our narrative about the interaction of science, society, and changes in the patient's worldview and the medical practices of physicians, we will focus on Paris, where a major revolution in medicine would occur and where by the second half of the eighteenth century, many of the *philosophes* were physicians. It is of course too simplistic to say that the Enlightenment was responsible for the French Revolution, but it "certainly helped to create a situation in which ideological loyalty to the old regime was steadily and almost entirely eroded." The old regime was not only the political regime but the social and medical regimes as well. The shadow of the Enlightenment has been seen by many in the Reign of Terror that followed the Revolution, but as we will now see, it can also be seen in the revolution in medical practice initiated in France after the Revolution. A quarter of a century later, it can be seen again in the revolution in sanitation in England: Both were changes that had profound effects on health. The point to remember is that the profound changes that so altered how we frame health and disease and what we expect from medicine were driven by changes in society. Only later would medicine become scientific. At the start of the nineteenth century, social developments were the engine driving the changes in medical practice and the general improvement in health we automatically associate with scientific medicine. One aim of the French Revolution was to give medical care to all citizens, and to do this meant that the hospitals had to be changed from repositories of society's outcasts to places where ordinary citizens could be treated. Historians see the French Revolution as the start of what they call "hospital medicine," the mode of practice that replaced "bedside medicine."

Hospitals have a long history in human civilization and tell us a good deal about how we have looked at people and their illnesses through time. For example, the plans for the equivalent of a hospital in the fifth century B.C. at Pergamon, the site of the sanctuary of the healing god Asclepius and the birthplace of Galen, still exist. From them scholars have been able to deduce a great deal about the way the sick were treated in that time and place. The main feature was a long room, open along one of its long walls, oriented toward the sun, with pillars through which the patients could see the temple. This main "treatment room" was a place where the attendant priests converted the *dreams of the patients into therapeutic regimens.* True, there were sacrifices, bed rest, baths, exercise, and perhaps attention to the patient's diet, but this was chiefly a place where the therapeutic word of the gods was interpreted through the dreams of the patient. If the patient was too sick to be there himself, he could send a surrogate to dream his dreams for him.

The Romans set up hospitals for sick and wounded soldiers throughout the empire. These consisted of light and airy rooms with courtyards, good plumbing, and a remarkable amount of privacy, a commodity that even most well-born Romans did not have. This treatment shows us that soldiers were valuable to the Romans (remember that Galen's first job was as physician to the gladiators, who were also valuable property). We don't really know what kind of therapies were given in these institutions, but there is no reason to suppose it was anything other than the accepted Hippocratic and Galenic medicine of the time, with perhaps some religion thrown into the mix.

The word *hospital* comes to us from the Latin word *hospes,* which means "guest" or "host," and the hospital as we know it comes from Scripture, specifically the Christian "acts of mercy": "For I was hungered, and ye gave me meat: I was thirsty, and ye gave me drink: I was a stranger, and ye took me in: naked, and ye clothed me: I was sick, and ye visited me: I was in prison, and ye came unto me" (Matt. 25:35–36). Early Christian hospitals were places where these acts of mercy could be carried out, repositories for all of kinds of social relief to the aged, infirm, dying, diseased, wounded, blind, crippled, and insane. Orphans, paupers, wanderers, and pilgrims could all be served in the same structure, and the more miserable the sufferer, the greater glory to the giver of the charity. Many of the earliest hospitals were set up along the routes taken by pilgrims, who were almost by definition sick, having undertaken a long journey as a form of penance, wearing sackcloth and, occasionally, pebbles in their shoes while traveling over primitive roads through strange lands with new diseases.

Through the Middle Ages the monasteries served as infirmaries and centers for healing, their gardens the source of healing herbs and the monks an important source of medical knowledge and care. In time, as population and urbanization increased, hospitals moved to the secular world of the cities, but they still housed the same mixture of miserable souls. While retaining their character as places of religion, where the salvation of the soul of the poor wretch was often more important than healing his or her body, they became death traps and hotbeds of infection.

But slowly the characteristics we know in our modern hospitals began to emerge. In eighteenth-century England, for example, an increasing number of hospitals were run by the state to serve the "deserving poor"—working-class people who were able to secure a letter from an upper-class sponsor attesting to their good character and financial plight. These were mostly young people suffering from non-life-threatening ailments, for whom coming to the hospital was often a welcome relief from the soiled garments, wretched living quarters, and deficient diets they knew at home. In France the tradition of the hôtel-Dieu went back to medieval times as an institution that took in the sick and abandoned but excluded the incurable or those suffering from venereal diseases. The conditions of the French hospitals at the time of the Revolution (1794) were appalling.

> The general policy of the Hotel Dieu—policy caused by the lack of space—is to put as many beds as possible into one room and to put four, five, or six people into one bed. We have seen the dead mixed with the living there. We have seen rooms so narrow that the air stagnates and is not renewed and

> that light enters only feebly and charged with vapors. We have
> seen the convalescents together with the sick, the dying, and
> the dead, forced to go barefoot to the bridge in summer and
> winter when they want fresh air.

The conditions in the hôtel-Dieu are horrid to read about, but what they tell us about European life at the eve of the French Revolution is even more horrid. The life of the common person was as miserable as it had always been. When we read about the Revolution, we read about Robespierre, Marat, and Sade; only in fiction do we get some insight into the suffering of the common people. The Revolution may not have been caused by the *philosophes* of the Enlightenment and they may not have been thinking about those wretched souls in the hôtel-Dieu when they wrote their high-flown talk about progress, but the common people finally had their say, at least about health care and hospitals, after the Reign of Terror.

The revolutions in the British colonies in 1776 and the revolution in France in 1794 together signaled a change in the way ordinary people looked at themselves in relation to the state. But the change was brought about with blood. "While banks of roses perfumed the air at one end of Paris, puddles of blood contaminated it at the other end." In 1794, the guillotine was so busy in the rue Saint-Antoine, where it had been moved from the place de la Revolution, that the local residents complained about the "mephitic odors" from the bodies rotting in the June heat. On July 28, Robespierre, the tyrant himself, "was thrust onto the plank by Sanson, blood smeared over his coat and blotching his nankeen breeches. To give the blade of the guillotine an unobstructed fall, the executioner tore away the paper bandage that had been holding his jaw together [after a botched suicide attempt the night before]. Animal screams of pain escaped, silenced only by the falling blade."

The Reign of Terror was over, but in the zeal that had led to it, the National Convention suppressed all corporations and faculties as part of its plan to abolish all the hated bastions of privilege and oppression. This included both the faculty of medicine and the hospitals! Since one of the social changes driving the society to the turmoil of Thermidor was the desire for health care for all, this was an action that could not have come at a worse time. The ordinary people who had converted themselves into a murderous mob wanted to change the way medical care was parceled out to the poor and would no longer tolerate horror chambers such as the hôtel-Dieu, but they wanted *something*. The system had been demolished, and clearly it now had to be rebuilt. In that process of the rebuilding, both the system of health-care delivery and the training of doctors were reformed, a change that would have far-reaching effects on how medicine is practiced.

The first significant change in the Paris hospitals was to put only one patient in a bed. Of course this meant smaller beds and more beds crowded into the existing space, but nevertheless it was a beginning of social change in which the health and welfare facilities of the country were to be extended to the poor. Of equal interest is the not-so-obvious effect this admirable goal had in changing the relationship between doctor and patient. We have already seen that doctors and patients were of similar social classes, and because medical knowledge was not arcane, the well-to-do were active participants in their own treatment. It was really a system of patronage in which the patient, and not the doctor, determined the conditions in which medical service was rendered. Under the new plan, it was not the social outcasts and refuse of society who would be treated in the hospital, but ordinary working people, for whom the state now provided medical services. There was no possibility that the patient would be the patron in this new system of *hospital medicine*.

Unfortunately, the conditions in the hospitals improved only slightly, so that even by 1836 Florence Nightingale complained that hospitals did not meet the minimal requirements of doing no harm to the sick. The patients in the new hospitals were not used to the same living conditions as the wealthy, who had been patrons of their doctors; these ordinary people came from homes as crowded and rank as the hospitals into which they were crammed. They were accustomed to seeing people urinating, defecating, and having sexual intercourse, and the need for what we consider proper sanitary conditions was alien to them, as it was to most of society at the beginning of the nineteenth century. The poor were now treated by doctors in the hospitals, but according to an English observer of the Parisian hospitals in 1843, the patients were never allowed to forget their social place. They were "always required to conduct themselves in an orderly and respectful manner; they are aware on entering the hospital that they must comply, unhesitatingly, with [the doctors'] advice, and abide by the directions of the medical officers; if the slightest difficulty occurs they are immediately discharged."

The second crucial change brought about by the Revolution was in the training of physicians. In the law of *14 Frimaire an III* (December 4, 1794) three new "schools" (not faculties) of health (not medicine) were created. Students and faculty alike would be chosen through open examinations, and the students would come from all over France, not just urban centers, so that physicians would now be a more representative cross-section of French society. An even more crucial change was bringing together the training of physicians and of surgeons—the "poor man's physician"—for the first time. What may appear a minor and even logical academic reform was neither. Surgeons were of a lower social status (although they often made much more money than physicians) and were anxious to gain the prestige of being associated with the physicians, people with whom they had up to now had little in common professionally. After all, surgeons dealt with *localized* disturbances in the body such as boils, abscesses, and accessible tumors. Physicians, who had great social prestige, were willing to share some of it with the less prestigious surgeons if they could make more money by the association. What the surgeon did was professionally alien to them because as physicians they dealt with disease as a *generalized* phenomenon: the humors went throughout the body and their job was to reestablish the general balance. Social revolution forced them together. This seemingly subtle change was crucial for the rise of surgical pathology, the correlation of the sick patient's symptoms with the lesions in his organs at autopsy. The Parisian hospitals became places where for the first time the symptoms of many patients could be seen by many physicians and the physical lesions responsible for their diseases could be examined after their death. A new "road map" of the body came about, one that was intelligible to both the physician and the surgeon.

This was the atmosphere that allowed medicine to begin to become scientific. Until now, all of the debate by anatomists about the role of the humors and the solid organs in the body had been of little practical importance because patronage had essentially given patients veto power over the therapies they would receive. Furthermore, a single physician saw only a few patients and so had no way of correlating his diagnosis and treatment with the physical lesions in the person he was treating. Now the hospitals were filled with compliant patients, the physicians and surgeons were becoming united in their view of the "landscape of disease," and all the while, a religious belief in the value of science was in the air.

The bad news is that in the process, the common people became not *patients with diseases* but *subjects of disease*. A group of science-minded doctors in Paris began to take advantage of the fact that there were so many patients being treated in one place and started to compile systematic records of the symptoms of the patients in the hospital and the autopsy results after their death. The well-born private patient had been *observed;* the poor hospital patient was *examined* both when alive and dead; the subject (the "sick man") was turned into the object. In bedside medicine, the patient was an individual with individual symptoms; in the new hospital medicine, the patient was only one of many with this or that set of symptoms, an example of disease.

The proximity of the deathbed (and remember, mortality rates in the hospitals were very high) and the autopsy table worked to bring closer together the symptoms of the living patients and the lesions in their organs after death. The craze for statistics in the nineteenth century could be easily met, and the state helped. In the Paris hospitals the *Conseil Général d'Aministration* was responsible for providing a decent burial for anyone dying in the hospitals, but if the relatives did not claim the body and the 60 francs the state provided for burial within twenty-four hours, the body became the property of the administration and was immediately sent to the dissecting room. Until as late as 1840 each practitioner had the right to perform the autopsy on his own patients, so the connection between the symptoms and the lesions were now regularly seen by the same person.

What was the effect of all of this social change on medical practice? The solid parts of the body were being examined after death and the lesions correlated with the symptoms and treatment during life, but in fact therapy and outcome changed hardly at all. Disease was still thought of as an imbalance of humors. The imbalance might cause a change in the liver, lung, or kidneys, but the therapeutic strategy was still to reestablish the balance of humors. In 1833, well into the era of "hospital medicine," over 40 million leeches were imported into France for bloodletting, the infant mortality rate was almost unchanged, and the medical lot of the average person was not significantly improved. The structural organization of the medical care delivery system and the professional organization of the medical profession were changed, but the medical treatment of the sick changed little. Nor did the constant presence of death.

As we will now see, the changes that really had an effect on the lives of people were not coming from the growth of science, the professionalization of medicine, or the growth of hospital medicine. They were coming from industrialization and the social changes that led to improvements in housing, diet and, above all, sanitation.

Edwin Chadwick and the Sanitation Movement

The French Revolution and the Reign of Terror changed forever the character and social structures of France. The character and social structure of England was changed permanently during the Industrial Revolution, which lasted roughly from the middle of the seventeenth to the middle of the nineteenth century. Factories began to replace traditional handwork as the means of production of goods; water and steam replaced hand power, resulting in, arguably, the greatest change in the role of human labor in the production of goods in the history of the world. In a little over a century, England was transformed from an agricultural society into an urban, industrial one, because the factories became magnets for labor in the cities. The population of England more than doubled, going from 4.9 million to 13.3 million between 1680 and 1830 (a period that historians call the long eighteenth century). This rise in population was not due to a decline in infant mortality or increase in life span; surprisingly, it was due to an increase in fertility, the number of children born to each mother. The average age of death changed only from 32.4 years to only 38.7, and historians and demographers still do not agree on the causes for the increase in fertility. One fascinating theory by a scholar aptly named Abelove has it that changes in the productivity of the labor that came about during industrialization caused changes in productivity in sexual practices. He argues that as society became geared to production and efficiency in work (more product per working hour), so too sex became geared to production of children (more children per unit of intercourse). As intriguing as this notion is, it does not account for the fact that the population of the entire world began to rise at about the same time.

As people were attracted to cities, the combination of increasing population and urban crowding was ideal for the spread of infectious diseases. The countryside had always been known to be healthier than the cities, and so it is not surprising that the great population increase was in rural England, which sent much of its growing population to the cities to die. "Crowded together in such filthy environments, every city dweller was inevitably exposed to infection every day of his life. It is no wonder that the population of cities through all history has had to be recruited periodically from the country. Few cities were ever able to maintain their population by their reproduction, but the attraction of gregarious life has always been sufficient to bring a constant stream of the ambitious from the healthier, because less densely populated, countryside." By 1851 half of the population of England was urban, but what unimaginable hell that urban life was.

There was growing awareness in England that the health of the laboring poor was a social as well as an economic problem. As a legacy of the Enlightenment, some members of the upper classes in Victorian England were committed to social reform, not because they believed in the social equality of all people, but because they believed that the well born, by virtue of their social position, have an obligation to change social institutions to make life better for the poor. The idea that equality of society should be a social goal was unthinkable to the vast majority of both rich and poor. The fact that there was a growing need for the poor to work in the factories of the rapidly industrializing cities made the problem all the more urgent. One group of social reformers was interested in changing the sanitary conditions of the poor as a means of reducing the appalling death rate among the working class. The fact that the gentry lived on average to forty-three years of age, tradesmen to thirty, and laborers to only twenty-two (remember, these numbers are from 1840, not 1340!) suggested to them that either the upper classes were inherently healthier than their social inferiors—an idea that was not alien to many of them—or that social conditions were responsible for the gentry's living twice as long as the laboring poor. This group of people, whose intellectual roots were from the Enlightenment thinkers Jeremy Bentham and Robert Malthus, concluded that it must be the *conditions* in which the poor lived—dirtier houses, dirtier streets, dirtier districts—that were responsible for their early age of death. Eliminate the dirt, and the disease will go: It is this idea, that "death is a social disease" and is therefore preventable, that is the basis of what came to be called the Sanitation Movement.

From our present vantage point, all of Victorian English society lived in unsanitary conditions. Midway into the nineteenth century, building encyclopedias and manuals made no reference to ventilation, and the great mansions in Belgravia reeked with exhalations from defective house drains. Perhaps not one home in a whole street of middle-class residences possessed a bath. When we think of sewage disposal, we think of washing away the filth in a flow of water, but a constant source of water under pressure was not yet available; drains were only places where the excrement could be stored until it was collected and hauled away to be used as fertilizer in the countryside. The drains in Buckingham Palace were found to be so bad that the government didn't dare to publish the report. But while "the middle and upper classes lived in such splendid squalor, the lower classes seemed in danger of being engulfed and poisoned by their own excretions."

In London and the industrial towns, one room was often the sole accommodation for the entire family of a laborer. It was "their bedroom, their kitchen, their wash-house, their sitting-room, their dining-room; and, when they do not follow any outdoor occupation, it is frequently their workroom and their shop. In this one room they are born, and live, and sleep, and die amidst the other inmates." But how did the followers of the Sanitation Movement, who were called sanitarians, think that the filth caused the disease? Remember, microparasites were unknown even in 1840. Ideas about contagion similar to ours have surfaced from time to time throughout history, but they have been so counter to the senses that ordinary people did not accept them. Most people made the common-sense correlation between filth and disease and assumed that correlation is the equivalent of causation. Disease, of course, was an imbalance of the humors, so what they were addressing were the causes that put the humors out of balance. The sanitarians were not reframing disease, they were attempting to prevent it within the framework that people had had about disease for two thousand years.

The sanitarians worked on the assumption that disease was caused by an unknown "something" in the atmosphere. This "something" could react with the gases from the decomposition of animal and vegetable matter in places like a stagnant sewer, a graveyard, or a slaughterhouse, so that if the proper "epidemic influence" was present, an epidemic of typhoid or cholera could be generated. Their faith in the association of filth and disease remained intact even in the face of the Great Stink of 1858, the year the stench of the polluted Thames was so great that the Law Courts had to be closed. The sanitarians had predicted that these "mephitic vapors" would lead to an unprecedented outbreak of disease, but even though fewer people than usual succumbed to disease that year, few seriously questioned the basic assumption.

T he best window into how the Enlightenment understood and dealt with the poor in Victorian England and how this view led to the dominance of the sanitarians is through the person of Edwin Chadwick. The leading figure and guiding force of the English Sanitation Movement, Chadwick can be considered one of the last men of the Enlightenment in England, a man who embodied all of the traits of the Enlightenment thinkers we have come to think of as good and bad. Edwin Chadwick was not a likeable man; his biographer R. A. Lewis says that he was not only a bore but "a really outstanding specimen of bore in an age when the species flourished." In 1831 he became secretary to the Enlightenment political philosopher Jeremy Bentham, and throughout his life Chadwick was to be associated with Bentham and Benthamism. This political philosophy argued that the state has "indefinitely extensible" powers to ensure the interests of the individual and that in gaining the maximum happiness for the individual, the state must promote the welfare of the many.

In his last great work, *The Constitutional Code*, Bentham had laid the ground for the actions that Chadwick and the sanitarians would follow. Here was the justification for the state "to protect factory children and railway labourers; to supply a legal minimum of relief for the able-bodied pauper and institutional care for the sick, orphaned, and aged; to put under public regulation the supply of water and the burial of the dead; to cleanse parishes and municipalities of corruption and central departments of nepotism and patronage; to destroy, adapt, create institutions as the principle of utility might dictate . . . the new ministries of Health, Education, Justice, Indigence Relief, and Interior communication." All of these Chadwick, as Bentham's disciple, tirelessly pursued. Yet in doing so he became one of the most hated men in England, because for all of the good that he did in raising the level of existence of the poor, he is remembered mainly for the way in which it was carried out. The lot of "the poor" was to be made less horrid, but they were still to be "the poor." Edwin Chadwick is still held primarily responsible for the odious New Poor Laws.

By modern standards, most of British society in the nineteenth century was poor. In a society with such clear class differences, there was enormous disparity in wealth, and the average laborer or artisan was at the mercy of economic swings, having to rely on the income of his children and friends, and credit from local tradesmen, during hard times. The upper classes, very much afraid of the effects of "idleness and profligacy" in the laboring class, felt that this state of affairs was right and proper, because it inspired the laboring poor to work. From the time of Elizabeth (1533–1603), English society had built an elaborate system to control pauperism in the form of the Poor Laws. The intent of these laws was that no person should starve or be homeless; each parish was responsible for providing assistance and even work for the destitute or orphaned or those incapable of providing for themselves. Over the years, however, the administration of these laws grew to be complex, and many thought that the Elizabethan Poor Laws had become a part of the problem rather than the solution. By the beginning of the nineteenth century, pauperism continued to rise at a faster rate than the money available for relief. We don't know how bad the problem really was, because at the time the rhetoric on both sides was very strong, but there is no question that there was a strong movement from the emerging middle classes to have the laws revised. The crucial step in this direction was taken in 1832 with the formation of a royal commission to institute changes in the Poor Laws.

The establishment of the Poor Law Inquiry Commission can be considered the first great public victory for the political philosophy of Jeremy Bentham. We have already mentioned the Benthamite vision of government regulation of all aspects of society, but at this juncture we must also mention Bentham's contemporary Robert Malthus, because the views of these two men were at the very heart of the workings of the commission. Malthus, an Enlightenment political economist, had concluded that population growth was the factor that had to be controlled for government to give the maximum happiness to all citizens, so he was *against* guaranteed relief for the poor. He felt that if their poverty was removed or even alleviated, the poor population would rise because they would enter into improvident marriages and have children without thinking about their future support, which in turn would lead to the need for more relief, which would result in more children, etc., etc. Moreover, the growing industrialization of the country created a need for labor; by providing relief, the poor were being discouraged from finding jobs in the new factories.

So all but the poor seemed to agree that a radical revision of the Poor Laws was needed and Edwin Chadwick, a known disciple of Bentham, was appointed first an assistant to the commission and then a member. He was soon to become its most influential, visible, and feared member. Chadwick knew that to completely abolish relief to the able-bodied poor would be politically impossible. The solution was to make the choice of relief worse than the choice of work. To convert this idea into action, he devised a scheme called the "less eligibility principle." Under the less eligibility principle, the relief that could be given to a person must not allow him to live any better than an "independent worker of the lowest class." So no matter how dreadful life was for a poor laborer, by accepting relief, it would automatically become worse.

And how would these principles be put into practice? By the expedient of making sure that all relief to able-bodied persons or their families that was not provided in a state-regulated workhouse was unlawful. Instead of the local parish's aiding an able-bodied pauper, as had been the case under the old Poor Laws, now he must either find work or go to a workhouse. These workhouses came to symbolize the horror of the laboring classes in Victorian England that were shown to the world in the novels of Charles Dickens. For all of the good work that he was to do in sanitation reform, it is with the workhouse that the name Edwin Chadwick has always been associated.

If the conditions in the workhouses were so deplorable that they would be only the last resort of the poor, what were the conditions of the alternative, the "independent worker of the lowest class"? Whether or not by design, the poor who were removed from the previous forms of parish relief now had to find work in a factory in one of the industrializing cities. In this way there would continue to be a source of labor needed for the great "progress" that was the essence of the industrialization. The population of the industrial cities had already begun to grow, and the influx of new workers would only increase the crowding. Manchester became a city that has come to symbolize all that was wrong with the Industrial Revolution, a city where "we observe hundreds of five- and six-storied factories, each with a towering chimney by its side, which exhales black coal vapour." With the growth of industrial cities, change in the modes of power, and the unceasing disease in these newly industrialized cities, industrialization caused a change in the organization of society as profound as those of the Neolithic age.

To the government and the industrialists, labor was an important commodity in the industrial process, one that must be kept functioning, just as the machinery in the factories had to be maintained. But if the average laborer died at twenty-two, the commodity was not being used efficiently. In 1838 the Poor Law Inquiry Commission under Chadwick reported to the Home Secretary that three medical inspectors had been employed to look into disease in London. Two of them, like Chadwick, were disciples of Bentham. In 1840 this Select Committee on the Health of Towns reported that "measures are urgently called for, as claims of humanity and justice to great multitudes of our fellow men, and as necessary *not less for the welfare of the poor than the safety of property and the security of the rich*" (author's emphasis). In 1843 Sir Robert Peel appointed a royal commission to investigate health conditions throughout the country. Chadwick was disappointed that he was not a member of that commission, but he soon took over its operation and leadership. With his sanitarian allies and his not inconsiderable political skill, he attempted to guide the royal commission to propose rigorous measures that would affect sewage, water, housing, the workplace, and anywhere else that the filth was present. The sanitarians had no doubt that the living conditions of the poor, especially the pervasive filth, were responsible for their ill health and short life spans, just as they had no doubt that it was the fate of the poor to labor and the responsibility of their "betters" to keep them alive so that they could continue their labor. With the institution of sanitary reform, the causes of illness and early death would be removed and the poor could continue to work in the factories and generate goods for those who could afford them and profits for the owners and investors.

The political battle of course was to convince Parliament that these ideas made sense. Even well-intentioned people had justifiable doubts that the large investments in sanitation would indeed raise the workers' level of health. In 1845 the royal commission presented to Parliament two very large reports, containing a number of recommendations for legislation. The members of Parliament, while they may have been shocked by the facts, resisted the plans because of the costs. However, after several setbacks in parliamentary maneuvering, the Public Health Act of 1848 passed. It was not the bill Chadwick would have wanted (for one thing, he did not have personal control over the execution of its provisions), but it was nevertheless the first public health bill. It provided for a central board of health that could introduce the machinery of local sanitary administration into any district that wanted to institute any aspect of sanitation. It would then advise the local boards and carry out other central administrative functions to assist them in actually carrying out the sanitary reforms. While this was not rampant Benthamism, it was an important compromise, one that would set in motion the changing of the conditions of life.

What specific things could be done? There was power to compel owners to provide house drains; to ensure a constant water supply, even if it meant purchasing the existing waterworks; to force the reconstruction of the sewers; to pave the streets; to make regulations for the disposal of filth; to provide places of public recreation. In retrospect we see, of course, that for those communities that chose to make the changes, the bill would give them the living conditions that we now associate with civilized society. But considering how in our enlightened time we still have government subsidy of tobacco, which we know causes thousands of deaths each year, and toxic emissions from cars and factories, we would be wise to resist the temptation to pity the shortsightedness of those who did not believe that adding drains and removing filth was worth the money invested and who chose not to avail their communities of the reforms for which the act provided.

In 1853, only five years after the act had passed, the central board could report that 284 towns had applied for its intervention, which meant that a total of 2.1 million people had been brought under the act. In these towns, the annual death rate of the working class had already fallen from 30 to 13 per 1,000! The social arithmetic was simple: If this rate was applied throughout England, 170,000 lives could be saved per year and the average age of death would go from twenty-nine to forty-eight. In London alone there would be 25,000 lives saved per year.

A common theme begins to appear in the middle of the nineteenth century in France and Germany, as well as in England: the need to raise the living standards of the poor so that they will not foment social unrest or cause disease among the rich. But in each of these countries there was the same problem—the enormous cost. How could the leaders of industry and government be sure that the outlay of vast sums of cash would indeed quiet these strange stirrings for social justice among the poor and keep them healthy enough to work the mills?

The solution was made easier for the good burgers of Hamburg in 1842. A fire broke out at one o'clock in the morning on May 5 and burned until eight o'clock in the morning of May 8. This was followed by so much looting and rioting that the merchants of the town realized they had to rebuild quickly to reestablish social order, but the cost of sanitation was too high for them. Four years earlier, in 1838, these same influential merchants and council members of Hamburg, who were as uncertain about expenditures for sanitation as their English counterparts, had had no doubt about the benefits of a rail line between Hamburg and Bergedorf and had brought in an English engineer named William Lindley to supervise the work. After the fire, Lindley, who had spent some of his youth in Hamburg and spoke fluent German, was called upon to help rebuild the city. As it happened, Lindley was a disciple of Chadwick and he, naturally, turned to questions of sanitation in the rebuilding of the city. His arguments for sanitation measures was one of self-interest of the wealthy: "Lack of cleanliness makes the population all the more receptive to devastating epidemics such as cholera, smallpox, fever, etc., and encourages such diseases to become endemic or to return again. Experience shows that when these epidemics have reached a certain degree of severity they also reach the dwellings of the well-off." Not only that, but "lack of well-being encourages the pathological lust for destruction which, given the opportunity (e.g., during the Great Fire) turns against the possessions of the better-off." Lindley tried to have an extensive sewer system built, but the city administration and business interests balked at the cost; they finally compromised by building a system of about fifty kilometers of sewage pipe, which was installed by the end of the 1850s. The death rates due to tuberculosis and typhus/typhoid began to decline in Hamburg after that time, and although there is no way to prove that this decline was due to these improvements, they certainly didn't hurt. Sewage disposal in the rest of Germany was another story. It was not until 1870 that Berlin had a comprehensive sewage system of underground pipes. Before then human waste was disposed of in open gutters that were flushed with running water into the river.

The story in France was a bit different; here the sanitation movement was considered a branch of political economy. Like the English sanitarians, the French, led by René Villermé, collected statistics on the living and dying conditions of the poor, and concluded that death was more prevalent among the poor and that the conditions of life among the poor were horrid. But unlike Chadwick and the English, who argued that the state had an obligation to improve housing and eliminate the filth, which they saw as the causes of the early death, the French sanitarians argued that the problem was a social one, created by the improper functioning of both society and especially the economy: "by favoring instruction, work, and liberty by means of wise laws and protective institutions, industry, wealth, and sound behavior are encouraged and, like a second providence come to this world, an [able] administration at its pleasure creates virtue, happiness, and men themselves."

Rather than the state imposing itself with engineering projects, the French believed a healthy nation must be built first of all on a vigorous economy and only secondarily should it worry about sewers. If the economy grew, "civilization" would grow; as poverty, the reason for the greater death among the poor, was eliminated, early death would also be eliminated. Since "death is a social disease," it could be cured by social means.

By the end of the nineteenth century, infant mortality was beginning to decline and the average age at death was beginning to increase in the industrialized world. Even though we focus today on the horrors of industrialization, we would be wise to focus also on the fact that it did begin to reduce poverty, so that the average worker could better feed, clothe, and house his family. In places where sanitation reforms were instituted, the improvements were often dramatic. All of this should have been a story of the triumphant success of the Sanitation Movement, and yet how many people today have heard of Chadwick? Flushing away our waste in sewers that do not contaminate our drinking water is such a common-sense notion that we do not even think twice about it; to ventilate our houses is required by law; our dead are interred in a way that neither offends our sensibilities nor harms our health. All of these are reforms that the Sanitation Movement argued for, so why do we not know about them and honor them?

Most of us have learned that it was science that brought about these changes, but as we have seen, the Scientific Revolution had not yet changed medicine; Enlightenment thinking was the driving force behind the social reforms of the sanitarians. The reframing of disease had also not yet occurred; it was still a condition resulting from an imbalance of humors, and as a result, therapies had not changed. Death and disease became a less constant presence but not, as we have been taught, because of the triumph of science. To be sure, science and technology worked together to bring about industrialization, better transportation, and better food. It would be wrong to say that science played no role in the profound changes in the living conditions and health of the population. But it is equally wrong to claim that these changes are due to changes science had brought about in medicine. That change would begin only after the changes in social structure and sanitation were well under way.

Chapter

4

"Pasteur" and the Authority of Science

The "new philosophy" of science may not have had much effect on either the constant presence of death or the way people thought about disease, but it was beginning to permeate the thinking of almost everyone by the start of the nineteenth century. Two Enlightenment personalities, one virtually unknown today who appears at the beginning of the "Age of Reason," the other a well-known figure who lived just before the French Revolution, serve as examples of the extent of the rise of science during the eighteenth century.

In the early part of that century, Julien Offray de La Mettrie (1709–1751) was a physician and *philosophe* who railed against the theoretical training in Galenic medicine that physicians received; to him the preeminence of physicians was not only useless but downright harmful. Surgeons, Mettrie argued, did far more good for people, and he called for the application of the new philosophy of science into medicine. He died early, and although his name is hardly known today, his ideas can be found again and again in the medical ideas of the *philosophes*. "Medicine is philosophy at work; philosophy is medicine for the individual and society." Yet for all of this radical talk, Mettrie was not advocating that disease be reframed. After all, he pointed out in his book *L'homme machine* (1747), an obstructed spleen was all that was necessary to turn a brave man into a coward; the human body was a "machine which winds its own springs" and, by implication, balances its own humors.

The second character, much more colorful and far more influential, appeared by the end of the century. When Franz Anton Mesmer (1734–

1815) arrived in Paris in 1778, the goal of the *philosophes* to have science a part of life had reached dizzying proportions. Science was everywhere; the only problem was that there were no clear ground rules for deciding just what constituted "science." Parisians flocked to Mesmer, who claimed that he had discovered a superfine fluid surrounding and penetrating everything. An obstacle to the flow of this fluid through the body resulted in sickness, which could be healed by "mesmerizing" (massaging) the body's magnetic poles to induce a "crisis" (often in the form of convulsions). In the resulting cure, the harmony of man with nature was restored. These ideas seemed as natural to Parisians as Newton's gravity and Franklin's electricity, which were being talked about everywhere. Antoine-Laurent Lavoisier, who is celebrated today as one of the discoverers of oxygen and a founder of modern chemistry, had discovered an invisible gas with remarkable powers. All around them, Parisians saw science describing invisible forces, so Mesmer's invisible fluid was really not that special. Talk of science was so pervasive that one mistress asked her lover not to send her light verse, "because I only like poems when they are dressed up in a bit of physics or metaphysics."

And over and above all of these (literally) would be the ultimate proof that science was all-powerful. Using the new wondrous gases of science, the Montgolfiers made their first balloon ascent in 1783. It is very difficult for us, with supersonic travel on earth and landings on the moon, to understand the feelings of people as they watched a balloon slowly and majestically rise into the air: "[T]he women in tears, the common people raising their hands toward the sky in deep silence; the passengers, leaning out of the gallery, waving and crying out in joy . . . you follow them with your eyes, you call to them as if they could hear, and the feeling of fright gives way to one of wonder. No one said anything but, 'Great God, how beautiful!' Grand military music began to play and firecrackers proclaimed their glory." What late-Enlightenment and pre-Revolution France took for science is very different from what people would consider science half a century later, but then, late-twentieth-century science is almost certain to be very different from what science will be in the mid-twenty-first century. If we are not fools for believing in our version of what science is, then neither were they! The point is, when we look back at what people then believed to be science, we must work very hard to see the world in the same context in which they saw it. Why would someone *not* accept Mesmer's electric fluid and the therapies he devised to establish a balance when the humors of Hippocrates and Galen had been believed for millennia? Why shouldn't one believe in noxious odors and mephitic vapors causing epidemics any more than one should believe that an invisible force such as gravity causes objects to fall to earth and is responsible for the tides?

The hand of the Church, pointing the finger of divine punishment at the cowering faithful, had lost much of its power to blame people for their diseases by the beginning of the nineteenth century, but what replaced it? Hippocrates himself had stressed that variations in weather and the character of the seasons were the true elements that determined the rise and fall of epidemic disease and the idea resurfaced in Europe in the early 1600s. By the middle of the seventeenth century in England the renowned physician Thomas Sydenham (1624–1689), who was called the English Hippocrates, was claiming that epidemic diseases such as plague, smallpox, and dysentery were caused by atmospheric changes, while diseases such as scarlet fever, pleurisy, and rheumatism were due to some innate susceptibility of the individual. He wasn't sure exactly what it was about the atmospheric changes that led to "the epidemic constitution," but he believed that it was some kind of a miasma arising from the earth.* To have some perspective into the seventeenth-century scientific mind, Sydenham, like others at the time, including Newton, gave serious consideration to an astrological origin of disease.

An alternative view based on contagion had been put forward first by the German Paracelsus (1490–1541) and then the Italian Girolamo Fracastoro, who wrote a three-volume treatise called *On Contagion, Contagious Diseases and their Treatment* in 1546. Fracostoro had what was at the time the rather bizarre idea that epidemics were caused by minute infective agents that were able to propagate themselves and be transmitted between people. Moreover, he thought that these seeds, or *seminaria*, of disease were specific for individual diseases. To compound the problem, he claimed that the seeds could be transmitted not only by

---

* The *Oxford English Dictionary* cites the first use of the word *miasma* in English in 1665 by Needham, who talks of "The Miasma or Malign Inquination of blood and humors."

direct person-to-person contact, but also through intermediate agents, such as clothing, or through the air. During abnormal atmospheric or astrological conditions the air might become infected with these seeds, and great epidemics were the result. It is of course tempting to see the origins of our modern understanding of bacteria and the germ theory of disease in the writings of Fracostoro, but his ideas were no more related to our modern scientific view than were the views of Sydenham. How many who are willing to accept those of his ideas that fit into our modern view (the seeds) are also willing to accept the parts that do not (the astrology)? Picking and choosing ideas from the past to show the relentless march of progress is a tricky business.

To the populace, who knew they were at risk to epidemics, and to those responsible for their safety and the public order, theories were far less important than doing something to stop the spread of disease. Mephitic vapors, filth, and miasma might be responsible for disease, but it could do no harm to isolate people with plague, burn their clothing, and close down the theaters. By 1850, as a result of the Public Health Act in England, there were better sewers and water purification, and this gave empirical evidence that when the streets were not filled with dead and decaying animals, human excrement, and other things too horrible to contemplate, the amount of disease did in fact decline. So we see that by the mid-1800s, when science was beginning to permeate everything, it had contributed little to allow people to choose between ideas of how disease was caused and spread. But all of that would change because of the work and public figure of Louis Pasteur.

The Authority of Science: Louis Pasteur and "Louis Pasteur"

By the start of the nineteenth century, science was no longer the domain of a few philosophers and curious souls wealthy enough to indulge their fancy. The physical sciences (chemistry, physics, astronomy) had become part of the technical advances upon which all industrializing societies depended, even though most laypeople made no distinction between Newton's force of gravity and Mesmer's force that penetrated everything. In contrast, those who were responsible for moving industrial society forward had a very good way of distinguishing between different scientific claims; if they could *apply* a scientific "fact," it was good science. Mesmerism may have captivated the minds of many and fulfilled the radical political ends of a few, but in the end it did not prove to have a useful end and it faded from the scene. The Revolution may have sent Lavoisier to the guillotine in 1794 with the statement that "the Republic is in no need of chemists," but those responsible for conducting the French revolutionary wars soon discovered their loss and reestablished French chemistry for the good of the war effort. When James Watt, who was not a scientist, improved the primitive steam engine, it gave physicists such as Joule, Kelvin, and Helmholz a practical reason for deriving theoretical information about the relationship between heat and power, making it possible to harness steam power for transportation and industry with even greater efficiency. When it was found that an electric current became twisted around a magnet, the interaction between currents and magnets led Ampère, Faraday, and other physicists to show that this phenomenon could be used to create the telegraph and the electric motor. The English chemist Humphry Davy is known to scientists as the discoverer of twelve elements, but he was known in his time as the man who invented the miner's safety lamp and a device that prevented mine explosions, making mines safer places to work and ensuring a supply of coal to fuel the factories of industrialization. The role of science was so important that in 1807, when France was at war with England, Napoleon presented a medal to Davy and later, in 1813, allowed him to visit the volcanoes at Auvergne. By the nineteenth century, what today are called the "hard" sciences had gained great authority because their value to society had become so evident.

But it is painfully clear that this was not the case with medicine and biology. One of the reasons science came so late to medicine was that the fundamental assumptions of biology and medicine were the deeply rooted in the idea of *vitalism*. This is the belief that some kind of mysterious "vital force" separates living things from nonliving matter. It was an idea of so much inherent attraction that it would change only when the functioning of living organisms began to be looked at as a collection of chemical reactions and processes. These reactions differ in no way from chemical reactions and processes that are not associated with life, so the thing that makes life unique is the particular *combination* of reactions. This was a hard idea to take hold, given the fact that any particular society has a religious explanation for the uniqueness of life, the obvious similarity between animals and humans, and the mystery of the growing cycle of plants. So it is perhaps characteristically human for most people to believe that evolution through natural selection has been pointed toward the evolution of humans, the "highest" of the animals. And it is only natural that philosophers, scientists, and ordinary people for a very long time resisted the idea that *L'homme machine* is really no different from the steam engine.

One of the first chemists to study processes that directly affect living things was Justis von Liebig (1803–1873). As a means of improving the agriculture in the rural area of Germany in which his laboratory was established, he began to elaborate the scientific principles of soil fertility so that fertilizers could be used in a more rational way. By the 1830s he was one of the world's leading chemists, and although he studied living entities, as a chemist it was unthinkable for him to invoke the concept of a "vital force." Chemists could describe reactions in strict quantitative terms, so there was no need to explain any fundamental part of the chemistry, even of living things, as being due to something as nebulous and philosophical-sounding as "vital forces." For example, since the beginning of time everyone knew that yeast were associated with the fermentation of wine and beer and the rising of bread. In the new era of science there was no reason to think that this was an especially wondrous thing; after all, both fermentation and bread making were only the production of alcohol and carbon dioxide by simple chemical conversions of sugar. Chemists knew that yeast were necessary for these chemical conversions to occur and assumed that they must play some role in the chemistry, but there was no reason to think that they are living creatures.

One of the goals of Liebig and the other great chemists of his time, in addition to explaining chemical reactions, was the destruction of the old-fashioned idea of vitalism. But in 1839 two Frenchmen and one German independently published the results of experiments which they claimed showed that yeast were in fact living creatures and not simple chemical entities. The great arbiter of the chemical world, the Swedish chemist Jöns Jakob Berzelius, treated these reports with incredulity and disdain. In response, the French Academy asked one of its members to attempt to repeat the finding (after all, the honor of France was at stake) and he was able to do so. But rather than rethinking their assumptions, Leibig and his equally famous chemist colleague Friedreich Wöhler joined in the ridicule by publishing an elaborate and cruel parody of the idea that yeast were alive and could ferment sugar to alcohol. In one of the most prestigious chemical journals, they published a cartoon that showed yeast looking like eggs that developed into minute animals shaped like the familiar distilling apparatus used by chemists, taking in sugar as food and excreting alcohol. This should have been enough to scare off anyone who wanted to champion an idea the chemists considered to be vitalism.

But why, the modern reader asks, should the result of bona fide scientists, repeated at the request of a prestigious academy of science, be ridiculed? Why indeed. It did not have sufficient authority! To the chemists, the question of how the sugar in grape juice became the alcohol in wine was one that was already closed. Lavoisier, before he lost his head, had "solved" the problem using the methods of quantitative chemistry. He had reached a conclusion so exact that for the chemists of the day, the fundamental nature of the phenomenon was solved. Granted, Lavoisier's equations made no provision for the yeast that were known to be present during the process, but they could be explained by assuming that they were nonliving "catalysts," substances that speed up chemical reactions without actually taking part in them. In the chemist's view of the world, there was no place for vitalism or living entities being a part of a chemical reaction, so even sound and repeatable experiments were rejected and ridiculed by the leading chemists of the day. The most Liebig was willing to admit was that *if* yeast were alive, it was only in their dying that they contributed to fermentation, because, as all chemists knew, fermentation was the process of breaking things down.

As strange as it might seem, this was the backdrop to the beginning of the changes in how we frame disease. To the laborer in the factory, the farmer in the field, the merchant selling the goods from the factories, vitalism, the touch of the divine—or whatever explanation professors, clerics, or divines discussed—was of only passing interest unless it could change the way disease was framed and treated. It took a Frenchman named Louis Pasteur to put the last nail in the coffin of vitalism and usher in a new era of medicine.

Pasteur's life, from 1822 until 1895, spans the century that he did so much to shape. His work and the force of his personality have formed our understanding of the nature of normal living processes and enabled us to reframe the concept of disease. Bruno Latour, a noted sociologist of science, recently wrote a book entitled *The Pasteurization of France*, in which he wonders why in the popular mind Pasteur has received credit for all that the sanitarians did to eliminate infectious disease. Every village in France has a street named after Pasteur, but are there very many in England named after Chadwick? Why science was "triumphant" in the mind of the public and of scientists themselves, and why a myth developed in France around Louis Pasteur, becomes clear when we look at Pasteur's role in reframing disease. He brought the "hard" science of chemistry together with medicine, so for the first time it was possible to see how the hope and promise of science could be applied to medicine. It was Louis Pasteur who dealt the final blows to vitalism and turned the tide against miasmas as the cause of infectious diseases. The start of the reframing came when Pasteur showed that not only are the yeast that carry out fermentation living things, but that the *living creatures in the microscopic world first opened up to us by Leuwenhoek can be responsible for disease.* Few scientists have the emotional stamina to stand up to the established power structure of science to fight for their seemingly heretical viewpoints, but Pasteur was one of them. Fewer scientists really change the way ordinary people in future generations will look at the world as Pasteur did. In the process, Pasteur the scientist became "Pasteur" the symbol of science. To understand the grandness of Pasteur's accomplishments, it will be necessary for the reader to set aside the fact that he or she knows the "correct" answer, that specific microbes cause specific disease. That idea was unthinkable at the start of the nineteenth century, and by changing it, Pasteur was changed into "Pasteur."

Pasteur and the Reframing of Disease

Born in the eastern part of France and raised at Arbois, the son of a former sergeant in Napoleon's army who owned and managed a small tannery, Louis Pasteur was an ordinary, earnest, provincial young man who gave no early indication of future greatness. An admiring biographer (until it recently became fashionable to deconstruct science, Pasteur had only admiring biographers) points out that when he came to Paris to enroll in the Ecole Normale Supérieure, only his interest in portrait painting separated him slightly from the other good students. After receiving his doctorate in chemistry Pasteur taught chemistry at the University of Strasbourg between 1848 and 1854, where he made his early reputation with a striking chemical discovery that two crystalline forms of a molecule can be identified and isolated. By the age of thirty-three he had already received the Legion of Honor and was appointed professor of chemistry and dean in the newly organized Faculté des Sciences at Lille. So Pasteur's first work gained him standing and fame as a chemist, an important point in the scientific-political struggles for authority that are to follow, but gave little indication that he would go on to become anything but a well-respected member of the establishment.

Shortly after he came to Lille in 1854, Pasteur was approached by the owner of a sugar-beet distillery who was having trouble with the fermentation of beet sugar to alcohol. When the juices of grapes or sugar beets are placed in vats, they begin to undergo characteristic changes that lead to the production of alcohol, a process we still call fermentation (and which was then called alcoholic fermentation). Everyone knew that milk left standing in a warm place would begin to sour, resulting in a dreadful mess or yogurt, in a process that was called lactic acid fermentation because lactic acid is produced during the process. Alcohol could be converted to vinegar, a process called acetic acid fermentation, because vinegar is acetic acid. From this we can see that chemistry was an advanced enough subject by the middle of the nineteenth century to be able to identify the products of all of these processes; and because the beginning material and the end products were really simple chemicals, chemists were certain they had the explanations for how they were produced. Every chemist knew that fermentation was a chemical process caused by chemical agents called ferments, which brought about the conversion, so when Wöhler and Liebig ridiculed as being benighted "vitalists" the biologists who claimed yeast were living, they had the authority of "hard" science behind them. The chemistry of fermentation had been adequately explained, with yeast serving as nonliving catalysts.

This, of course, is why the owner of the sugar-beet distillery came to Pasteur, the professor of chemistry, rather than to the professor of biology. The distillery owner's problem was that the alcohol was being converted into acetic acid (i.e., vinegar) before it could be distilled and marketed as pure amyl alcohol. The amyl alcohol was used for commercial purposes rather than drinking, but the same kinds of problems regularly occurred in the wine and beer industries. Pasteur was attracted to the problem because of its economic importance, but he soon realized that the problems at the sugar-beet factory were also of fundamental scientific importance.

The nonscientist can get an insight into how scientific debates come about by understanding why Pasteur took a different tack than a chemist would have been expected to take. Even though he and Liebig were both chemists, they disagreed on a fundamental technical point of chemistry because of the different kinds of chemical work they had each done before. Both agreed that the amyl alcohol that was a product of fermentation of sugar could assume two forms, which differed in how they refracted light in a certain laboratory apparatus (very much like right-handed and left-handed versions of the same molecule). Liebig assumed that the two forms of the end product (right-handed and left-handed amyl alcohol) represented two forms of the sugars that were present at the *start* of the fermentation process and so was not surprised that they were there at the end. Pasteur's experience with optically different molecules (he had made his reputation for this kind of work) was quite different. In his experience, the optical activity of the starting molecule was immediately lost when a molecule underwent the kind of chemical changes sugar had undergone when it was converted into alcohol. From this experience he assumed that the optical activity of the amyl alcohol at the end of the process could *not* have come from the optical activity of the sugar at the start, but must have been acquired along the way. He had already begun to suspect that living organisms can bring about chemical changes, and the only mechanism he could think of that would result in two optically different forms of amyl alcohol arising from the same molecule of sugar at the start was that a living process was involved. For two well-known chemists to disagree is "science as usual"; for one to explain the difference in a totally new way is either brilliant or ridiculous. It would not have been unusual for Pasteur to propose a new *chemical* explanation, but he chose to propose a *biological* one. It was an explanation that was, understandably, unthinkable and ridiculous to Liebig and his cohorts.

The first hint of what would be called the germ theory can be seen in the way Pasteur framed his discovery that yeast are responsible for alcoholic fermentation. He considered alcohol's conversion to vinegar a "disease" of alcoholic fermentation. "Disease" clearly signifies more than benign chemical reactions, and Pasteur had noticed that in the cases where there was a "disease" in the fermentation process, he could see other forms besides yeast when he examined the material from the vats in the microscope. He went on to prove that these other things were bacteria that had "infected" the fermentation process and were carrying out an acetic fermentation. It was an *infection* that was converting the alcohol to vinegar!

This was too much for Liebig and the other chemists, who rejected the idea of living agents being responsible for fermentation, let alone causing disease. Not only was Pasteur saying that yeast carry out alcoholic fermentation, but that other microbes carry out acetic fermentation. Liebig showed his scorn in no uncertain terms, claiming that the idea that fermentations of any kind could be carried by "microscopic animalcula . . . may be compared to that of a child who would explain the rapidity of the Rhine current by attributing it to the violent movement of the many millwheels at Mainz."

But Pasteur was more than a match for the members of the pantheon of chemistry. Slowly, and with much heated debate over the period of several years, the chemists came around to his viewpoint on the idea that microscopic living organisms can carry out specific chemical reactions. Pasteur went on to show that the noxious putrefaction of protein materials was also a form of fermentation due to living agents. *This idea that specific organisms cause specific kinds of fermentation paved the way for the idea that specific organisms also cause specific diseases.*

The battles with Liebig had crossed the boundaries of science and become personal, but in 1872, shortly before his death, Liebig wrote, "I would be much pained if M. Pasteur took in a disparaging sense the observations in my last work on fermentation. He appears to have forgotten that I have only attempted to support with facts a theory which I evolved more than thirty years ago, and which he had attacked. I was, I believe, in the right in defending it. There are very few men whom I esteem more than M. Pasteur, and he may be assured that I would not dream of attacking his reputation, which is so great and has been so justly acquired. I have assigned a chemical cause to a chemical phenomenon, and that is all I have attempted to do."

I t is one thing to show that microscopic living things carry out fermentation processes; it is quite another to ask where these living things come from. Darwin published *Origin of Species* in 1859; the important lesson from evolution was that species are not constant, and because they undergo changes, there is a continuity between existing species. Microbial life should not be an exception, and Pasteur, as the leading microbiologist, became involved in this question. In 1861 he published a monograph called *Memoir on the Organized Bodies Which Exist in the Atmosphere,* in which he described experiments that are now universally recognized as having sounded the death knell for spontaneous generation, the idea that living things appear spontaneously from non-living matter. If Leeuwenhoek's "animalcules" were alive, they had to come from somewhere, and although it had been several centuries since serious people thought that mice developed spontaneously in piles of old rags or maggots spontaneously appeared on meat, the origin of microbial forms of life was not clear. After all, Pasteur himself had shown that the fermentation of the sugar in grape juice to wine is caused by specific yeast and the fermentation of wine to vinegar by specific bacteria. Did the bacteria causing the acetic acid fermentation come from another place, or were they spontaneously generated in the wine vat? Some of Pasteur's most ingenious experiments were carried out to show that the microbes that "infected" wine were present in the air. In every case where it seemed that they had appeared spontaneously he showed that they were introduced from some clearly identifiable source. All life comes from life, and the air around us teems with microscopic forms of life, most of which are harmless, some of which are useful, and some of which can do grave harm.

Between 1866 and 1870 Pasteur demonstrated that it was bacterial infection that was causing the silkworm disease that was ruining the French silk industry. In short, he had convincingly demonstrated that microbes can be the cause of disease and that these microbes do not appear spontaneously. They are in the air, in the water; they are everywhere. In England a young British surgeon named Joseph Lister was especially impressed with the practical medical implications of Pasteur's demonstration. With the introduction of anesthesia around 1840, the need for speed in surgery had been eliminated, so surgeons could now undertake long and very complicated procedures. But in the process of keeping the surgical site open for a long time, the already existing problem of infection of the wound, technically called sepsis, became exacerbated. From the concepts of Pasteur, it was now clear that bacteria growing in these septic wounds were responsible for the putrefaction and that they had come from the air, the surgical instruments, and the hands of the surgeon. Based on this, Lister concluded that if he washed his hands in a strong solution that would kill microbes, sterilized his instruments, and kept the surgical wound clear of microbes, he would reduce the chance of sepsis during long surgery; he even began to use disinfectant-soaked dressings and to carry out the surgery under a spray of disinfectant. In short order he was able to reduce dramatically the incidence of sepsis during surgery, and after the usual initial skepticism that greets new ways of doing things, these methods were quickly and widely adopted, making surgery one of the most powerful tools of medicine and Joseph Lister a hero.

The advances Lister made in surgery dramatized the more far-reaching implications of Pasteur's discovery. The realization grew that if there are microbes in the air that can cause diseases of wine and silkworms and sepsis in surgery, there must be microbes that cause cholera, tuberculosis, or any other infectious disease. There was no longer any need for vague talk of miasmas, mephitic vapors, or "germinating" factors. The authority of science had now been firmly brought to medicine, because now science could be converted into things that really mattered—the way we frame disease and what we can do about it. From this point forward, disease would be framed in terms of specific living causes, an idea that was called the *germ theory of disease*.

Robert Koch and the "Microbe Hunters"

Robert Koch was a modest man whose only ambitions in life seem to have been to practice medicine in rural Germany and indulge his passion for nature study. All of that changed when, because of Pasteur's discoveries, Koch turned the microscope he had been using for his nature studies to look into a local outbreak of anthrax, a disease of sheep and cattle that can also infect humans. In April 1874, Koch first saw bacteria in the blood of a sheep sick with anthrax and, following the new idea of the germ theory, thought they might be responsible for the disease. By December 1875, he had completed all of the work necessary for the proof that there were specific kinds of bacteria that were able to cause anthrax, and his life was changed forever. From a modest rural physician with an interest in nature studies, Koch would become a world-famous bacteriologist and disease hunter, sharing for a while the world spotlight with the great Pasteur himself. Koch is still today a widely known and respected name, but he never became "Koch."

In the isolation of his rural medical practice, Koch first had to figure out a way to grow the bacteria that he saw in the blood of the diseased sheep. He saw in his microscope that there were many different kinds of bacteria in the diseased sheep, but if the germ theory was correct, only one specific kind was causing the disease and the others were probably harmless. Pasteur grew his bacteria in liquid culture, but this would not have allowed Koch to separate the culprits from the bystanders, so necessity forced him to devise a way to grow the bacteria on a solid-culture medium to tell the difference. Once he was able to do this, he carried out a very thorough sequence of steps to separate the different kinds of bacteria and find the ones that caused the disease. It is clear from this earliest of his scientific work that he was a naturally gifted scientific thinker, but we will see how his lack of rigorous training in the self-skepticism of scientific thought would hurt him in later years.

The steps he used to show that anthrax was caused by a specific kind of bacteria would later be formulated as "Koch's postulates." They are an instructive and easy-to-follow example of how science is really a logical and often remarkably common-sense way of solving problems (although the answers are seldom what one would have come up with using only common sense). Reasoning that if the microbes he saw in the blood of the diseased sheep really caused anthrax they might also kill rabbits, he began by injecting a rabbit with blood from an infected sheep. When the rabbit became ill and died twenty-four hours later, he removed various organs to see if he could grow bacteria that looked like the ones he had seen in the blood of the diseased sheep on his solid-culture medium. He found that when one kind of these bacteria were injected into another rabbit, it came down with the same kind of disease as the first rabbit, strongly suggesting that these were the bacteria responsible for the disease. Of course to complete the experiment, Koch would have to inject the bacteria into healthy sheep and show that they came down with anthrax. Koch did not do this part of the experiment, but we will see later on that when it was done, the sheep did in fact come down with anthrax. The clarity of the experiment should be evident to everyone. It would serve as the model for proving that bacteria suspected of causing human disease were indeed the culprits.

Perhaps the most striking thing about this obviously first-rate piece of science was the fact that he had done it in complete scientific isolation. Pasteur and Liebig were in the mainstream and had fought their battle on the stage of science visible to the whole world, but here was a physician in rural Wollstein who had carried out a scientific *coup*. Arthur Conan Doyle, himself a physician, in a character sketch of Koch in 1890, wrote that "[n]ever, surely, could a man have found himself in a position less favourable for scientific-research—poor, humble, unknown, isolated from sympathy and from the scientific appliances which are the necessary tools of the investigator. Yet he was a man of too strong a character to allow himself to be warped by the position in which he found himself, or to be diverted from the line of work which was most congenial to his nature."

The reality of his isolation struck Koch when it came time for him to publish the work. Pasteur, remember, had already received the Legion of Honor and was professor and dean when he published his work on fermentation and so Koch was seized with the natural fear that he might have made a blunder. He finally summoned up enough courage to have his work evaluated by Ferdinand Cohn, the director of the Institute of Plant Physiology at the University of Breslau, which was only a few hours' train ride away from his home. Without too much armchair psychology, it might be thought that Koch was able to gather the bravery to approach Cohn because even though Cohn was a world famous botanist and expert on microscopic life forms, he was a somewhat marginalized person in German society and science. Though universally recognized as brilliant, and a native of Breslau, Cohn had been forced to go to Berlin to complete his scientific training because Jews were not allowed to study for doctorates at Breslau. He returned to Breslau, and even though he finally was appointed professor, it took the university twenty years to get around to providing him with the laboratory facilities that should have accompanied the title. Finally in 1866 he was given his "Institute" in some rooms on the second floor of an old student dormitory.

In a modest letter to Cohn stating that he thought he had discovered the bacterial cause of anthrax, Koch asked that "before I publish my work, I would like to request, honored professor, that you, as the best expert on bacteria, examine my results and give me your judgment on their validity." Koch traveled to Breslau to show his work to Cohn, who was impressed by the science and, realizing that the work was of great medical importance, immediately sent word to the Pathology Institute that there was something of great importance here. As luck would have it, the director of the Pathology Institute, Julius Cohnheim, came to see the rural doctor his colleague and friend Ferdinand Cohn seemed so taken with. Cohnheim, who was one of the world's leading pathologists, had studied with one of the central characters in the scientification of medicine, Rudolf Virchow, whom we will meet shortly. A battlefield conversion to Christianity during the German-Danish war had made it possible for Cohnheim to obtain both his professorship and a place at the institute at a young age. He was the perfect person to spread the word that Robert Koch had made a discovery of the highest importance. "He has done everything himself and with absolute completeness. There is nothing more to be done. I regard this as the greatest discovery in the field of pathology, and believe that Koch will again surprise us and put us all to shame by further discoveries."

The anthrax paper was published in December 1876, and by April 1880 Koch was no longer a rural physician. He moved to Berlin as a member of the staff of the Imperial Health Office, and in August of the next year he demonstrated his techniques to Pasteur and Lister. At that meeting Pasteur, then at the height of his fame and powers, paid him an honor: "*C'est un grand progress, Monsieur,*" but a few months after this meeting Koch, along with other German bacteriologists, attacked Pasteur's work on anthrax (of which we will see more presently). Pasteur had never said a disparaging word about Koch or his work; indeed, he had called the original paper "remarkable." Now, taking advantage of his newfound fame, the formerly humble country doctor wrote of Pasteur's work on anthrax that "there is little which is new, and that which is new is erroneous."

Koch's modest and humble demeanor had changed, but Cohnheim's prediction that he would make even greater contributions was fulfilled.

In early 1882 Koch electrified the world with the announcement that he had isolated the bacteria responsible for tuberculosis, and in 1884 he traveled to Egypt to head the German expedition to isolate the organism responsible for cholera. The following year he was appointed professor and director of the Institute of Hygiene in Berlin. French "microbe hunters" under the direction of Pasteur and Germans led by Koch were isolating and identifying the bacteria that were the cause of virtually all of the important infectious diseases. Koch may have disparaged Pasteur's work on anthrax, but he was one of the people most responsible for making the germ theory displace miasmas as the cause of disease. We will return to both Pasteur and Koch later, but this was to be the peak of Koch's career.

The nineteenth century began with the promise that science would change people's lives and it ended with the promise about to be fulfilled. While the world was not yet free from disease, it most certainly was becoming a world without the constant presence of death, and science held the hope of the eradication of even more disease. In the popular mind, "Pasteur" had been the reason for the change. We have seen, of course, that it was public health, sanitation, nutrition, and better housing that were responsible for the changes, yet as Edward Kass noted in his lecture at the Society for Infectious Disease in 1971, science received the credit. This is a very important point, not because the placing of credit is important in itself, but because if we have a false understanding of the past, we are liable to have false hopes for the future.

Chapter
5

Rewriting History:
The Triumph of Science

By the nineteenth century science was not only in the air, it represented two of the most powerful of modern ideas—progress and faith in the power of humans to change the world. The germ theory of disease was a radical new way of framing disease and represented the fulfillment of the faith in the power of science; and while the conditions of life were actually being improved by better sanitation, housing, and nutrition, science received the credit. The triumph of science over public health is an important issue to examine because it is on the basis of this misconception that we have set the goals for what we want from science in the twenty-first century. Oddly enough, it was the appearance of two new epidemic diseases, cholera and polio, that brought together ideas of civilization and social justice, and of science and medicine. In its responses to these new diseases, the public health movement wholeheartedly adopted the germ theory and in the process gained the authority of science, but in doing so, it abdicated to "Pasteur" the credit for the eradication of disease for which it was primarily responsible.

Today, with the germ theory of disease firmly entrenched in our thinking, we know that cholera is a disease caused by infection with bacteria called *Vibrio cholera*. But before the acceptance of the germ theory, what we today consider a basic and obvious fact was neither. The truth of this message is dramatically seen when we examine cholera in the period just before and just after the germ theory was gaining acceptance.

Cholera was the classic epidemic disease of the nineteenth century. It had a profound emotional impact, but one that was quite different from plague or smallpox. About half of those who came down with it died in a few days, suffering from particularly terrible gastric symptoms leading to coma and death. The initial outbreak was in India in 1826. From there it moved to Persia in 1829, Russia in 1830, then westward through Poland, Hungary, Prussia, Germany, Austria, and England in 1831. By 1832 it reached Paris, where it killed 25 out of every 1,000 inhabitants (18,000 out of a population of 785,000). By 1860 its cause and cures were being thought about in what we would now recognize as something like modern terms, and by 1883 its submission had become one of science's great triumphs. So the changing ideas about cholera through the middle fifty years of the nineteenth century give us a window into the changing ideas of the cause and control of infectious disease and the role of science.

The Hippocratic and Galenic traditions dictated that to understand what was happening to patients, it was necessary to be aware of the role played by the seasons of the year, winds, drinking waters, site, elevation, soil, climate, astrological signs, and diet. That medicine had changed little since Galen became starkly clear as cholera spread west from India through Russia, Poland, and Germany. Each country set up a medical commission to report on the progress of the epidemic, and make recommendations about how to stop it, while it moved inexorably across Europe. Even a brief look at these reports and responses tells us a great deal about how disease is framed in social, religious, and economic terms and how these both reflect and shape the scientific stance we take at any time in history.

As the epidemic approached France, for example, the citizens were told by one expert that there was no chance that a disease that had started in "fetid, marshy areas in certain parts of Asia Minor" could possibly arrive in France, where "civilization" had attained "a higher degree of perfection." The experts saw little chance that cholera would enter France by way of the seaports, because of the enlightened sanitary measures observed by the country. At any rate, even if it did enter the country, "the disease would quickly be confined to the ports and treated with such success by rational medicine known to all French physicians, that there need be no fear of its spread to the interior. . . ." But a few months later, when all of France was in the terrible grip of the disease, another expert proclaimed that "the people of Paris were not made to serve as fodder for the cholera of Asia and to die like slaves in pain and terror. . . . What good, then, are all its hospitals, its doctors, its science, and its public administration? Is civilization incapable of compensating mankind for all the harm it had done through its laws, its institutions its errors, and its injustices?" The French sanitarians had seen death as a "social disease" and here was the proof that this was the case; there was still too much dirt, too much poverty, too much human suffering, and too much human greed. Until these were changed, death from cholera and other diseases would continue to plague the high "civilization" of France.

One of the fathers of modern physiology and one of the most famous physicians in France, François Magendie (1783–1855), studied the disease and reported to the French Academy in 1831 that cholera was neither imported nor contagious: It was due to "filth." Horrid housing conditions, lack of ventilation and light, and humidity were the causes of cholera and quarantines were of no use. In the next ten years virtually all the physicians who were revolutionizing medicine in the Paris hospitals would publish various declarations and reports arguing against contagionism not only in cholera, but in leprosy, yellow fever, typhus, and plague as well. They may not have agreed on what caused cholera, but they were in perfect accord on what did *not:* It was not a disease caused by a unique living entity.

In Germany the presence of the epidemic rekindled the old moralistic fervor that disease was divine punishment for personal and collective sins. The citizens of Hamburg were told, "Just don't be afraid!": The thing to do is be "moderate and sober." Ministers and physicians agreed that those who succumbed to cholera had weakened their constitutions and thereby predisposed themselves to the disease. Drinking, overeating, sexual excess—all could dissipate the vital forces, leaving the sinner susceptible to whatever the cholera-causing forces were in the atmosphere. But there was no unanimity on this point. One German authority at the time argued that cholera was due neither to miasma nor contagion, nor necessarily to moral dissipation; if the disease was caused by miasma or personal sin, why had it not broken out before? Conditions had not changed that visibly and people were no worse now than they had ever been. No, he claimed. Cholera was due to unknown "repeated cosmic-telluric influences," which caused the nervous system to become "feverishly overexcited." It was the fear caused by seeing victims of the disease that caused the observer to come down with it: "Contagion is only *psychological*" (author's emphasis). Another authority claimed it was "sadness and fear" that caused people to succumb to cholera, and yet another argued that "the claim that cholera only seizes those who are predisposed by a

faulty diet or depressed emotions . . . is completely without foundation";
instead, he argued, it is a question of "polarity": Cholera affected people by
changing the balance of "sympathies" and "antipathies" within the body.

So just as science had not yet established its authority in medical matters to allow physicians to distinguish between the ideas that disease
was caused by *miasma*, atmospheric effects, contagious *seeds*, or other
reasons, so too religion had lost enough of its authority to assert its
moralistic views on how the public responded to the advancing new disease of cholera. In a time when no one idea had authority, all were open
for consideration.

During the cholera outbreak in England in 1831, an eighteen-year-old
apprentice to a Newcastle surgeon was sent to help with the victims of
the disease at the nearby Killingworth Colliery. John Snow, the son of a
farmer, had been apprenticed at the age of fourteen and would soon be
ready to go to London to take his exams and become a member of the
Royal College of Surgeons; years later he would become the leading
anesthetist (he administered chloroform when Queen Victoria gave
birth) and one of the most respected surgeons in London. Snow was a
man of strong moral character, an active vegetarian for many years, and
a lifelong, vocal advocate of the temperance movement.

His experiences with cholera as a young man made him a lifelong student of the disease, and Snow concluded that cholera "travels along the
great tracks of human intercourse, never going faster than people travel,
and generally much more slowly. In extending to a fresh island or continent, it always appears first at a seaport. It never attacks the crews of
ships going from a country free from cholera to one where the disease is
prevailing, till they have entered a port, or had intercourse with the
shore. Its exact progress from town to town cannot always be traced; *but
it has never appeared except where there has been ample opportunity for it to be
conveyed by human intercourse*" (author's emphasis). This, as we have seen,
was quite contrary to the general thought.

Even though disease was associated with dirt and poverty, it was common knowledge that in a crowded tenement some people came down
with cholera and others did not. While the "miasmists" invoked individual differences, moral character, or any number of other things to
explain this fact, Snow's explanation was different, and also very much
at odds with the prevailing view: "[T]he communicable diseases of
which we have a correct knowledge spread in very different manners.

The itch, and certain other diseases of the skin, are propagated in one way; syphilis, in another way; and intestinal worms, in a third way." Because cholera is a disease of the intestine, he concluded that the agent of infection must be present in the discharge from the intestinal tract, and those people who ingested food or water that was contaminated with this agent would come down with cholera, while those who did not would remain disease-free. Again note that Snow is at a divergent pole from the accepted explanation; he sees disease as specific in a time when all others see it as general.

When cholera returned to London in 1853, Snow made a remarkable study in which he examined the distribution of the disease and the distribution of water by the private water companies of London. The history of London's water is fascinating, but all we need to know for the present is that between 1849 and 1853, when London was free of cholera, one of the private water companies, the Lambeth Company, moved the source of its water from Hungerford Market to Thames Ditton because the original source of water was so visibly and grossly polluted that people were beginning to complain of the odor and color. In much of London it was easy to identify which of the companies supplied the water, but in other areas, the pipes of the Lambeth Company and those of the Southwark and Vauxhall Company ran down the same streets and any given house might receive water from one or the other company. Snow was convinced that by moving its source of water, the Lambeth Company had contributed to a lowering of the number of cholera cases in the 1853 epidemic, but the fact that some districts were served by both companies made this difficult to test. In Snow's words, "In consequence of this intermixing of the water supply, the effect of the alteration made by the Lambeth Company on the progress of cholera was not so evident, to a cursory observer, as it would otherwise have been." It was clear that in areas where Lambeth was the sole supplier, there was virtually no cholera and in areas where Southwark and Vauxhall was the sole supplier, there was a great deal. The question was how to determine the role played by the water supply in the areas where the pipes ran side by side. In those areas Snow made a careful study of which households received water from which company and could show that if a household had its water supplied by the Lambeth Company, there was little or no cholera. Most of the cholera in these mixed areas was due to water from the Southwark and Vauxhall Company. So Snow's contention that cholera is transmitted by something in the water was fulfilled from this "experiment."

John Snow is a hero among modern public health professionals. His studies on the distribution of water and the spread of cholera are taken as the forerunner of modern scientific public health and vivid proof that the germ theory has its origin in this field. This idea draws its greatest support and has its greatest appeal in the story of the Broad Street pump, which has become legendary. In the Golden Square area of London, in the six weeks between August 19 and September 30, 1854, there were 616 fatal attacks of cholera, 369 of them in a four-day period between August 30 and September 4. It was common knowledge that the Golden Square area, one of London's poorest, was the hardest hit by the epidemic, a fact that was consistent with the idea that the cause of the disease was the filth, poverty, and overcrowding of the area. But Snow sought a cause that was based in the water, and so he requested permission "to take a list, at the General Register office, of the deaths from cholera, registered during the week ending September 2, in the subdistricts of Golden Square, Berwick Street, and St. Ann's, Soho, which was kindly granted." Using the same plan he had used in showing that the Southwark and Vauxhall Company's water was implicated in the earlier outbreak, he placed a black mark on a map of the area at the residence of each person who had died during the period. A glance at the map shows that the deaths were clustered within a radius of 250 yards, and at the center of the circle is a public water pump, the now infamous Broad Street pump.*

But some deaths occurred in houses that were not in the immediate area of the pump. For these he was able to determine through interviews with the family members that the victims had drunk water from the Broad Street pump. One family that lived a few blocks away preferred the taste of the water from that same pump to the taste of the water from its local pump. One case of cholera in a small town outside of London could be traced to the Broad Street pump: A young woman had come to Broad Street to visit a relative dying of cholera and had taken a drink of water from the fateful pump. When he realized that the pump was at the epicenter of the epidemic in Golden Square, he received permission to

---

* Today, if they look hard, visitors to London can find the spot of the pump marked by red paint on the curb in front of the John Snow Pub, at the corner of Broadwick and Lexington streets, not far from the fashionable shops of Carnaby Street.

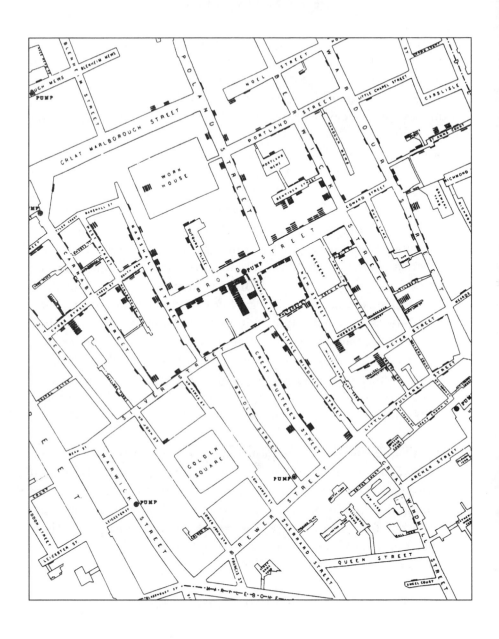

The Broad Street Pump, responsible for spreading cholera in London. Illustration from John Snow's Snow on Cholera, *reprint of a 1936 facsimile edition. Hafner Publishing Company, 1965.*

remove the handle of the pump, and tradition has it that there were no further cases, but this is not true. Even he realized that new cases of cholera were already on the decline when he removed the handle; "the attack had so far diminished before the use of the water was stopped, that it is impossible to decide whether the well still contained the cholera poison in an active state."

It would seem from this true medical detective story that science pure and simple had won the day. But this is not at all what happened. John Snow used methods that we today recognize as scientific, but it will be instructive for the reader to take a short break in the narrative and take another look at Snow's map of the area. Try to put yourself into the times. It is 1854, the same year Pasteur is beginning his studies on the diseases of fermentation. Science is "in the air," but there is nothing in science to argue against cholera being caused by filth and poverty, moral weakness, or mephitic vapors and miasmas. If John Snow had not been looking for a source of water as the cause of the outbreak in Golden Square, would he have noticed that the cases clustered around a water pump? There were pumps nearby in Little Marlborough Street, Marlborough Mews, Warwick Street, and Bridle Street, so why even notice the Broad Street pump? There was a brewery near Golden Square and not near the other pumps; why not assume that it was the production of beer that was responsible for cholera?

A short while later, when the pump was excavated it was found to be contaminated by sewage from the local houses, but this was only learned retrospectively and we can't be sure that the other pumps were not also contaminated. The lesson is that science is always part of its time. It is extremely rare for a scientist to see the world very differently from his or her fellows and to convince them of a radically new view.

Who Made John Snow a Hero?

It would seem by logic and the fact that John Snow is a public health hero that he had put the case for contagion in a manner that even the most recalcitrant opponent could not resist. Indeed, the mythology that has arisen around John Snow and the Broad Street pump is that the city of London, indeed the whole world, immediately recognized that cholera was a contagious disease transmitted by something in the water. It could not be entertained for a moment longer, given Snow's brilliant detective work, that cholera was due to miasmas or mephitic vapors. A scholar who has looked deeply into the reception Snow's reports received has concluded that Snow was not a hero in his time. Quite the contrary; if people actually paid any attention to his studies, they probably regarded him as "a holder of eccentric views that went back to the dark sixteenth-century theories of contagion of Fracestorius." He asks the question, "Who made John Snow a hero?"

It is clear that in the 1850s there was little support in medical and scientific circles for the idea that diseases were contagious. The voice that dominated the discussions of the cause and prevention of cholera for a quarter of a century was not John Snow's, but that of the German Max von Pettenkofer (1818–1901). Pettenkofer has been cast as the fool to Snow's hero, but from 1855 until the 1880s, crucial years in the development of our ideas of what causes infectious disease and how the diseases are transmitted, he was a dominant force.

Pettenkofer's idea was that a "cholera miasma" arose because of a series of changes in the level of ground water: It is the water table that determines if cholera will come to a community. When the water table suddenly rises, the moisture content of the soil is increased; if the water table falls in a dry period, the moisture content falls, leaving a layer of soil above the water table in which cholera can "germinate." Even when the idea that specific bacteria were responsible for specific diseases such as cholera began to gain acceptance, Pettenkofer would continue to argue that such organisms could contribute to disease only if they were present under the proper atmospheric conditions. Under these conditions, a proper "miasma" would be created and the disease could then be transmitted through the air that had been polluted by the germination process. This may look a bit like a view that is in keeping with the germ theory, but Pettenkofer was one of the most vocal of the anticontagionists in a period that was full of them.

Given his background, it is no accident that Pettenkofer resisted the growing trend and held to his ideas. The ground-water theory can probably be traced to the fact that after he received his medical degree in Munich in 1843, Pettenkofer went to study organic chemistry with none other than Justis Liebig himself. Liebig was then championing the idea that decomposing matter contained "ferments," chemical entities that caused the breakdown of organic matter, and was a vocal opponent of

Pasteur's idea that living organisms carry out specific fermentation. Liebig had begun to advocate the idea that these ferments in decomposing matter somehow could determine whether a geographical area would be receptive to endemic disease, and Pettenkofer, who was trained in medicine as well as chemistry, put Liebig's ideas into a clearer medical framework.

To understand the events of the time, try to conjure up a picture of Pettenkofer the man. He was not only a physician and an organic chemist, he was also partly responsible for developing the method of preparing meat extracts that eventually led to bouillon cubes; he devised a copper amalgam for filling teeth; he created a new kind of "good German cement"; he invented a practicable way of producing gas from wood which was used to light the theater and the main railway station in Munich; he improved the Bavarian method of coinage by improving assays for gold, silver, and platinum; he devised ways of restoring cracked varnish on the paintings in the Munich Pinakothek; and much more. Clearly, this was a mind and an energy to be reckoned with, especially when we consider that all of these inventions were done in his spare time; Pettenkofer's real interest and main work was in public hygiene. His was the voice that was heard when public hygiene and cholera were discussed, not that of an English surgeon who dabbled in epidemiology. In 1854, the same year Snow implicated the Broad Street pump, Pettenkofer wrote in a report on cholera, "I have disposed, once and for all, of causation by drinking water."

But how could such a statement have been listened to in the face of John Snow's evidence? The answer is painful: because Pettenkofer was in a position to be listened to by the people who mattered (other hygienists and people in political power) and Snow was not. Pettenkofer had become the court apothecary to King Maximilian II of Bavaria in 1850 because of the work he had done in devising a method for the manufacture of reproductions of antique stained glass and his assays for precious metals. By 1855 he had become a full professor at Munich and by 1864 he was rector of the university. Using his influence in both the academic world and at court, he was able to get hygiene recognized as a full subject in all three Bavarian universities, and he took the chair of hygiene himself at Munich. The Bavarian government was forced to build him his own Institute of Hygiene in 1878, when he threatened to accept the directorship of a newly built Institute of Hygiene in Vienna. In 1890 he was elected president of the Bavarian Academy of Sciences, and by the turn of the century virtually every major director of a hygiene institute or professor of hygiene in Germany and in much of Europe was a former student of his. He and his disciples controlled the two major journals in which hygiene research was published, so they effectively controlled the terms of the scientific debate. But like Miniver Cheevy, Max von Pettenkofer committed suicide in 1901.

So here was a man who was at the top of his profession, had the ear of the government, and controlled what was taught and what the professionals in the field read. Because Pettenkofer was in a position to have his ideas put into practice, something Chadwick was less than successful at and which Snow could not do at all, Munich developed a reasonably safe water-supply system. The system Pettenkofer devised to ensure that the citizens of Munich would be free from cholera was based not on water filtration (as would a system that had been built based on Snow's ideas) but on keeping drinking water separate from ground water. Pettenkofer thought it was necessary for clean, fresh water to be delivered to every house and garret in Munich so that people could wash—he was a vocal advocate of cleanliness, good diet, and ventilation—and then, after the water was used, remove it before it could contaminate any surfaces or become mixed with the ground water. The system brought water in from the mountains, delivered it to houses, and removed it by a sewage system that channeled it far downstream before it could allow disease to "germinate" and create a miasma.

It is obvious that Pettenkofer's solution would have differed only slightly if he had been a full convert to the germ theory. Pettenkofer was a famous scientist who used his science to clear up the dreaded cholera in a major city. The fact that he did it for the wrong reason has cast him in history as a fool, while John Snow, who had absolutely no effect on the course of history, has been cast as a hero. *Sic transit gloria.*

During this same period, because of advances in methods of performing chemical analyses on water, many people in England were focusing on the role of inorganic chemicals in water, trying to find correlates with disease. With the development of chemical methods to measure the content of inorganic salts in water, the chemical water analysts became authorities about the safety of water in England, even though they did not know that what they were measuring had anything to do with disease. The case should be a cautionary one for the present day, when the front pages of newspapers and television stations carry news stories of breakthroughs and miracles in biotechnology and gene cloning or dangers from small amounts of pesticides or voltage transformers. Each of these stories, of course, has commentary from an authority, a scientist working in the field who is certain that he or she knows the deep significance of the most current breakthrough or miracle. The layperson accepts the word of these authorities. Obviously, we must rely on authorities, but it takes a scientifically literate populace to be aware that even scientific authority is ephemeral, and a scientific community that must learn to temper its certainty when discussing with the public the social implications of science.

Disease Reframed and the "New" Public Health

By the end of the nineteenth century, the great change had been completed: There was no question now that specific microbes cause specific diseases; they could be identified and grown in pure culture. In the roughly half century since Chadwick stressed that it was the duty of well-born society to remove the disease-producing miasma from the environment of the poor to the triumphant identification of the causes of the two great scourges, tuberculosis and cholera, the idea of the nature of infectious diseases was turned on its head. But by this time, death no longer had a constant presence. Slowly but surely, major cities had been adding sewers and providing clean water to their inhabitants. Despite the horrors it brought, industrialization was improving the economic lot of the poor, and with it came better nutrition and housing. We were beginning to see a glimpse of the world as we know it.

The germ theory was accepted at about the time when the effects of the sanitation and public health reforms instituted to fight miasmas were becoming obvious to everyone. Pasteur became "Pasteur," and Koch and the other microbe hunters isolated new kinds of specific bacteria responsible for the old dreaded diseases. The idea became planted in the minds of physicians, scientists, and the public alike that the science of medicine, epitomized by "Pasteur" and the new field of bacteriology, was doing what the science of chemistry and physics had done before: improving the lives of real people. The great benefits that came from improved sanitation and nutrition were assumed to be the fruits of the progress promised by science.

The acceptance of the germ theory and the developments in bacteriology in the 1880s that resulted from it—the identification of the specific bacteria that caused the great diseases—were embraced by the advocates of public health and disease prevention in the 1890s. The intellectual basis of the public-health and sanitation movements had been the institution of *general* methods of disease prevention, so when disease became framed by *specificity,* these movements found a way to gain scientific authority and separate themselves from "mere social reforms." As two modern authorities of the subject put it, bacteriology sharply differentiated the "old" public health, the province of untrained amateurs, from the "new" public health of scientifically trained professionals. William Sedgwick, who used bacteriology to study the water supplies of Massachusetts, said, "Before 1880 we knew nothing; after 1890 we knew it all; it was a glorious ten years." The "everything" scientists came to know in those ten years was that infectious diseases are specific and that unique diseases can be transmitted in unique ways. Public health had become a legitimate arm of scientific medicine.

In the new fervor of specificity, some took on the ardor of converts. In a 600-page handbook for public-health officers in 1915, J. Scott Mac-Nutt devoted about half to contagious diseases, four pages to industrial hygiene, and gave "only passing notice to housing, water supplies, public education and environmental health." But others worked very hard to incorporate the new, powerful idea of specificity into the more traditional aims of "preventing disease, prolonging life, and promoting physical health and efficiency thorough organized community efforts for the sanitation of the environment, the control of community infections, education of the individual in principles of personal hygiene."

The "new" public health urged on the public the acceptance of the idea of specificity and the germ theory of disease. But the association of dirt and disease that the "old" public health had done so much to establish remained fixed in the public's mind, and while officials tried to make germs as fearful as filth, it was a difficult task, because "unlike garbage and overflowing sewers, germs were not readily visible."

America, where public-health laboratories had been opened in the 1880s in Rhode Island, Michigan, New York, and Massachusetts, had opened its gates to the poor and hungry, "the huddled masses yearning to be free." Though they might have been free, they were still poor, hungry, huddled masses crammed into teeming tenements. The immigrants' overcrowding and subsequent lack of sanitation caused the native-born middle classes to link them with disease, so that by the early 1900s, even though the germ theory had permeated scientific medicine and the "new" scientific public health, the power of the old way of framing disease remained when polio appeared on the scene.

While the polio epidemic struck many of the industrialized nations, it was especially bad in the United States; between 1905 and 1909, two-thirds of the over 8,000 cases of polio reported worldwide occurred in America. In 1916 there were 27,000 cases in the United States, with 6,000 deaths. Between June and December in New York City alone, there were 2,400 deaths from the 8,900 cases. While the death rate for that horrid epidemic year was 25 percent, many of the three children in four who survived were paralyzed and would remain so for life. The disease became known as infantile paralysis, the very name freezing the hearts of parents.

The new public-health laboratories set about isolating the "germ" that caused the disease, feeling, in all probability, that this would be yet another triumph of microbe hunting. But no bacterial cause could be found and the public, which had just begun to grasp the reality of disease caused by things that were invisible but could at least be grown in the laboratory, was informed that this new disease was caused by agents that could be neither seen nor grown. The great leap into the era of science in the new century was not proving to be easy; science, which had delivered so much, was proving sluggardly in isolating the cause and eradicating infantile paralysis. The same public that had gladly given credit to science for the dramatic reductions of tuberculosis and cholera was now demanding the same for polio. Scientific medicine made pleas for patience; miracles after all don't come quickly.

The new public health took an approach very similar to the old public health. Disease might be caused by specific agents (in this case a virus), but these agents have always been associated with dirt and poverty; therefore Americans must redouble their efforts to eliminate this breeding ground of the terrible new virus. Campaigns against flies, dirt, and crowding were carried out in earnest. One unfortunate outcome of this well-meaning program was that the new immigrants were singled out as the visible source of dirt, disease, and ignorance. How could the children of clean, well-nourished, middle-class Americans with the best of sanitation and the cleanest of water be struck by this new disease? An era of scapegoating of immigrants began out of the frustration that science could not control and eradicate this terrible disease.

Science was triumphant in the minds of the public, medical scientists, and even public health officials. The answer to the question Why does "Pasteur" get the credit for that which the sanitation movement and public health were primarily responsible? is that public health was happy to cede the credit to gain the authority of science. The same answer applies to the question of who made John Snow a hero: He became a convenient icon to show that public health was aware of germs before the advent of germ theory. The changes in living conditions brought about by public health in the nineteenth century were very dramatic, and since they coincided with the reframing of disease, brought about by bacteriology, in an era when science was "in the air," how could anyone resist bringing the two together?

It is ironic that science was given so much credit for the disappearance of disease but so little has been said about it's most important contribution to medicine, the idea of specific causes of disease. Without this profound change in how we view disease there would be no movement to specific therapy.

Part

II

Reframing
the Internal
World

Chapter

6

"Never to Die of a Disease in the Future"

B
y making the invisible world of disease-causing microbes accessible to both our understanding and our manipulation, bacteriology in the 1870s provided the scientific basis for specificity. In the 1880s Pasteur set in motion the scientific thinking that led to the idea that there can be specific *prevention* of disease. The development of specific vaccines to prevent specific diseases, and immunology, the science that studied how they work, only became possible when disease had been reframed, yet we will see that the promise of specific prevention was probably one of the most powerful forces leading to the full acceptance of germ theory and the idea of specific therapy for disease. Pasteur became "Pasteur" because of this promise, yet this was not the first time disease had been conquered and the conqueror made a hero. Successful, albeit risky, methods to prevent smallpox, one of the great scourges of the world, had been available for at least two centuries in Europe and perhaps much longer than that in China, India, and Persia. Edward Jenner had become a hero a century earlier, when he devised a much less risky method of preventing smallpox, called vaccination.

People in antiquity knew from repeated observation that those who recovered from some diseases were likely not to contract them again. Thucydides, the Greek chronicler of the Peloponnesian Wars, was probably the first to record it.

> Yet still the ones who felt most pity for the sick and the dying [in the plague of Athens] were those who had had the plague themselves and had recovered from it. They knew

what it was like and at the same time felt themselves to be safe, for no one caught the disease twice, or, if he did, the second attack was never fatal. Such people were congratulated on all sides, and they themselves were so elated at the time of their recovery that they fondly imagined that they could *never die of any other disease in the future* [author's emphasis].

The lucky survivors were indeed protected from dying from a second bout of the plague that raged in Athens at the time (we don't know what the disease really was), but they most certainly could die of *other* diseases in the future. It took a long time for people to realize that the protection possessed by the survivors of one disease was specific to the disease from which they recovered and did not protect them from getting other diseases. So when disease began to be reframed in terms of specificity, the idea of specific cures and specific preventions came with it.

"The Small-pox . . . Is Here Entirely Harmless ": Jenner and Vaccination

Smallpox is an ancient disease, dating in Europe at least from the sixth century, and perhaps to A.D. 1000 in the Orient. By the seventeenth century it had replaced the plague as Europe's most devastating and feared disease; there are reports, perhaps somewhat exaggerated, that at that time only five out of every one thousand people *escaped* infection with smallpox. There is good reason to believe that one out of four died of "the Scourge" in seventeenth-century England. "The smallpox was always present, filling the churchyard with corpses, tormenting with constant fears all whom it had not yet stricken, leaving on those whose lives it spared the hideous traces of its power, turning the babe into a changeling at which the mother shuddered, and making the eyes and cheeks of a betrothed maiden objects of horror to the lover."

Over time, people began to notice that second attacks of smallpox were rare, and it became the practice in many areas for people who had recovered from smallpox to nurse those who were suffering from the disease. Probably on the basis of this folk observation, long before modern science, a means of protecting people from the ravages of the disease was developed in China, India, and Persia. The practice was to intentionally induce a mild case of the disease in a person so that he or she would not develop a severe case later. This was done by the rather dangerous and unappealing means of inoculating a healthy person with small amounts of disease material from someone who was suffering with the disease. Lady Mary Montagu, the wife of the British ambassador to Constantinople in the early 1700s, is usually credited with introducing this practice into European society. One wonders why Europeans, who were so sure that their culture was superior to any others that they spent a great deal of effort forcing it upon those others, had not made the same observation themselves. At any rate, Lady Mary wrote to a friend in England, "I am going to tell you a thing that I am sure will make you wish yourself here. The small-pox, so fatal, and so general amongst us, is here entirely harmless by the invention of *ingrafting . . .*"

The "ingrafting" consisted of "opening the pustules of one who had the Small Pox ripe upon them and drying up the Matter with a little Cotton . . . and afterwards put it up the nostrils of those they would infect" or poke it into the skin. Those who were ingrafted showed some mild symptoms, but not the tragic disfigurement suffered by those who had a full-blown case of smallpox. Lady Mary had her children ingrafted by the English physician of the embassy, Dr. Charles Maitland, and was obviously convinced of the efficacy of the procedure. Lady Mary was not optimistic, however, about the practice being instituted in her native land. She was "patriot enough to take pains to bring this useful invention into fashion in England; and I should not fail to write to some of our doctors very particularly about it, if I knew any one of them that I thought had virtue enough to destroy such a considerable branch of their revenue for the good of mankind. . . . Perhaps if I live to return, I may, however, have courage to war with them." There truly seems to be nothing new under the sun! But we must remember that the doctors Lady Mary was talking about did not have the same kind of relationship with their patients we are accustomed to in the twentieth century. Recall that at the time doctors and patients were social equals, and the patients often were almost as sophisticated about medicine as the physicians; they were not people who would for one moment consider being a guinea pig for some "foreign" treatment.

During the smallpox epidemic of May 1721 in England, Princess Caroline, wife of George I, wanted the royal children to be "inoculated." Of course, heirs to the throne are not lightly subjected to unfamiliar and "foreign" medical practices, so it was decided to see if the procedure was indeed safe enough to be used on the royal children. The king sought advice from the royal attorney and solicitor-general on the legality of his granting a pardon to several condemned criminals in Newgate prison if they would agree to be inoculated. It probably should come as no surprise that the king's legal advisers found that the king could do what the king wanted to do . . . "the Lives of the persons being in the power of His Majesty, he may Grant a Pardon to them upon such lawful Condition as he shall think fit; and as to this particular condition We have no objection in point of Law, the rather because the carrying on this practice to perfection may tend to the General Benefit of Mankind."

Three men and three women prisoners were inoculated on the morning of August 29, 1721, in front of twenty-five physicians, surgeons, and apothecaries, as well as representatives of the press, who covered the story because of the interest in the royal children. All but one of the subjects developed mild symptoms of smallpox, and that person was later found to have had a slight case of smallpox the year before (a fact that will become important to this story in a very short while, when we meet Edward Jenner). They all recovered, showing no ill effects of the inoculations and, true to the royal word, were pardoned on September 6.

This experiment convinced Princess Caroline that the procedure was safe, but it did not address the question of efficacy. Would these prisoners really be as protected if they came into contact with an infected person as if they had contracted a "real" case of smallpox, or could they still get the disease? The physician who carried out the inoculations was the same Dr. Charles Maitland who several years earlier had inoculated the children of Lady Mary Montagu in Constantinople. To show that the inoculation of smallpox material in small amounts was not only safe but really did protect against future infections with smallpox, he arranged for one of the survivors of the Newgate inoculations, a nineteen-year-old woman, to come to a small town near London to act as the nurse and lie in the same bed every night with a ten-year-old smallpox victim. So much for royal pardons! Fortunately, after six weeks of exposure, she still had not contracted the disease and, we hope, lived happily ever after. One can only be thankful that the good doctor didn't think— or didn't tell the queen—that the proper control for this experiment should have been to have an uninoculated nineteen-year-old woman also share the bed with the diseased boy to make sure he really had smallpox.

This cruel experiment convinced the queen that inoculation could protect against the disease. But apparently one could not be too careful with royal children; the question was raised that the procedure might work in adults but still be dangerous for children, so Princess Caroline asked that a list of orphans who had not had smallpox be drawn up so that they might be inoculated. (To show that even royals have feelings, she asked that the entire procedure be carried out at her expense.) In due course the orphans were inoculated and showed no ill effects, so it was now deemed safe for the royal children to be inoculated. None of them contracted smallpox in later years.

But even though the safety of inoculation had been so publicly demonstrated, there was little movement of the general public to avail themselves of it. The way medicine was organized was one possible reason, but given the general ideas of how disease was framed, it is not difficult to see that there was little reason to think well of such an obviously damn-fool idea as intentionally putting miasma-containing pus into a normal person. There were in fact enough cases where the procedure was not carried out properly—with the result that people developed severe cases of smallpox—that the idea, which was repulsive at best and dangerous at worse, fell into disuse in Europe. Three quarters of a century later, Edward Jenner was able to make the procedure less dangerous and a bit more aesthetically pleasing.

Edward Jenner (1749–1823), like Robert Koch a century later, was a country practitioner with an interest in natural history. In fact, his observations on natural history had been important enough for him to be elected a member of the Royal Society. Like all important historical events, those leading Jenner to his great discovery have become a story so often told that it might as well be true. The story is that he diagnosed a dairymaid in his Gloucestershire practice as having smallpox, but she told him (with a girlish shake of the head? a shocked look of incredulity? an exasperated sigh?), "I cannot take the smallpox because I have had the cowpox." Cowpox, as the name implies, is a disease of cattle, so why should a person who had a cattle disease consider herself unable to contract smallpox? It was known to all rural people that those who had the scars of cowpox on their hands did not have the scars of smallpox on their faces. We now know that the disease of humans (smallpox) and the disease of cows (cowpox) are caused by very similar viruses, and the pustules that are one of the major symptoms of both diseases are similar. It must have been known by everyone in rural Gloucestershire that cowpox can infect and cause a mild disease in humans. The great insight of Jenner, who knew nothing about viruses, was to realize that the scars of cowpox on the hands of local milkmaids, and the slight illness that came with them, gave these women the same kind of protection as an inoculation with human disease material. Perhaps these women had unintentionally received some relatively harmless disease material from a cow with the same result as if they had undergone the more dangerous procedure of intentional inoculation. If that were the case, then Jenner should be able to show that *intentionally* inoculating someone with the cowpox material might prevent him from contracting smallpox, just as the accidental infection had protected the milkmaids.

The approach Jenner took fit into the way of thinking of the new philosophy of science; it was a systematic and logical way of testing a prediction. First, he knew that in the old method of inoculation, people who had never had smallpox always showed local swelling at the site where the pus was placed under the skin. This is one of the mild symptoms that folklore dictated was necessary in order to avoid contracting the disease again. We already saw that the one prisoner in the royal experiment who had recovered from an earlier case of smallpox did not have this kind of reaction when he was inoculated during the experiment. So Jenner knew that one sign that a person is protected from smallpox is that he does not show swelling at the site of inoculation; but to make sure that this was correct, he inoculated a small amount of pus from *smallpox* patients into some uninfected people and into some people he knew had previously been infected with cowpox. He then waited to see if there was swelling at the site of inoculation. No swelling at the site of inoculation in the people who had already had a slight case of *cow-*

pox would show him that, indeed, infection with cowpox prevents the swelling from *smallpox*. This is exactly what he found: The naturally cowpox-infected patients showed only a transitory local reaction and no characteristic fluid-containing pustule at the inoculation site. In contrast, those people who had never been naturally infected with cowpox all showed the characteristic pustule.

This little experiment was a strong argument that the folklore had a basis in fact (as it so often does) and that "the cowpox protects the human constitution from the infection of the smallpox." In passing, it is worth noting that this is also a good experiment by modern ethical standards. Jenner was not subjecting the patients to anything that was unduly harmful, because inoculation with smallpox pus was already an accepted, if not popular, medical practice. To carry out his experiment today, he would have to go before his institution's ethical-standards board, at which he would no doubt argue that the royal smallpox experiment, which probably would not have been allowed by the ethics board, showed that inoculation with smallpox can be both safe and efficacious and that he was not putting his patients into any unusual or unnecessary danger.

Now Jenner began the real test to see if someone *intentionally* inoculated with cowpox would fail to develop pustules when he or she received an inoculation with smallpox a little while later. He inoculated an eight-year-old boy named James Phipps with cowpox and several months later inoculated him with smallpox. Again remember that even if the experiment failed, Joseph Phipps would not have come down with smallpox; he would only have had a strong reaction at the site of the smallpox inoculation, as did the prisoners in the first royal experiment. The results were all that Jenner could hope for: "[O]n his being inoculated some months afterward, it proved that he was secure." Jenner called the procedure vaccination from the Latin word *vacca*, for "cow."

The original report that Jenner sent to the Royal Society was rejected for publication with the friendly admonition that such an incomplete study would injure his reputation. In fact he did have very few subjects and the claim was so very important that it merited more evidence. On those grounds we can forgive the Royal Society for rejecting one of the most important medical papers ever submitted to any journal. By 1798, Jenner had completed more studies and had them privately published as a pamphlet, with the catchy title *An Inquiry into the Causes and Effects of the Variolae, a Disease Discovered in Some of the Western Countries of England, Particularly Gloucestershire, and known by the Name of Cow Pox.* With the publication of the pamphlet, the importance of Jenner's discovery of vaccination to protect from smallpox was recognized.

The procedure of vaccination was somewhat controversial for a while, as most important discoveries are. But it gained in acceptance and its effects were so clear that by 1802 Parliament voted Jenner £10,000, and in 1806 £20,000, as recognition of the importance of his achievements. In America, Thomas Jefferson had his whole family and some of his neighbors vaccinated. But even though the dreaded smallpox was now on its way to becoming a preventable disease, a significant number of people were opposed to vaccination. Antivaccination societies were formed in England (see the famous 1813 print by the satirist James Gilray showing the dire consequences of vaccination). As late as the end of the nineteenth century, which he called the Wonderful Century, Alfred Wallace, the codiscoverer of evolution, while recounting the wonders of science, called vaccination a hoax and a dangerous procedure. But even with the opposition, it was clear to most people that vaccination worked and the procedure was gradually accepted universally.

Because communicable diseases were still not considered separate entities and only cranks believed in the idea of contagion, there was no attempt to derive a *general principle* from Jenner's work, to try to develop vaccination procedures for other diseases. All of that changed, of course, when the germ theory of disease became accepted in the middle of the nineteenth century and so many agents of infectious disease were identified during the golden age of bacteriology. When that happened, there were many proposals to try to use the principles of Jenner's vaccination (causing a mild form of a similar disease to induce protection) against other diseases. The problem was to find something comparable to the harmless form of similar disease that Jenner had found with cowpox.

"Well then! men of little faith!": Pasteur Generalizes Vaccination

The mythology of "Pasteur" has it that he was so fascinated with the idea of generalizing Jenner's cowpox work that he recalled farmyard experiences—seeing animals naturally infected with bacteria that cause only mild symptoms passing on the bacteria to other animals in which the bacteria are lethal. Supposedly, he realized that this was analogous to the cowpox-smallpox story. Whether this is true or not is not too important, but it does fit into Pasteur's well-known dictum of science: "In the field of experimentation, chance favors only the prepared mind." Pasteur's ability to generalize Jenner's vaccination certainly shows that his mind was "prepared."

Pasteur had begun to work with the disease of chickens, called chicken cholera, in 1879, about the time he started intense studies on the bacteria responsible for several human diseases. Even though it shares the name with the dreaded disease of humans, this disease of chickens has no relation to the cholera of humans. The bacteria that cause chicken cholera were routinely grown in cultures in Pasteur's laboratory, and when a sample was inoculated into chickens, they inevitably contracted the disease and died. However, after returning from summer holiday in 1879, Pasteur found that the cultures that had previously proven virulent for chickens had now lost their lethal effect. Pasteur then isolated a fresh culture from an infected chicken during a natural outbreak of the disease, and as expected, normal chickens succumbed when injected with the new cultures. Perhaps for reasons of frugality, Pasteur decided to inject the new cultures into some of the chickens that had survived the inoculation with the cultures that had lost their virulence. To his surprise, the chickens remained free of disease! Although he was looking for harmless, naturally occurring bacteria that were *similar* to the dangerous ones that caused disease, this chance observation with chicken cholera gave him something even better—a less virulent form of the *same* bacteria. Just as the harmless contact with cowpox protected from the dreadful effects of smallpox, the harmless chicken-cholera organisms seemed to have protected animals from the lethal effects of the virulent ones.

The brilliance of Pasteur's association of the two phenomena is his recognition that even though they were specific, infectious agents could change: They could lose their virulence. The idea of specificity of microbial life forms, an idea that Pasteur had introduced, had taken hold so firmly that Koch was arguing that microbial life was absolutely invariant. Now here was Pasteur, the father of specificity, saying that the specificity was not absolute. If Pasteur was correct, the advantage was obvious. To develop protection, one would not have to look for analogous diseases in some other species, one only had to look for ways to make changes in the infectious agents themselves to render them harmless. If bacteria have properties that can change or be changed, he could take advantage of this and make them as harmless as Jenner's cowpox and his avirulent chicken cholera. It was clear to him that if he could really do this, he could "vaccinate" against all diseases! But Pasteur had to find a way to make virulent microbes harmless and still retain their mysterious ability to protect the body. Anthrax was to be his first great success.

Soon after Koch discovered the bacillus that causes anthrax, Pasteur began his studies on the disease. He knew that there was a high incidence of anthrax in the Beauce country of France and that the local shepherds and farmers thought some fields were "accursed." They knew that even years after the last outbreak of anthrax, sheep grazing in these "accursed fields" could mysteriously come down with the disease. This inexplicable fact was actually used as an argument *against* the microbial cause of anthrax until Koch showed that the bacillus responsible for anthrax can exist as a spore, able to lie dormant for years. Pasteur had also discovered that spores can lie dormant for long periods of time when he had studied the diseases of silkworms plaguing the French silk industry, and in what we can see as his typical style of thinking, he realized that the two situations could be analogous. The sudden reappearance of the disease of silkworms after long periods free of disease and the sudden reappearance of anthrax in a fallow field was just too much to be coincidence. It seemed reasonable to suppose that spores were making the fields "accursed" because the sheep were being infected by them.

Because the portraits always show him in his laboratory, most people don't know that Pasteur's work style was a combination of laboratory and fieldwork. His practice of taking on problems that had both practical importance and theoretical significance meant that he often set up a laboratory at the site, so it was natural that he set up a field station in the Beauce area among the "accursed fields." One day while walking through the fields shortly after the harvest, he noticed a patch of soil with a slightly different color. The owner told him this was where sheep that had died of anthrax had been buried the year before. Poking around the soil, Pasteur noticed that it was rich in earthworms and, according to yet another admiring biographer, realized on the spot that these earthworms could be responsible for bringing the anthrax spores from the carcasses of the dead sheep to the surface, where they could infect the sheep grazing in the field. In short order he was able to show that guinea pigs injected with soil from these earthworms came down with anthrax. It appeared that the spores came to the surface in the gut of the earthworms and, once above ground, infected the sheep through small abrasions on their legs caused by the dried stubble in the fields. The reason that some fields were "accursed" seemed to be solved.

But one more piece of folk knowledge stuck with him: Everyone knew that not all of the sheep grazing in the "accursed fields" contracted anthrax. When Pasteur injected some of these animals with pure cultures of the anthrax bacilli, he found to his surprise that some of them did not come down with the disease, while sheep from other fields injected with the same pure cultures died of anthrax. This happened a few years before the chicken-cholera episode and at the time there was no reason for him to think that the lucky sheep that did not get anthrax in the "accursed field" may actually have recovered from a mild case of the disease. But he filed the observation away in his mind to draw upon later. When he made the chicken-cholera discovery, his "prepared mind" saw the similarities among the sheep recovered from anthrax to withstand a lethal injection with anthrax bacilli, the chickens to withstand a lethal injection of chicken cholera, and the people vaccinated with cowpox to withstand the ravages of smallpox. Like the chickens that had been initially treated with the culture that had lost its virulence, those sheep that had recovered from the infection with the anthrax spores were protected from a further infection. This became the impetus for Pasteur to begin a search for ways to remove the disease-causing properties from virulent cultures of anthrax bacilli, a process known technically as attenuation. (It now should be obvious why it was important for him to think that the bacteria could change their properties.)

Probably reasoning that it was the searing August heat of Paris that had caused the cultures of chicken cholera to lose their virulence, Pasteur tried a similar trick with cultures of anthrax. He was lucky, because he found that by growing the anthrax bacilli at a slightly elevated temperature, they too became attenuated; they lost their virulence and could no longer cause disease. But would the attenuated bacilli protect animals from lethal injections with virulent anthrax? He injected guinea pigs, rabbits, and then some sheep with the attenuated anthrax bacilli and found that they were indeed protected when he challenged them with virulent bacilli. It appeared that he had found what so many had been ardently seeking, a way to generalize Jenner's principle of vaccination.

Pasteur's great discoveries, which led to the acceptance of the germ theory of disease and the phenomenal rise of bacteriology, were not without detractors. In our Whiggish way of looking at scientific history, it seems inconceivable that events we now see as historically significant could not have been obvious to everyone at the time. But as we saw with John Snow and Pettenkofer, there are always well-established and respected authorities in the field who see things differently, and they do not hesitate to defend the positions they feel to be correct. We are fortunate that the middle of the nineteenth century was a time when internecine battles were conducted in a much more visible manner than they are today and that language was still used with flair. A scientist had to be a talented debater and polemicist to make sure that his views would prevail. As an example of what Pasteur had to contend with, one Dr. Rossignol, a leader of the medical community that was still wedded to balance of humors and miasmas, wrote of him:

> Microbiolatry is the fashion and reigns undisputed: it is a doctrine which must not even be discussed, particularly when its pontiff, the learned M. Pasteur, has pronounced the sacramental words, *I have spoken*. The microbe alone is and shall be the characteristic of a disease; that much is understood and settled; henceforth the germ theory must take precedence over the clinical art; the microbe alone is true, and Pasteur is its prophet.

124

Remember, Pasteur was a chemist whose work and thinking were having a profound effect on the field of medicine, which was Rossignol's turf. This confrontation of authorities resulted in a highly publicized and famous public test of Pasteur's claim that he could protect animals from anthrax by using the same principles as Jenner's vaccination. In the spring of 1881 Rossignol organized the financial support of farmers at Pouilly le Fort in the Brie district and used his own farm as the location for the large-scale test. He knew that many of the physicians and veterinarians who were involved were hoping this would be a public humiliation for the theory, the discipline, and "the learned M. Pasteur." The event was highly publicized, probably by those who were sure it would fail even more than by those who had confidence it would work. The press would be there in force, including the Paris correspondent of *The Times* (of London).

Pasteur and the skeptical committee came to an agreement that twenty-four sheep, one goat, and six cows were to be inoculated with the heated anthrax cultures and then, after an interval of time, injected with virulent anthrax bacilli. This is a standard procedure, a variant of the one Jenner used with young James Phipps, but it needed more than this to be a proper experiment. Pasteur had to prove that the virulent anthrax bacilli with which he was challenging the "vaccinated" animals really were able to cause disease. (Remember the young woman who recovered from the royal smallpox experiment and was made to sleep in the same bed with the smallpox-infected boy?) So at the same time that the first group received the challenge of virulent organisms, a "control" group of twenty-four sheep, one goat, and four cows that had not been "vaccinated" were also challenged with the virulent anthrax. In two ways the experiment was quite different from Jenner's. First, if the "vaccination" failed, all of the animals would die; if it worked, the vaccinated animals would live but the control group would die. Second, the field trial at Pouilly le Fort was being carried out before the public. While Jenner was a respected physician in his local area, Pasteur was a world-famous scientist who was putting his own authority and reputation, as well as the reputation and authority of bacteriology, on the line.

On May 5, 1881, the first group of animals was vaccinated with the attenuated anthrax and the control group remained unimmunized. All of the animals were challenged with virulent cultures a few days later. Pasteur had his most trusted assistant, Dr. Pierre Roux, make the inoculations. Later Roux related how as he left the laboratory in Paris for Pouilly le Fort, Pasteur, in a gay mood, told him, "be sure not to make a mistake with the bottles." The story, perhaps apocryphal, is that several days after the challenge with the virulent organisms a message was brought to Pasteur advising him that some of the vaccinated sheep looked sick. He turned on Roux in a rage and accused him of having spoiled the field test by his negligence. Madame Pasteur attempted to calm him and get him ready for the journey to Pouilly le Fort the next day, but he would have none of it. He would not go! He would not expose himself to the ridicule of the public! Roux should go alone and suffer the humiliation, since it was all his fault!! However, a telegram came during the night telling him that all was well—the vaccinated animals were free of disease. The next day, knowing the trial was a success, Pasteur stood in his carriage, turned to the crowd, and exclaimed in a triumphant voice, "Well, then! Men of little faith!"

The results of the trial were astonishing. All of the immunized sheep were free of disease. Twenty-one control sheep were already dead and two others died before the very eyes of the spectators. The last of the unvaccinated sheep died the next day. All six vaccinated cows were normal, but all four of the controls had severe symptoms of anthrax. A few weeks after this triumph, Pasteur was the undisputed hero of the International Medical Congress in London and it was here that he proposed the use of the words *vaccine* and *vaccination* as generic terms as homage to "the merit and immense services rendered by one of the greatest men of England, your Jenner."

Five years later, in 1885, Pasteur would once again astonish the world by announcing that he had created a vaccine for the dreaded disease rabies. He had been working on a method of attenuating the agent that causes rabies (it would later be found to be caused by a virus and not a bacterium) but did not know if the method really worked. In a report to the French Academy, he related how nine-year-old Joseph Meister had been bitten on the hands, calves, and thighs by a ferocious dog. Young Joseph had been pulled from beneath the dog covered with foam and blood. The dog, which was killed by its master, appeared to be rabid, and the boy was taken to Paris. Pasteur, who was not a physician, had him examined by two medical colleagues, who confirmed what everyone had suspected: There was a very good chance that young Joseph Meister would come down with rabies. Because rabies is virtually always fatal, Pasteur decided to treat him with the attenuated rabies vaccine that he had been testing in animals. "The death of the child appearing to be inevitable, I decided, not without lively and cruel anxiety, as one could imagine, to attempt on Joseph Meister the method which for me was constantly successful with dogs . . ."

Joseph Meister was inoculated with a solution of dried spinal cord of rabbits that had been inoculated with material from rabid dogs and had been allowed to dry in a flask for fifteen days. This was the method Pasteur had developed to attenuate the agent of rabies. Joseph Meister did not contract rabies and it was concluded that the vaccine had worked. "Since the middle of August, I have looked forward with confidence to the future good health of Joseph Meister. Again at the present time, after three months and three weeks had passed since the accident, his health leaves nothing to be desired."

Joseph Meister later became gatekeeper at the Pasteur Institute. There is a widely told story that on the day the Germans invaded Paris during the Second World War, he committed suicide rather than see them force their way into the crypt of his beloved Pasteur. This crypt, which can be visited by appointment at the Pasteur Institute, is a mixture of religion and science, the two strong elements of the life of Louis Pasteur, and is vivid proof of the reverence in which he was held.

The very next year, in 1886, a young American named Theobald Smith showed that Pasteur's method of attenuation for bacteria (not viruses like rabies) could routinely be achieved by heating cultures of various different bacteria at 58° C (about 130° F) for ten minutes. This meant that the principle of attenuation, like the principle of vaccination, was a general one. It now seemed possible to prevent any disease caused by bacteria with a specific vaccine. A new horizon had been revealed. Sanitation and public health prevented disease by keeping the agents that cause them away from people; vaccination would protect people from a specific disease even if the causative agent was present. A new scientific discipline called immunology had been born, and with the promise of prevention through vaccination, the "Pasteurization" of our views was complete: Science and medicine had given us bacteriology and immunology, which had conquered death!

Koch and the False Cure for Tuberculosis

The time we are describing was, like our own, a time when scientific and medical advances were treated as news, and the great promise of the power of scientific medicine was constantly before the public. And as in our own time, the public expected delivery on the promise. The ability of Pasteur to actually save people with the rabies treatment, even though it was beginning to meet the same kind of opposition in some quarters that Jenner's treatment had met, was widely seen as the first of a hoped-for series of vaccines that would be used to prevent human disease. Certainly, scientists believed this and Robert Koch, perhaps not to let his rival Pasteur have all the glory, was the first to act upon it.

Around 1886 Koch was becoming increasingly depressed. His marriage was failing, his beloved daughter had become engaged, and he had become an administrator who no longer carried out his own experiments. In the fall of 1889 he took a long holiday in Switzerland and when he returned to Berlin isolated himself in his laboratory and began working away at a project he kept secret even from his closest colleagues. In August 1890 the results of this solitary research were made known in a paper he delivered at the Tenth International Congress of Medicine in Berlin. Koch announced to the world that he had found a cure for tuberculosis, the single largest killer, which was responsible for almost 15 percent of all reported deaths in Europe! Koch reported to the Congress that

> my experiments with these substances, though lasting more than a year, are not yet concluded, so that all I can say at present is that if guinea pigs are treated they cannot be inoculated with tuberculosis, and guinea pigs which already are in the late stages of the disease are completely cured, although the body suffers no ill effects from the treatment. From these

> experiments I will draw no other conclusion at present than that it is possible to render pathogenic bacteria within the body harmless without ill effect on the body itself.

Imagine the effect of such an announcement by the great Koch. Despite the disclaimer that his work had been done only with guinea pigs, the tone must have struck everyone as one of modesty becoming a medical hero. Surely Robert Koch would not lightly announce at an international congress that it is possible to render pathogenic bacteria inside the body harmless without ill effects on the body itself if he did not believe this was true for people as well as guinea pigs. Understandably, tuberculosis patients from all over Europe descended upon Berlin, hoping to be cured with the miraculous treatment. Lister came from London to witness the cure firsthand because Koch had not revealed to the congress how he prepared the material. *The Lancet* said that Lister "compared the action of Koch's fluid with that used by Pasteur in the case of anthrax, *an injection of which gave complete immunity from this disease . . .*" (author's emphasis). If Lord Lister held such high promise for the treatment, it must be correct. Unfortunately, Lister never got a chance to actually talk to Koch or see any of his data; he was simply caught up in the excitement of the times.

An English magazine sent Sir Arthur Conan Doyle, himself a physician, to Berlin. Doyle reported that when he visited Dr. Libbertz, whom Koch had entrusted with the preparation and distribution of the mysterious material, he saw a "pile of letters upon the floor, four feet across, and as high as a man's knee" from tuberculosis patients asking to be treated by the method. And that pile represented only a single day's post. Pasteur and the heads of the departments of the Pasteur Institute sent Koch a congratulatory telegram, and at a meeting of the French Academy there was extensive discussion of the new therapy. The result appeared to be so conclusive that Pasteur, when asked to comment, said, *"Cela y est, cela y est, il n'y a pas à discuter"* (That is it, that is it, there is nothing to discuss).

But the euphoria was short-lived. It soon became painfully clear that Koch's treatment of tuberculosis in humans was not comparable to Pasteur's treatment of anthrax in sheep. It did not cure patients of their tuberculosis. The material, which he called tuberculin, was an extract made from the culture fluids in which tubercle bacilli had grown. The principle

Koch had used is clear; as with Pasteur's vaccination against anthrax, he was attempting the treatment of an individual with material from the disease-causing agent. The same elements of specificity were there, only this time they did not work as a therapy; in fact, many of the people who were treated became more seriously ill. After the disappointment died down, it was realized that the rather severe reaction at the site of injection of tuberculin into the skin of a person who has been infected with tubercle bacilli but who still does not exhibit symptoms could be a valuable diagnostic test for tuberculosis. It is still used for this purpose today.

We now know that Koch had really discovered a whole new part of the immune response but of course had no way of knowing it. The "Koch phenomenon," the reaction around the site of the injected tuberculin in a patient or experimental animal that is infected with tubercle bacilli, is a form of "hypersensitivity" or "allergy." By injecting the material into the body, Koch was inducing a generalized allergic reaction with severe consequences. Koch's fame kept him from a total disgrace, but he never again held the esteem of the world he had at the height of his microbe-hunting days.

Behring and the Real Cure for Diphtheria

The near fiasco with tuberculin set back the hopes that all infectious diseases could be treated by the principle of vaccination, but it did not destroy them. So high were the hopes of the populace that it was considered just a matter of time before the new science of immunology, moving hand in hand with bacteriology, would discover dramatic new vaccines.

In 1889, an ambitious young German army doctor named Emil Behring was assigned to Koch's Institute for Infectious Diseases in Berlin. He was to direct the first successful application in humans of the new discipline of immunology against the widespread childhood disease diphtheria. The bacteriological discoveries that set the stage for the immune therapy came, not surprisingly, from people in Paris and Berlin who were working at the institutes that had been built for Pasteur and Koch in those cities. Two years before, Emil Roux in Paris made the remarkable discovery that diphtheria could be induced in experimental animals by injecting them with the liquid that the diphtheria bacilli had grown in after the bacteria had been removed. He grew the diphtheria bacilli in liquid cultures and then passed the material through a series of filters whose pores were increasingly smaller and smaller. Eventually, only the liquid could pass through the filters because the pores were too small for the bacteria to pass through, a method that was already used in the sanitation of water. The surprise, of course, was that the fluid was able to cause the disease even after the bacteria were removed, which meant that diphtheria bacilli cause the disease by producing a liquid *toxin*. In Berlin in 1890, Shibasaburo Kitasato discovered that the bacillus responsible for tetanus also produces a toxin.

Just as the bacteria that cause these diseases are specific for each disease, so too are the toxins. The toxin from *Corynebacterium diphtheria*, the bacteria that cause diphtheria, does not cause tetanus, and the toxin from *Clostridium tetani*, the bacteria that cause tetanus, does not cause diphtheria. About the only thing that diphtheria and tetanus have in common is that they are both caused by the toxin produced by the bacteria responsible for the diseases. In a brief but epoch-making paper in December 1890, Behring and Kitasato reported that by injecting a rabbit with an amount of toxin of tetanus bacilli so small that it did not cause disease, the animal was able to survive greater and greater amounts of toxin. The first dose of the toxin, which is too low to cause visible disease, somehow allows the animal to withstand the injection of a slightly higher dose. Eventually, "the degree of immunity of this animal was such that it would stand a dose of 10cc of a bacteria-containing culture of virulent tetanus bacilli, while a normal rabbit would always die from a dose of 0.5cc." Obviously, this method of inducing protection is too dangerous to be used in humans, but it dramatically showed that the promise of using vaccination for other diseases was a real one.

One week later, Behring, this time writing alone, reported the same results for the toxin of diphtheria. Behring and Kitasato had a very clear idea that the injections of the increasing doses of tetanus or diphtheria had caused something to happen in the animals that could specifically neutralize the toxin. They called the material that protected against the lethal effects of the toxin *antitoxin*, a term that continues to be used to this day. The implications for therapy were obvious: If one could only figure out a way to attenuate the toxin—i.e., render it harmless but have it retain its ability to induce the animal to make the antitoxin—protection against diphtheria would be a reality.

Behring and Kitasato had made another discovery that was of equal importance and led to an immediate application. They found that if they mixed a small amount of diphtheria or tetanus toxin with some blood from an animal that had been specifically protected, the toxin was neutralized. Clearly the antitoxin was in the blood. It now became perfectly clear that while it might be dangerous to try to protect children by injecting them with small amounts of the dangerous toxin, they might be able to be protected with antitoxin that was already present in the blood of some other animal. First the idea had to be tested in experimental animals, so Behring and Kitasato injected mice with ever-increasing doses of toxin and then they transferred a small amount of the "protected" blood to disease-free mice. When these mice were injected with enough toxin to kill unin-jected control mice, they survived. This was a momentous experiment for two reasons. On the practical level, it made clear the avenue to be taken for human therapy. On the theoretical level, it focused attention to "something in the blood" that was responsible for the protection.

These results made possible the first human therapy to come from the new science of immunology since Pasteur's rabies treatment. Now that everyone knew diphtheria was caused by the toxin produced by the bacilli found growing in the throat of children with the disease, and that animal experiments showed that serum containing antitoxin could pre-vent the disease from developing in experimental animals, it was a simple step to injecting children who had contracted diphtheria with antitoxin to neutralize the toxin and save their lives. On Christmas night of 1891, a child in Berlin was treated with diphtheria antitoxin produced in a rabbit and lived. By the most dramatic means possible, Behring showed that serum therapy could be used to prevent death in children who had already contracted diphtheria. During the next three years, it is estimated that 20,000 patients, mostly children, were treated with anti-toxins, with a very high recovery rate. Following the lead of Behring and Kitasato, Roux and Louis Martin at the Pasteur Institute inoculated a horse with graded doses of diphtheria and in February 1894 they treated all of the diphtheria patients at the Hospital for Sick Children in Paris with this antiserum. They all recovered. The Trousseau Hospital, the only other hospital in Paris that admitted children with diphtheria, was not using antitoxin and the mortality rate remained the same. The news-paper *Figaro* started a subscription to provide funds for the production of antitoxin and gave the money to the Pasteur Institute to build stables to house horses for immunization. In a matter of a few months, over 50,000 doses were given away free.

The effect on the mortality rate of children with diphtheria was dramatic. In Paris the rate at both the Hospital for Sick Children and the Trousseau had been around 50 percent (55 deaths per 100 cases). When the children at the Hospital for Sick Children were given the antitoxin, it fell to 24 percent, but remained at 55 percent at the Trousseau. While the disease could not yet be prevented, the chance of survival of a child that had contracted it was doubled. There was no question in anyone's mind that a means of vaccinating children to give them "active immunity" would soon follow. The disgrace of Koch and his failed tuberculin therapy was blunted and the future of immune prevention of disease still looked bright. Kitasato would return to Japan as an honored scientist, to found a bacteriological institute in Tokyo that would later bear his name. Behring was the recipient of the first Nobel prize in Medicine, in 1901. By then he had been ennobled and was von Behring. The citation for the prize reads, "For his work on serum therapy, especially its application against diphtheria, by which he has opened a new road in the domain of medical science and thereby placed in the hands of the physician a victorious weapon against illness and death."

Pasteur died four years after the first child was saved by the diphtheria antitoxin, but the myth of "Pasteur" remained fixed in the minds of the public and the medical scientists.

Chapter

7

Reframing the Internal World

There is another set of historical threads that must be examined to understand how science enabled us to reframe health and disease. Pasteur's role was in reframing the external world, conceiving the microscopic agents that cause the body to malfunction. But it probably has not escaped the attention of the reader that as important as it was, just knowing that certain symptoms and death are caused by certain specific living microbes does not give us any new way of responding to them other than avoidance (public health) or prevention (vaccination). This is another version of *scientia* and *techne*, knowing and doing, that we first encountered in the earliest days of science. Unless the knowledge of science could be converted into the technology of therapy we would have changed our ideas about disease, but little would have changed in what we could do about it. However, science in the nineteenth century was also moving in the direction that allowed the knowing and the doing to come together in the twentieth century to give us specific therapies.

A new way of framing the way the body functions under normal conditions and how it responds to disease had begun. Once again reverting to the Great Men approach to history, we will take a short look at Claude Bernard and Rudolf Virchow, two figures equal in importance and visibility in their lifetimes to Pasteur, whose part in changing the very way we look at health and disease was crucial.

We have already seen that by the beginning of the nineteenth century, hospital medicine in Paris was bringing together the clinical observation of the sick person and the result of the autopsy of the dead subject. From this came the realization that to explain disease, it was necessary to explain what was going wrong in the solid tissues of the body. Pasteur had been the great force in convincing scientists that a chemist could study living systems, but we saw the reluctance of Liebig, Wöhler, and other famous chemists to become entangled in anything that smacked of "vitalism." It would take the work of Claude Bernard to convince the world of the importance of the *milieu intérieur*, the idea that the functions of the body "varied as they are, have only one object, that of preserving constant the conditions of life in the internal environment." And it would take the work of Rudolf Virchow to convince the world that the symptoms of diseases are the result of alterations and damage to the cells of which the tissues are composed.

The last half of the nineteenth century was a veritable intellectual three-ring circus of scientific medicine. We think of the twentieth century as the age of science, and twentieth-century science has certainly changed our lives and our expectations, but it was nineteenth-century science that changed the way we look at ourselves and empowered us to expect longer and healthier lives. The science of the nineteenth century allowed us to frame health and disease so that the twentieth century could be an era of medical technology.

Claude Bernard and Rudolf Virchow

While Louis Pasteur was showing that the physiological processes of microbes are responsible for fermentation as well as disease, his contemporary Claude Bernard was showing that the normal functions of the body are a delicately balanced set of chemical interactions. Together they were demonstrating a unity of biological functions from the microbes to humans which, when added to the new theory of evolution, changed the way we look at the functions of the body and the place of humans in the biological world. The results of the dissection room and the observation of the physician at the bedside at the end of the eighteenth century had brought together symptoms and pathology. Now in the nineteenth century the study of the normal functions of the body in the laboratory would enlarge this emerging picture. This powerful scientific combination, along with the nearly universal acceptance of the germ theory of disease, all but sounded the death knell for two thousand years of Galenic medicine. There would be little room for the balancing of humors in the new scientific medicine; diseases had specific causes and the symptoms were the result of specific changes in the organs and chemistry of the body. Disease was beginning to be framed in the laboratory.

In Paris, the first laboratory devoted to physiology, the study of normal functions of the body, was established at the College of France for François Magendie. In our modern mind, the word *laboratory* conjures up visions of clean, well-lit rooms filled with equipment, but Magendie's lab, as described by Claude Bernard, who was his assistant for several years and who would succeed him as director of the laboratory, shows a very different kind of place. It was "a sort of small closet where we two could scarcely fit ourselves in," so damp that in later years, when Bernard was the professor, he worked wearing a hat and muffler. In fact, Magendie claimed that Bernard's later poor health was due to the early years he spent working in that laboratory. But it was in laboratories such as this that modern science began and in which the fundamental discoveries we build on today were made.

Magendie was a powerful figure in Parisian medicine in the first half of the nineteenth century, when conflicts between the old and the new medicine were beginning to develop. As we have seen, Enlightenment philosophy and Revolutionary sentiment had changed the social order, and these changes were beginning to percolate into the consciousness of physicians. Most of the disagreements between the old and the new were not about changing therapies; we have already seen ample evidence that there was little alternative to bloodletting, emetics, and the other treatments derived from Galenic medicine. The disagreement was about the degree of scientific rigor that could be brought to the diagnosis of the patients in the new setting of the hospital. By more rigorously relating the symptoms of their patients to what was being learned about the changes in the organs of the body as a result of those symptoms, Magendie and the other medical visionaries were making the first steps toward scientific medicine.

Magendie was a physician who happened to be a scientist, while Bernard was a scientist who happened to be a physician. Magendie carried out physiology experiments in the dank laboratory, and he also treated patients and taught clinical medicine in the hospital ward. His clinical battles were not about *whether* to bleed but *when* to bleed. He once boasted in the Academy of Sciences that he never bled his pneumonia patients at the hôtel-Dieu, yet they recovered with a more rapid convalescence than the patients of those who practiced bloodletting in their pneumonia patients. "It is true that you do not bleed your patients, but your interns bleed them behind your back," he was told by another physician, and the general snickering told him this was true. Heads rolled the next day, and from then on the only bleeding of Magendie's pneumonia patients was done to obtain material for physiological experiments.

Magendie is remembered because he was most influential in bringing experimental animals into physiology. The idea that we can learn about how humans function by using animals was not new; after all, Galen had dissected animals to learn about human anatomy. What Magendie did, and Bernard raised to the highest levels, was devise clever ways of determining on living animals how the body functions. Both Magendie and Bernard had to contend with strong antivivisection sentiment in France. In Bernard's case it was even more difficult because his wife held strong antivivisection sentiments, and as their unhappy marriage headed toward separation, she became more publicly vocal in her opposition. Magendie was a scowling, curt, and sarcastic man when he was dealing with his students and colleagues, but Bernard learned from Magendie that the feelings of the antivivisectionists must be respected and dealt with. He told the story of a Quaker who visited Magendie's little laboratory, dressed in characteristic Quaker garb of wide-brimmed hat, coat with upturned collar, and knee breeches. "I have heard thee spoken of, and I see I have not been misinformed; for I have been told thee does experiments on living animals. I have come to see thee to ask thee by what right thee does so, and to tell thee that thee must stop experiments of this kind because thee has no right to cause the death of animals or to make them suffer, and because thee sets a bad example and accustoms thy fellows to cruelty." Magendie ordered the experiment in progress to be stopped and the animal to be taken away, and then he pointed out to the man that his aim was to benefit humanity; war was cruel but may be necessary, and hunting inflicts more suffering on animals than does physiology. The Quaker replied that he was opposed to both war and hunting, and it was clear that neither man would convince the other, but the lesson of Magendie's consideration of the sincere beliefs of the Quaker was an important one to Bernard.

Claude Bernard was a man of quite different temperament than Magendie; his quiet dignity served him as well as Magendie's curled lip or Pasteur's killer instinct in debates served each of them. In fact, a personal diffidence always marked Bernard's bearing, even when he was at the very pinnacle of world acclaim. His modest, almost shy public demeanor was very different from Pasteur's, because while Pasteur could go for long periods of time in his laboratory without speaking to anyone, in public he could be voluble and charming. When Bernard was invited to spend a long weekend at the court of Napoleon III and the empress Eugénie, he explained his work to the emperor and then faded into the scenery. When Pasteur received his invitation, he engaged the emperor and even sent back to Paris for his microscope (which the empress herself carried to the tea table, declaring that she was Pasteur's *garçon de laboratoire*), and delivered an informal lecture on microbes, using fermented wine from the royal cellars as examples. He charmed everyone. When the emperor offered a personal gift after Bernard's visit, he reluctantly asked for one year's salary for a low-level laboratory assistant; Pasteur in contrast asked for a six-month leave (with pay) to continue his studies on silkworms. These two scientific giants shared with everyone in the second half of the nineteenth century the common sorrow of the death of children. Two of Pasteur's daughters had died in infancy and a third died of typhoid at the age of twelve; Bernard had lost two sons in infancy. Even though Paris was the epitome of modern life, death among children was still ever-present.

Bernard was born in Saint-Julien in the Beaujolais region of France in 1813 and, like Pasteur, gave no indication as a young man of the scientific greatness he would achieve. In school, the local priests considered him rather ordinary but of serious enough manner to be enrolled in a Jesuit college in the hope that he would enter the service of the Church. But the rather ordinary young man had ambitions of becoming a playwright and not a priest, and when he was apprenticed to an apothecary at the age of eighteen, he was much more interested in writing drama than in concocting drugs. In fact, the pharmacist was forced to ask Bernard's father to relieve him of the responsibility for his young apprentice. Bernard returned home, where he continued to write a "masterpiece" historical drama and prepared to take the entrance examinations for admission to the university, where he intended to fulfill his ambitions as a dramatist. In November 1834 he arrived in Paris, with his examinations passed and a letter from M. Millet, the apothecary, stating that "M. Claude Bernard . . . aged twenty-one years, entered my employ in the capacity of apprentice, January 1, 1832, and left it July 30, 1833, and during these eighteen months he served with honor and fidelity." No mention of distinction, let alone interest in his work. Shortly after his arrival in Paris, Bernard somehow arranged to have his play read by the professor of French poetry at the Sorbonne. The verdict, alas, was that young M. Bernard lacked the temperament to be a dramatist, but after talking to him and learning of his experience in the pharmacy, the professor convinced him to remain in Paris and to study medicine. After all, medicine was a profession that could give him a decent livelihood and also provide the leisure time for literary pursuits. Bernard would always have an interest in the theater, which would be virtually his only diversion outside of science once he began his steady rise to the top of his profession.

As a medical student, Bernard began working as an assistant in Magendie's little laboratory, and slowly his life became more and more focused on his physiology experiments. His talent for designing good experiments on living animals and his extraordinary technical ability to carry them out became obvious to everyone, so when he finished medical school and qualified as a physician, he chose to remain associated with Magendie and follow a life of research. He soon became the rising star of Paris physiology and eventually succeeded Magendie as professor of physiology.

The major accomplishment of Bernard's life in physiology research was to bring about the realization that the internal environment of the body is a delicate balance among nutrients entering the body, the specialized functions of each of the organs, the chemicals they produce, and the elimination of the waste products generated during these processes. All of this was encapsulated in the phrase *le milieu intérieur*—"the internal environment." It might appear at first glance that because the blood is the vehicle for transporting nutrients and signals from one organ to another that Bernard was merely enshrining the traditional Galenic view of the body, but nothing can be further from the truth. "The blood contains all the elements necessary to life, elements which it obtains from outside by means of certain organic mechanisms. . . . [It] serves as a *vehi-*

cle for all the influences which, coming from without, act upon the fibers of the tissues. . . . [T]he blood comes into contact with the air and obtains from it oxygen which is subsequently carried to the whole organism. . . . [B]y the mechanism of alimentary absorption the blood obtains from without all the liquids which are subsequently furnished to the organism to serve as nourishment for the tissues. . . . [A]ll the products of organic decomposition are collected in the blood and circulate with it to be excreted, either in the form of gas through the skin and lungs or in the form of liquid by the kidneys." This could be a concise synopsis of physiology as we know it today! One biographer claims that this notion of the constant and controlled internal environment, which Bernard first published in 1859, was to physiology what Darwin's *On the Origin of Species by Natural Selection*, published in the same year, was to evolution.

The idea that the body was a complex integrated whole, with the blood serving as a means of distribution and communication between the organs and tissues, represented a powerful new way of thinking. It left no place for such vague concepts as the humors. Specific molecules made by specific tissues carried out specific functions; the blood was crucial but no longer mysterious. So between them, Pasteur and Bernard, the two giants of French nineteenth-century scientific medicine, set the ground for the use of rigorous science to describe the processes of life involving cells, tissues, and the chemical signals they make and receive. The way we frame the body in health and disease would be fundamentally changed for the first time since antiquity. The new philosophy of science had at last reached medicine.

The changes in the organization of medical-service delivery and education in Paris also affected German medicine. While Pasteur was showing that microbes carry out normal physiological processes that are useful and can cause disease, and Bernard was showing that the balance of chemicals between the tissues of the body determines health, Rudolf Virchow in Germany was studying the changes in the cells of the body during disease. The union of the bedside symptoms of the patient in life and the changes seen in the body at death had only reinforced the long-held belief that *inflammation* was at the center of disease. Cohnheim, the pathologist who was so impressed with the young Robert Koch, wrote in his definitive textbook of pathology that the interpretation of inflammation "has formed the starting-point and goal of all the systems and schools of medicine that have, in the course of centuries, succeeded one another." Most people who died in the hospitals did so as a result of surgery at a time before Lister was to make it safer or from infections incurred during the process of therapeutic bloodletting, and many of course died in childbirth, which was a positively horrifying experience in a hospital. Little wonder that the subjects who turned up on the autopsy table were riddled with abscesses, their veins filled with disintegrating clots. Before Claude Bernard, few questioned that health was the balance of the humors, so it was only natural to them that they found the blood vessels of those who had recently died full of these obvious impediments to the flow of the blood (the ultimate result of an imbalance of humors). We can readily understand why one credo of French hospital medicine was, "*la phlebite domine toute la pathologie*" (phlebitis, inflammation of the blood vessels, dominates all pathology).

The cell had been identified and named in the late 1600s by Robert Hook, who used a microscope modeled after one of Leeuwenhoek's, but it was not until the modern microscope was developed around 1830 that the revolutionary idea that these cells are the basic unit of life was put forward by a German botanist and a physician, the same two who were ridiculed by Liebig and the chemists at the time of their battle with Pasteur about the role of yeast in fermentation. So in 1844, when the twenty-three-year-old Rudolf Virchow was assigned his first research task, it was to look at the cells involved in the inflammation of the blood vessels. The theme of the cellular processes of disease stayed at the center of Virchow's work throughout his active, almost fabled life. It was his research that would set the stage for the revision of our understanding of the role of the cells seen in inflammation.

In the early years of his cellular approach to the pathology of disease, Virchow would resist Pasteur's claim that specific microbes are responsible for specific diseases, because the local cellular changes he saw in many different kinds of diseases seemed so similar. Today we regard a disease such as tuberculosis as almost exclusively a chronic disease of the lungs, but in the mid-1800s it could also be systemic (miliary TB) or located in the lymph glands of the neck (scrofula). If the tubercle bacillus was causing both, how could such different symptoms represent the same disease? Scrofula, in turn, showed very similar cellular pathology to glanders, a disease of animals that caused swelling of the glands. So to Virchow disease was clearly associated with the cellular changes seen in inflammation, but rather than each disease being a specific entity, it was classified according to the cellular changes in the kinds of inflammation that were involved.

R udolf Virchow was born in 1821, the son of a failed farmer and small-business man and his wife, of whom "nothing is known but an inclination to worrying and complaining." The Prussian state at the time provided a means for talented children of the poor to be trained as army doctors, and at the age of eighteen Rudolf enrolled. It was a time, his biographer says, when German "medical science had reached an all-time low ... reactionary German medicine had lost itself in the jungles of romantic speculation or the deserts of naked empiricism." But Virchow rose above the rigid barracks atmosphere of the army medical school, the philosophical attraction of an almost primitive belief in vitalism, and the hierarchical structure of German medicine to become a liberal political leader, a medical visionary, a leader in public-health reforms, and a renowned anthropologist. Quite remarkably, from the very beginning of his career he took to lecturing the entrenched establishment, asserting that the future of medicine depended on clinical observation, animal experimentation, and a reliance on pathological anatomy (especially microscopic pathology). This message would have been hard enough to swallow if it only meant that the establishment had to look at itself as being hopelessly dated and out of touch, but it meant something even worse: German medicine must become more like French medicine! The amazing thing is that he was listened to; in general, this confident young man was taken seriously from the very beginning.

With the improved microscopes of the day, all pathologists saw cells in the sites of inflammation, so the question for young and old alike was not *if* cells were there but how they got there and what they were doing. The leading anatomical pathologist in Europe at the time was a Viennese, Karl Rokitansky, who claimed that during disease, changes in the blood led to the production of some kind of amorphous material at the site of inflammation, which was then converted into cells. This kind of thinking is what Virchow's biographer meant by German medicine's being lost in the jungles of romantic speculation; the growing tide of opinion against spontaneous generation had clearly not penetrated their thinking. Germany was undergoing revolutionary, democratic ferment, and Virchow was at the center of the revolution he believed would change not only the social structure of the country, but medicine, public health, and health-care delivery as well. He publicly took issue with Rokitansky and the old order, claiming that spontaneous generation was dead and that cells, rather than being the byproduct of some nondescript forces, *were the basic unit of both normal life and of disease.* Cells could not develop spontaneously from amorphous material any more than mice could come from dirty rags; it was time to use modern thinking. The leading journal, run by the establishment, of course would not publish his claims, so he and a few like-minded young friends decided to create a journal of their own, leading his admiring biographer to declare that "this somewhat [sic!] overwhelming complete confidence in himself sustained Virchow throughout his life."

That same year, 1846, the twenty-five-year-old Virchow began a series of lectures on anatomical pathology that attracted not only the young, idealistic, and revolutionary doctors but even some of the veritable establishment *Geheimräte.* It is amazing as we look back to see how rapid his rise was, but his biographer points out that at the time there were a great many young brilliant German medical and political revolutionaries, many of whom died in their thirties and forties. (Again we see the constant presence of death and the effect it had on everything.) Virchow may have been outspoken, but he was brilliant, and furthermore, had the talent of not making personal enemies of his scientific foes. Of course, it didn't hurt that he was a product of the military school; if he was a radical, he was *their* radical.

The occasional liberals in the Prussian bureaucracy did little to help his career, and the revolution of 1848, rather than speed the acceptance of his views and his career, led to an extreme reactionary backlash, so that in 1849 he lost his position in Berlin. That year he took a professorship in rural Würzburg and for the moment immersed himself in his scientific work. Virchow's withdrawal from political life was temporary, but it was not unique. Ferdinand Cohn (whom we met with Koch) wrote in his diary on September 25, 1849, "Germany dead; France dead; Italy dead; Hungary dead; only cholera and court-martials immortal. I have retired from this unfriendly outside world, buried myself in my books and studies; seeing few people, learning much, only inspired by nature. . . ."

Although he was exiled to Würzburg, politics still remained an integral part of Virchow's life and thinking; he would describe the body as composed of equal individuals (the cells) within a free state, or as a federation of cells. And just as he saw the importance of political process, he also saw *disease as a process*. Disease to him was only "life under changed conditions," and in the political calm of the Würzburg years he developed these ideas into a new way of looking at disease with cells as the centerpiece. It is important to realize that the shift of focus of pathology from tissues to cells was not original with Virchow; by the late 1840s, the wide availability of good microscopes and the acceptance of the idea that cells were the basic unit of life made it natural and fashionable to look at them in disease. But Virchow was crucial in establishing the relationship of the cells to the *pathology* of the tissues.

At the same time, Virchow was in the vanguard of those pathologists who were applying the methods of chemistry to studying diseased tissue. This combination of microscopic examination of the lesions of disease and the chemical changes that occurred during the process of disease formed the basis of the next profound change in medicine, which would now move into its new era of "laboratory medicine." But more immediately, as we will shortly see, Virchow's breadth of thought and his position of power in the medical-science world allowed him to respond quickly to a truly revolutionary way of looking at the role of the cells in inflammation when it was introduced to him forty years later.

Elie Metchnikoff, Phagocytosis, and the Idea of Immunity

By the 1880s hardly any scientific physicians would disagree that bacteria were the cause of infectious disease, but hardly any of them would agree on what the bacteria were doing to the body that resulted in disease. At its foundations, science is a form of debate, a state of mind that requires the scientist to look at the world and design experiments to find out how it works. A common misconception about science is that it is value-free—that facts are facts and that once one is confronted with them, understanding follows. Nothing can be further from the truth: The facts that come from scientific experiments are always understood within the context of the assumptions the experimenter made when designing the experiment. The bacteriologists at the close of the nineteenth century assumed that bacteria are responsible for disease because they cause the pathological changes in the body of the infected person. The pathologists, looking at the same "facts," saw bacteria as agents that initiated changes in cells and tissues in the body that resulted in disease. Because science is really a value-laden intellectual exercise in which the participants are constantly striving to turn the "facts" into "truth," it almost always takes on the characteristics of a debate, and in special cases can look like a courtroom drama. The role of the bacteria and the cells was one of those scientific debates that determines the framework in which generations of scientists would look at the "facts."

Both the pathologists and the bacteriologists saw degrees of specificity in disease; diseases of the lung, for example, may have common features, but they were diseases of the lung and did not reflect a *general* condition implied by an imbalance of humors. They most certainly disagreed on what the basis of the specificity was, but the "fact" of specificity was inherent in each of their arguments. They also agreed on the "fact" that inflammation was synonymous with disease. Physicians since antiquity had seen that the accumulation of pus was a hallmark of many diseases, just as fever and swelling (two of the cardinal signs of inflammation) were the hallmarks of others. When anatomical pathologists began correlating the lesions at autopsy with the symptoms in life, they saw the obvious correlation between inflammation and disease. The microscope allowed these observations to be extended to the cells in lesions and it became a "fact" that they were part of the disease process. Virchow, as the father of cellular pathology, was one of the leading exponents of the idea. It is ironic, then, that Virchow would be instrumental in bringing about a total reversal of this idea during one brief encounter with a fantastic Russian zoologist named Elie Metchnikoff.

Elie Metchnikoff was the person who realized that the cells seen in inflammation were the body's way of *combating* the infecting bacteria, a concept of such monumental importance that all of modern immunology and much of modern medicine is built on it.

I f Elie Metchnikoff had never existed, we would surely have had to invent him. He has been characterized by the great popularizer of the golden era of microbiology, Paul de Kruif, as something between a mad holy man and a fool. He was neither. As a recent biography makes very clear, he was a complex, intense, probably brilliant, often infuriating man who was spectacularly correct about some things and equally spectacularly wrong about others. His childhood years resemble a Chekhov play: his father serves in the Imperial Guard and marries the sister of a fellow officer; the couple quickly become part of the high life of St. Petersburg society until their money runs out and they must retire to a boring provincial life on the family estate. It was in this provincial atmosphere of *The Cherry Orchard* and *Uncle Vanya* that the very bright and moody Metchnikoff grew up. When it came time for him to go to university, his mother thought he was of too delicate a temperament to study medicine, so, because of the interest he had shown in botany from an early age, he studied natural science. But his career began as a series of unhappy events: mentors taking credit for his work; old professors who did not have his burning passion for science; inadequate salary—the whole litany of an unhappy life.

The pattern of Metchnikoff's life, and the future that he saw for himself, can be seen in the description to his mother of the woman he intended to marry: "She is not bad, but that is all. She has beautiful hair; her complexion is not pretty." The object of this passion, Ludmilla Federovitch, was suffering from a wasting disease and had to be carried to the church for their wedding. She died a few years later and, distraught at all of the failures of his life, Metchnikoff made a dramatic and probably intentionally ineffective attempt at suicide. A short while later he put his life together sufficiently to marry a very young student and tried to settle into an academic life at the University of Odessa. But this too was filled with unhappiness and distractions.

It was from this unlikely start that Metchnikoff made his revolutionary discovery. One might expect a brilliant insight from such a person, but who would have ever predicted that this unhappy, apparently unsettled man would be able to focus his attention on that discovery for the rest of his life! It was after he acquired a bit of financial security from his own family's estate and that of his new wife that Metchnikoff took himself, his wife, and some of her family off to Messina, in Sicily, in 1883, where he planned to do research on marine organisms. It was this research that changed the view of pathologists and all of medicine about the role of inflammation. Later, he wrote this much-quoted account of the great discovery:

> I was resting from the upheaval which had led to my resignation from the University and I was passionately working in the marvelous setting of the Strait of Messina. One day, as the whole family was at the circus to see some trained apes, I remained home alone with my microscope and I was observing the activity of the motile cells of a transparent starfish larva, when a new thought suddenly dawned on me. It occurred to me that similar cells must function to protect the organism against harmful intruders. . . . I thought that if my guess was correct a splinter introduced into the larva of a starfish should soon be surrounded by motile cells much as can be observed in a man with a splinter in his finger. No sooner said than done. In the small garden of our home . . . I took several rose thorns that I immediately introduced under the skin of some beautiful starfish larvae which were as transparent as water. Very nervous, I did not sleep during the night, as I was waiting for the results of my experiment. The next morning, very early, I found with joy that it had been most successful. This experiment was the basis of the phagocytic theory, to which I devoted the next twenty-five years of my life.

To be sure, Metchnikoff was a romantic and this is certainly a romantic view of an important event. There may even be a small element of truth in it, but that is doubtful. He had in fact been reading works by cellular pathologists, especially Julius Cohnheim's treatise on inflammation that we mentioned earlier, as well as the work of Darwin. The great intellectual leap Metchnikoff made was to see a universal biological phenomenon in the accumulation of cells that are able to ingest a foreign body in the larva of starfish. He realized that this resembled the accumulation of cells at an area of damage in the inflammation of disease and he saw in this something that had been conserved in evolution from the starfish to humans. It made perfect sense to him that the cells he saw attempting to engulf the rose thorns were the evolutionary precursors of the cells pathologists saw at the inflammatory sites of infections. If this was true, he thought it must then follow that the cells at the site of the inflammation were attempting to engulf and *destroy* the infecting bacteria. If they were trying to destroy the bacteria, then they were not causing the disease, they were trying to protect the body from it! It was an idea that set the whole idea of the pathology of infection on its head; what everyone had assumed was the *cause* of the disease and therefore had to be controlled and eliminated, this eccentric Russian zoologist argued, was the body's means of *curing* it. Since the time of the Greeks, people had talked about "letting nature take its course," or the "ability of the body to heal itself," but these things had been said only metaphorically. These cells at the site of inflammation could be the real thing!

In one of the wonderful ironies of history, Virchow was visiting in Messina at the time Metchnikoff had his insight, and Metchnikoff was able to describe his result and his ideas to him. The idea that the cells in the inflammatory site were ingesting the bacteria was not new to Virchow, but the idea that the body used these cells as its defense against disease certainly was. He was not convinced by Metchnikoff, but he was interested enough in the intellectual idea to be encouraging. Four years later he would still disagree, writing, with his usual style of political analogy, that he did not "regard the pus corpuscles as gendarmes ordered by the police-state to escort over the border some foreigner or other who is not provided with a passport." So while warning Metchnikoff that his ideas flew in the face of the current wisdom—especially of the very powerful Robert Koch, who was convinced that the cells at the site of inflammation were the vehicle for the *spread* of bacteria—he encouraged him to publish. Virchow at the time believed that the cells at the site of inflammation were local cells that had responded to the local irritation, and it was this response that we saw as disease, but he gave the necessary psychic encouragement to a man who wanted to overturn the accepted scientific truth of the day. Perhaps Virchow, the old social revolutionary, liked the idea of yet another revolution, and the idea that the cells in inflammation were neither passive responders to irritation nor spreaders of the disease but were the active defenders of the body was certainly revolutionary.

Metchnikoff's idea got enthusiastic reception from two zoologists, Nicolaus Kleinenberg, a German who was professor at Messina at the time, and C. Claus, the director of the Zoological Institute in Vienna, whom he visited on his return trip to Russia. In fact, Claus was so enthusiastic that he asked Metchnikoff to publish his results in his journal, and he and his colleagues even coined the term for the ingestion and destruction of bacteria by the cells. Metchnikoff had used the awkward German term *Fresszellen,* or "devouring cells," but the Viennese zoologists gave him the Greek term *phagocyte* (phaegin = "to eat"; kytos = "cell"). To this day we use the term *phagocyte* for cells that take in other cells or particles, and call the process *phagocytosis.* With the intellectual encouragement of the great pathologist Virchow and the enthusiastic encouragement of his fellow zoologists, Metchnikoff began the work that would engage him for the rest of his life, gathering the proof that phagocytosis is the mechanism by which the body defends itself from disease. The idea was so clearly correct to him that once one "accepts the concept that phagocytes fight directly against pathogens, it becomes understandable that inflammation is a defensive mechanism against bacterial invasion."

Metchnikoff returned to Russia in 1885. The city of Odessa had decided to open an institute to prepare anthrax vaccines in the manner of Pasteur, and he was to be the director. It is not clear why a man who could not get along with authorities and who had such little interest in organization would be chosen for this position, which required great skill at both. He was probably the worst person to hold such a position, and not surprisingly, the first batch of anthrax vaccine the institute produced was not properly tested and resulted in the killing of thousands of sheep. Metchnikoff left Russia forever in 1888.

When they left Russia, the Metchnikoffs went first to Berlin, where Elie presented to Koch and his colleagues the evidence for his idea that phagocytosis was part of the protective response of the body. His meeting with Koch, as one might suspect, was less than cordial; the great man looked at the microscopic preparations that showed bacteria inside the phagocytic cells of a lesion and told him, "You know, I am not a specialist in microscopical anatomy; I am a hygienist [sic]. Consequently, it is entirely indifferent to me whether [bacteria] are within or without the cells." The response of Pasteur was quite different. Pasteur was by then old and ill and probably took a fatherly interest in the energetic young Metchnikoff. There is also the possibility that his personal dislike of Koch may have made him a bit more receptive to both the idea and the person who was presenting it to him. He offered Metchnikoff a laboratory in the new Pasteur Institute, and here the turbulence that had characterized his life till now ended, and he found the environment that would give him peace to carry out his life's work.

Virchow was helpful but unconvinced; Koch was uninterested; Pasteur was interested, but his physical powers were fading. Elie Metchnikoff, who went on to receive a Nobel prize, has been called the founder of immunology and has become a thoroughly mythic character. But how did an obscure and unstable Russian zoologist become so famous? Indeed, we very well might ask, as we did of John Snow, Who made Elie Metchnikoff a famous man?

The Body Actively Defends Itself

The *fin de siècle* always brings hopes and promises of wondrous changes to come in the new century. The end of the nineteenth *siècle* showed that such hopes and promises could be fulfilled before the satisfied eyes of the observers who already thought of it as "the wonderful century." And to these satisfied eyes, it was science that made the century so wonderful. Science was the engine that drove the changes. It had brought electric lights, which freed people from the tyranny of the darkness after sunset. Science had given them transportation, which freed them from the confines of their local neighborhoods and villages; it brought them goods from distant places and allowed even the working class to share the bounty that had been available only to the wealthy before. Science had given them, through photography, images of places and people of which they had only dreamed. Science let them soar in balloons, send messages by telegraph, listen to the phonograph, see moving pictures and even pictures of their own internal organs through X rays. But most important in the mind of the public, science had eliminated the constant presence of death. Of all the wonders of science and its benefits, this was the most important. Is it any wonder that they were turning Pasteur into "Pasteur"? Their children could be saved from dying of diphtheria; the causes of tuberculosis, cholera, typhoid, and syphilis were known; surgery was now safer; and the constant presence of death was becoming a memory only of the old people.

These changes were there for everyone to see, but science was also bringing an important subtle change into the new century—the way we thought about how our bodies respond to disease. Since the time of the ancient Greeks, people did not "catch" a disease, they slipped into it. To catch something meant that there was something to catch, and until the germ theory of disease became accepted, there was nothing to catch. But by the middle of the "wonderful" nineteenth century, Louis Pasteur had provided both the something to catch and the demonstration that specific protection (immunity) was possible. Patients may not have known it, but Claude Bernard and Rudolf Virchow had changed the way they would look at the function of their bodies, because their physicians would know that the cells and the chemicals they produced maintain an internal environment in the body that is the basis of normal function in health and abnormal function in disease. They may have been curious, but unmoved, by the advances in science, but they were passionately interested in the practical results that followed. For the first time in history there was the certain knowledge that the thing in which they were most interested—their health and the health of their children—would be changed for the better.

Lister had been able to make surgery safe by eliminating the bacteria from the surgical site; Koch had discovered the cause of so many diseases; and Pasteur had shown that it was possible to give specific protection against them. They were famous men because they visibly and understandably personified the science that was bringing about the changes in the health of the people. Metchnikoff's contribution was not so obviously practical, but if one of the quiet messages of this book is that science is a way of looking at the world and understanding it, then the idea that the body actively fights the microbial invaders responsible for disease was one of the most important that the new century would build on to fulfill the promise of even greater advances in health. Things are only understood in the context of what is already known, and until that time, with death from infectious disease the rule, there was little reason to seriously think that the body had much of a defense mechanism. Now, when the promise of general vaccination against infectious diseases seemed about to be fulfilled and death was about to be conquered, science had to find the context in which to understand it all.

How does vaccination give specific protection? To Metchnikoff the answer was clear: Evolution had provided humans and higher animals with phagocytosis as a protection mechanism to destroy the invaders. To be sure, other factors must be important; in 1884 he wrote, "I believe that the bacilli are destroyed by the phagocytes although the influence of other factors that may hinder their development is not eliminated." Pasteur, the quintessential microbiologist, had explained specific immunity after vaccination by analogy with bacteria growing in a flask in the laboratory; the specific bacteria used up all of the specific foodstuff they needed to grow, so that if the person was infected after he had been vaccinated, the vaccination had used up all of the nutrients and the bacteria could not grow. But when someone showed that it was possible to vaccinate with dead bacteria, which obviously could not use up the specific nutrients, the idea faded away. Metchnikoff's answer that the phagocytic cells were responsible for immunity was appealing, but he obviously had difficulty connecting it with specificity. And this was something he had to do, because the idea that specific microbes caused specific diseases, and that vaccination gave specific protection, was now accepted. It is one thing to argue that the inflammatory response is a *general* defense against invaders; it is quite another to argue that it is a *specific* defense. And specificity was essential if the idea was to carry the day.

I n 1901 Emil Behring won the first Nobel prize because of the dramatic effect his antitoxin therapy had had in reducing fatality from diphtheria. Antitoxins fit into the ideas of Claude Bernard's chemical basis for the functions of the body, and they fulfilled the truly wonderful part of Pasteur's legacy of specificity. Behring had removed much of the terror from that awful childhood killer diphtheria, but to make his work on antisera practicable, he had teamed up with Paul Ehrlich, whom we will meet in the next chapter. Ehrlich had argued convincingly that diphtheria antitoxin protected children by neutralizing the diphtheria toxin in the same way an acid neutralizes a base. In short, it was all chemistry! And yet here was a person at the Pasteur Institute, appointed by Pasteur himself, who claimed that cells were responsible.

Scientific debate tends to begin at polar opposites and then move toward the middle ground. Only rarely does one side in a scientific debate get it totally "wrong," but it is even rarer that one side will admit to much reason in the arguments of the other at the time when the extremes are being defined. Metchnikoff had begun in 1884 by arguing that phagocytosis was important, but "other factors" also play a role. Neither Behring nor Ehrlich wanted to argue that cells played no role in normal functions and in disease, but how could the dramatic effect of diphtheria antitoxin be explained by cells? Their positions became polarized. Koch was becoming more and more vocally an enemy of Pasteur, and the conflict between the exponents of the role of the cells and the exponents of the role of antitoxins grew and took on an ugly, sometimes even nationalistic, tone. By 1901 Metchnikoff was saying "there is only one constant element in immunity, whether innate or acquired, and that is phagocytosis."

These cat fights run counter to the image of the dispassionate searchers for truth that scientists believe they are—and certainly want the world to believe they are—but they have always occurred. But if we keep in mind that Behring kept a picture of Pasteur in his office for all of his life and that Metchnikoff stood as godfather to one of his children, we see that to the really great scientists, polar debate and a bit of mudslinging are just the way business is conducted. It was necessary for someone to see that the middle ground was where truth could be found, and just such a man stepped in.

Sir Almroth Wright: The Great "Immunizator"

I f Elie Metchnikoff is a character out of Chekhov, Almroth Edward Wright is a character out of Dickens. Born in 1861 to a clergyman father and a Swedish mother (the daughter of a chemistry professor), Wright lived his early years in Dresden and Boulogne, where his father was first the chaplain of the English church and then founder of the British Seamen's Institution. As might be imagined from this background, he was reared in a strict Protestant home in which frivolity was frowned on; all of the blinds in the house were drawn on Sunday and the hours not spent in church were devoted to Bible study and meditation. The children were educated by the parents in classics, mathematics, and languages; one son became lord chief justice of Trinidad, another the first librarian of the London library and a translator of Tolstoy, another the major-general of engineers who overcame the formidable supply problems of Allenby's campaign in the Middle East in the

First World War. Although the family income never exceeded four hundred pounds per year, Wright would later say that he was brought up in an atmosphere of intellectual riches and material poverty "entirely favourable to the growth of the life of the mind." We will see later that he continued to lead "the life of the mind," but he more than overcame the romance of material poverty.

When his father was transferred to Belfast, Wright entered Trinity College in Dublin, where he read English, French, German, Spanish, and Italian literature and gained first-class honors and the gold medal in his B.A. degree in 1882. He read medicine at the same time and qualified in 1883, the same year as Metchnikoff's great insight. It was at Trinity that Wright learned about the new scientific medicine of specificity that was developing in France and Germany, and he adopted the concepts (as he did other things) with an evangelical enthusiasm. In 1884, at the age of twenty-three, he went to Germany to study with Cohnheim, where he learned to observe the cells of the blood in the inflammatory process. So he was well prepared for Metchnikoff's phagocytic theory when he learned of it, but when he returned to London in 1885 ready to do something about it, he found that British clinical medicine had been largely unmoved by the advances in pathology and physiology on the Continent. Not fitting into the clinical scene and unable to get a university appointment, Wright won a scholarship to read law! But after finishing the course, he decided that he did not want to be a lawyer after all, and took the civil service higher examination. Thus, qualified in two professions and passionate about medical research in the scientific mode, he became a clerk in the Admiralty. Even Dickens would not have used this as a plot!

Wright was able to carry out his duties as a bureaucrat with ease and began to do research at the Brown Animal Sanatory Institute, the first experimental pathology laboratory in Britain. Founded with a bequest from an eccentric Irishman named Thomas Brown as a center for investigating and curing "maladies of Quadrupeds and Birds useful to man," it had gradually turned into an institute of animal pathology. When the superintendent, who had also worked with Cohnheim, became professor of pathology at Cambridge in 1886, he offered Wright a post in the department. At last, it seemed, the brilliant but restless Wright would be able to do the research he was so passionate about. But Cambridge soon palled (he told a friend that Cambridge scientists did not "take him at his own valuation") and in 1888 he won a scholarship to study for another year on the Continent.

To make the story more Dickensian, he then spent two years in Sydney as a demonstrator in physiology, finally returning home in 1891, with no job, to spend two years working without pay in the Laboratory of the Colleges of Physicians and Surgeons in London. By 1892 he urgently needed a salary and when he was offered the post of professor of pathology in the army medical school at Netley Hospital, by Southampton Water, he accepted it. As professor of pathology, he was expected to teach and do research. The army was interested in the pathology of wound infections and infectious diseases because these were the major causes of deaths during wars. The success of Lister's antiseptic surgery and the acceptance of the germ theory had convinced army surgeons that harsh antiseptic treatment of wounds was the only way to prevent infections. Wright would later campaign against this practice, arguing that the strong antiseptics killed the phagocytes that were crucial for the destruction of the bacteria infecting the wounds.

But alas, the military life was also not for him; once when his military laboratory assistant was required to take part in a parade, Wright stalked onto the parade ground and plucked the man out of the ranks. Another time, when he was giving evidence to a military tribunal, the president asked him if he had anything more to say; Wright replied, "No, sir. I have given you the facts. I can't give you the brains." Having fit into the military no better than he had fit into the academic life at Cambridge or Sydney, Wright left Netley to become professor of pathology at St. Mary's Hospital in London in 1902. The post at St. Mary's may have gotten him away from the military, but it was far from a plum. The facility was run-down and decrepit, he had little space and no funds for research, and he had the responsibility for all of the routine hospital bacteriology and pathology, as well as teaching. The salary was far less than his salary at Netley (£300) and the department was housed in two rooms that were ill lit, ill equipped, and shaken every few minutes by the Underground railway. But Wright was a magnetic teacher who told students that the physician of the future would be an "immunizator" and probably had a vision of what he wanted to be in the world that could only be brought off in this situation at St. Mary's.

In his training, Wright had absorbed the emerging modern, scientific basis of medicine laid down by Pasteur, Bernard, and Virchow. The year before he went to St. Mary's, Behring had won the Nobel prize for his work on diphtheria antitoxin. The power of immunization was "in the air." Wright could not help getting caught up in this excitement, but being the quintessential independent spirit, he would not follow any party line. From his experiences in Germany and in dealing with the army surgeons, he had become convinced that phagocytes played a very important protective role in the body, but he also knew the importance of specificity in immunization. He turned his department at St. Mary's over to putting all of the principles into practice: He would *immunize to increase the power of the phagocytes!*

One of the first things Wright found was that if he mixed some blood from a patient recovering from a disease with bacteria that cause the disease, the bacteria were engulfed by the phagocytic cells much more rapidly than they were when they were mixed with the blood from normal people. Wright was never a clear experimental thinker, but he was a talented bench worker and soon developed methods for measuring this phenomenon; a drop of blood from a patient who was suffering from a bacterial disease was mixed with the bacteria that cause the disease, and after a set time, the average number of bacteria ingested per phagocyte was determined by examining the drop under the microscope. The same was done with the blood from a disease-free person, so he could determine what he called the "phagocytic index," the ratio between the cells of the patient and the normal person's ability to phagocytize. He claimed that as patients recovered from disease, their phagocytic index rose, indicating that each cell was able to phagocytize (and presumably kill) more and more bacteria, resulting in the recovery of the patient. He reasoned that if a person's phagocytic index could be raised artificially, his body would behave as if it were recovering from the disease, and immunization was the way to do this. Wright constantly harped on the phagocytic index throughout his career, even when it was becoming clear that this was not going to be the key to the secrets of immunity. He later was called, behind his back of course, Sir *Almost* Wright. The irony is that from the distance of almost one hundred years we can see that Wright overstated a case that we now understand as being essentially correct, once again showing that heros and fools are difficult to distinguish at the time.

Wright was quickly associated in a very public manner with the idea that immunization functions by stimulating the phagocytes. His friend George Bernard Shaw used him as the model for Sir Colenso Ridgeon in his play *The Doctor's Dilemma*. Shaw, in reality, was using this as part of his argument against vaccination, because he found the idea of injecting disease-causing agents into healthy people offensive. But what Shaw really objected to most was the idea of specificity of disease, and therefore the specificity of the protection. In the play, the character of Sir Ralph Bloomfield Bonington (known as B.B.) speaks the following lines:

> B.B. What! Ridgeon: did you hear that? Sir Patrick: I am more struck by what you have just told me than I can well express. Your father, sir, anticipated a discovery of my own. Listen, Walpole. Blenkinsop: attend one moment. You will all be intensely interested in this. I was put on the track by accident. I had a typhoid case and a tetanus case side by side in the hospital: a beadle and a city missionary. Think of what that meant for them, poor fellows! Can a missionary be eloquent with lockjaw? No., NO. Well, I got some typhoid anti-toxin from Ridgeon and a tube of Muldooley's anti-tetanus serum. But the missionary jerked all my things off the table in one of his paroxysms; and in replacing them I put Ridgeon's tube where Muldooley's ought to have been. The consequence was that I inoculated the typhoid case for tetanus and the tetanus case for typhoid. [The doctors look greatly concerned. B.B., undamped, smiles triumphantly.] Well, they recovered. THEY RECOVERED. Except for a touch of St Vitus's dance the missionary's as well today as ever; and the beadle's ten times the man he was.
>
> BLENKINSOP. Ive known things like that happen. They cant be explained.
>
> B.B. [severely] Blenkinsop: there is nothing that cannot be explained by science. What did I do? Did I fold my hands helplessly and say that the case could not be explained? By no means. I asked myself why didnt the missionary die of typhoid on top of tetanus, and the beadle of tetanus on top of typhoid? Theres a problem for you, Ridgeon. Think, Sir Patrick. Reflect, Blenkinsop. Look at it without prejudice, Walpole. What is the real work of the anti-toxin? Simply to

stimulate the phagocytes. Very well. But so long as you stimulate the phagocytes, what does it matter which particular sort of
serum you use for the purpose? Haha! Eh? Do you see? Do you
grasp it? Ever since that Ive used all sorts of anti-toxins absolutely indiscriminately, with perfectly satisfactory results. I
inoculated the little prince with your stuff, Ridgeon, because I
wanted to give you a lift; but two years ago I tried the experiment of treating a scarlet fever case with a sample of hydropho-
bia serum from the Pasteur Institute, and it answered capitally.
It stimulated the phagocytes; and the phagocytes did the rest.
That is why Sir Patrick's father found that inoculation cured all
fevers. It stimulated the phagocytes. [He throws himself into
his chair, exhausted with the triumph of his demonstration,
and beams magnificently on them].

Wright is reported to have stormed out of the theater, but it is not
clear if he objected to the characterization of his views on phagocytosis
and vaccination or to the parody of his personality. But the episode did
not seem to do much damage to his friendship with Shaw; friendship
with people of influence was a hallmark of his career.

When in 1907 he was given three wards in the Clarence Wing of St.
Mary's, which the hospital did not have enough money to equip, Wright
made the operation self-supporting through his access to private funds
from his rich and powerful friends. He then created the famous Inoculation Department, whose income came from the fees paid by private
patients and from the sale of vaccines prepared in the department.
Enough money came in to pay rent to the hospital for its accommoda-
tions, the cost of medical services, as well as salaries and laboratory
expenses. The Inoculation Department created special vaccines for
acne, pyorrhea, boils, pneumonia, bronchial colds, influenza, gonorrhea,
sore throats, intestinal troubles, tuberculosis, and even cancer. Adver-
tisements claimed that the vaccines had been "prepared in the Vaccine
laboratory of the Department of Therapeutical Inoculation, St Mary's
Hospital, London W1 under the supervision of the Director, Sir Almroth
E. Wright, MD FRS etc." The vaccines were distributed by the pharmaceutical firm of Parke, Davis and Company. Besides the large amount
of money that the vaccines brought in, there was an initial endowment
of £17,000 from members of the committee and other well-wishers. The
days of austere piety clearly were long gone.

But did Wright's vaccines work? If they did, it was not because vaccines had been made to the specific disease in most cases. More often than not, they were made using bacteria that we know are not associated with the diseases, and in others, we know the disease is not bacterial in origin. Was it a placebo effect, or did no one bother to examine the records of the outcomes of the patients? There seems to be no evidence that Wright was doing any harm. From our point of view, the most important thing about the Inoculation Department was that it was at the cutting edge of science in the early years of the twentieth century. It stands as a shining example of how strongly and suddenly the tide had turned away from disease being framed as a general imbalance of the humors of the body to a specific inciting agent causing a specific disease. Vaccination was the new cause célèbre, and the race was on to see who would grab the next Nobel for finding the next specific cure.

Chapter
8

Magic Bullets and the New Paradigm of Medicine

I t took Pasteur, Bernard, and Virchow to change the way we frame disease and, as a consequence, how we treat it. At the start of the twentieth century, *disease* still meant infectious disease, but it would now be framed by specific microbes causing pathological changes in specific organs resulting in specific symptoms. It was specificity that made medicine scientific, and it was specificity that captured the public's imagination the way Newton's gravity, Franklin's electricity, and Lavoisier's oxygen had a century before; the hunt for the microbes that cause disease replaced the thrill of seeing the balloons of the Montgolfiers. Scientific medicine was so successful in replacing Galenic medicine because finally, like the other sciences, there was the promise that it could *do something*. Bacteriology had identified the causes of the diseases and immunology had already shown that there could be specific prevention. Now the promise of specific drugs would be the goal.

Magic Bullets: Paul Ehrlich's Quest for Specificity

W hen Emil Behring was trying to convert his discovery that antitoxin could save a mouse from the lethal effects of diphtheria toxin from a laboratory experiment into a therapy that could be used on children, he kept stumbling over the difficulty of producing a serum of enough activity to be effective. Paul Ehrlich came to his rescue by applying the reasoning of chemistry to the production of antiserum. For well over a quarter of a century, the children who were saved by diphtheria antitoxin therapy owed their lives to Paul Ehrlich as much as to anyone; and the rest of us owe the idea of specific drugs to treat specific diseases to him.

Of the odd and fascinating characters who have populated this narrative, Paul Ehrlich is one of the oddest and most fascinating. He was born in Strehlen, in Upper Silesia, in 1854, the year Pasteur became dean of the faculty at Lille and began his interest in biological research. Much of what we know of Ehrlich's life comes from a biography written in 1949 by Martha Marquardt, an adoring secretary who often tells us more than she thought she did. We learn, for example, that Ehrlich's father, an innkeeper, was "a man of keen judgment, with a cheerful manner and full of good humour. But in spite of these lively characteristics he would sometimes sit at the window for hours talking to himself, accompanying his words with movements of the head, and gesticulations of the hand. When speaking to others he would put out his words and sentences in a strange hurry, introduce a jest, repeat it several times loudly in the conversation, and laugh over it." The reminiscences of some of his schoolmates make it clear that even at an early age Paul was his father's son, and Marquardt's descriptions of his everyday activities in his laboratory show a quirky, preoccupied genius given to talking to himself and repeating stock phrases. But we know from his colleagues and the scientists who dealt with him that Ehrlich was a man of the keenest scientific insights who could visualize chemical and biological structures in his mind and devise complicated theoretical explanations based on these visualizations.

As a student, Ehrlich was fascinated with the chemistry of dyes and especially their use in the staining of biological tissues, so after he passed his initial medical school exams, through the influence of his cousin, the pathologist Karl Weigert, he was able to work in the laboratory of Cohnheim at Breslau while preparing for his final examinations. In fact, when Koch made his first fateful visit to Breslau and was taken to see Cohnheim, he was introduced to the young man as "little Ehrlich," who is "very good at staining, but he will *never* pass his examinations." But he did pass his examinations and became doctor of medicine with a thesis on the theoretical and analytical basis of staining. In 1878 he became an assistant at the Charité-Hospital in Berlin, and was apparently present in the audience at the 1882 lecture to the Physiological Society of Berlin at which Koch announced that he had isolated the bacillus responsible for tuberculosis. Ehrlich had been staining the organs and sputum of tuberculosis patients and remembered that he had seen some strange rod-shaped bacteria, but they were so faint that he could not be sure what they were. The story, probably not true, is that he rushed back to his laboratory and stained up some new preparations, but because it was late and he was so messy, he put them on top of an iron stove to dry and then forgot about them. The next morning the cleaning lady lit the fire in the stove, and when Ehrlich came in and recovered the slides, he found they were beautifully stained and so he was the first person to see the tubercle bacillus in a specimen. The story probably grew out of the fact that to stain the tubercle bacillus, unlike most other bacteria, it is necessary to heat the slide slightly to facilitate the penetration of the dye into the organisms. Even though we now know that heating slides while staining them seems to have been a practice that "little Ehrlich, who was good with stains" did in a rather routine way, the story is too good not to retell. Koch would later write that "with Ehrlich's method of staining, the recognition of tubercle bacilli could readily be made use of in diagnosis. We owe it to this circumstance alone that it has become a general custom to search for the bacillus in sputum, whereas, without it, it is likely that but few investigators would have concerned themselves with tubercle bacilli."

The sudden death of his chief and patron at the Charité brought about a sudden and severe change in Ehrlich's life. The new chief was not as indulgent with the eccentric Ehrlich and began to make him feel unwelcome. It is not clear how much of the pressures Ehrlich began to feel were due to the institutional anti-Semitism in German academic medicine and how much was due to the fact that Ehrlich truly must have been a pain in the neck for any administrator, but his health began to suffer and he resigned his position at the Charité Hospital. He claimed to have developed tuberculosis during the course of his research on staining, but his closest associates thought it was nervous strain. His brother-in-law would later write in an obituary that Ehrlich could not stand the constraints put on him under the regime of the new director, and just "as a highly strung racehorse would end by quivering helplessly in the yoke, breaking down as a result of nervous excitement without advancing or making any effective effort, so Ehrlich's body would pine away when his spirit was fettered. . . . His illness was called tuberculosis of the lungs, and he had the clinical symptoms of that disease. But what he was suffering from mostly was constraint. The easily cured tuberculosis never troubled him again when once he had recovered his strength." Ehrlich spent two years in Egypt recovering from whatever it was that ailed him, and his life took a new direction when he returned.

He had married the daughter of a wealthy Silesian factory owner a few years before, and when they returned from Egypt, he was able to set up a small private laboratory in Berlin. Koch, who was grateful for Ehrlich's contribution of the staining method, offered him the chance to work in his new Institute for Infectious Diseases—with no pay. Shortly after he began working in the institute, Ehrlich began a collaboration with Behring, who was in the middle of his work on diphtheria antitoxins. In his earlier research, Ehrlich had found that when he injected experimental animals with small amounts of the plant toxins ricin or abrin, the toxic effects were neutralized by the blood of the injected animals. By increasing the amount of toxin injected, slowly over a period of time, he had been able to increase the amount of antitoxin in the blood. This was important because Behring was unable to reliably get active preparations of diphtheria antitoxin from the blood of the animals he was immunizing with diphtheria toxin. Ehrlich had not only solved that problem with the plant toxins, he had even worked out the test-tube chemistry to measure how much antitoxin there was in the blood of the animals. Koch's biographer, the American bacteriologist Thomas Brock, says that "[A]ll sources seem to agree that if it had not been for Paul Ehrlich, Behring's honors would have come to naught. For it was Ehrlich who first developed suitable quantitative methods for diphtheria antitoxin, thus permitting analysis of diphtheria antitoxin production and efficacy."

From his work with dyes and his early training, Ehrlich had the mindset of a chemist; he thought in terms of specific chemical groups interacting with each other and of their quantitative relationships. Diphtheria toxin and antitoxin, in his mind, could be treated like any other chemical interaction and so he quickly devised a method for measuring the amount of diphtheria antitoxin in the serum of a horse that had been immunized. The importance of this work in moving the antitoxin therapy process forward into a routine reality was recognized by everyone, and once there was no question that serum therapy worked, it did not escape the notice of commercial interests.

Behring was approached by the German chemical company Hoechst with an offer to enter into a commercial venture to produce diphtheria antitoxin. But Hoechst first required that the procedure for producing the antitoxin be patented, and Ehrlich's contribution was of course an essential part of the patentable process. In 1893, in the presence of one of the directors of the company at the Hoechst headquarters, Behring told Ehrlich that he had sufficient connections in high government places to assure him of both a professorship and the directorship of a government laboratory. For a Jew to gain a professorship was rare, but to run a government laboratory was more than Ehrlich could have ever dreamed of. There was a rub, however: Behring told his friend that if he accepted royalties from a company for the commercialization of his research, neither offer would probably be forthcoming. On the spot, Ehrlich chose the honors over the royalties, and mysteriously, Behring's director friend immediately provided a piece of paper for him to sign away his financial rights. Behring was unable to deliver either the professorship or the directorship and he and Ehrlich never spoke to each other again. Ehrlich would later write to a friend:

> I always get wild whenever I think of that dark period and the way in which B. tried to hide our scientific partnership. But the revenge has come. He can see how far he has got without me since our separation. Everything is blocked now: his work on plague, cholera, glanders, streptococcal infections. He makes no progress with diphtheria. . . . And all this with more than sufficient means in hand, and a swarm of collaborators. . . . Of course, you can imagine how filled with rage he is. He wanted to be the "All-Highest" who could dictate his laws to the entire world and who, in addition, could earn the most money. He wanted to be a Superman; but—thank God—he did not have the necessary super-brain. . . . Away with the mammonisation of science!

A few years later, without the help of his former friend, Ehrlich did receive the directorship of the government Institute for the Investigation and Control of Sera. Eventually, the institute was moved to Frankfurt and Ehrlich remained its director. But even here Behring, who was now von Behring, plagued him. He tried to get the state to pay for research to be carried out by Ehrlich in his institute for which von Behring would get the scientific credit and the financial reward. In a long and tightly reasoned letter in 1906 to the director of the Prussian Ministry of Ecclesiastical, Educational and Medical Affairs, Ehrlich described his role in the development of the first antitoxins, telling how in those early crucial days Behring had been unable to make an antitoxin that had any potency, and of his ignorance in the methods of going about doing it. "When we began working together he showed me a bottle containing five quarts of diphtheria toxin. He believed that this would be sufficient for fifty years of immunization work in a large factory. It would hardly have been enough for one horse!"

I f Ehrlich's experimental genius was the crucial factor in making serum therapy practicable, his theoretical genius was essential to making a chemical basis for specificity accessible to all of scientific medicine. Metchnikoff had laid the groundwork for the assumption that the body has an active mechanism for defending itself against the microbes that cause disease, and Behring's antitoxin treatment had shown that the protection was in the blood. Ehrlich, with his great facility in chemistry, carried out the studies that convinced everyone of the exquisite specificity of vaccination: Immunization with diphtheria toxin protected against diphtheria, not tetanus; immunization with ricin protected against ricin, not diphtheria. Now, in the closing years of the nineteenth century, he began to visualize (literally) how the body could produce specific antitoxins. In March 1900, Ehrlich was invited to deliver the Croonian Lecture to the august Royal Society in London, and he amplified his ideas of just how the body can fight disease specifically. The ideas in this lecture were important because they showed his reasoning, but its lasting value is that he set the intellectual basis for specificity of the reactions of the body.

Being a chemist at heart, Ehrlich believed that biological reactions such as those between toxins and antitoxins could be studied as pure chemical reactions. The success he had in making Behring's diphtheria antitoxin therapy a useful one certainly showed that the idea had merit. But he was also convinced of the correctness of Metchnikoff's ideas that the body has an active defense system, and of Virchow's idea that the cell is the basic unit of life in both health and disease. He needed a way to bring these ideas, which seemed to be mutually exclusive, together while retaining the essential features of each. Using his unusual ability to visualize structures, he created an ingenious explanation that was to be the basis for his thinking as he moved beyond specifically curing disease through the use of antitoxins (immune therapy) to curing them through the use of chemically specific therapy, which he called "magic bullets."

The basis of this wonderful idea, which led his major antagonist to call him Dr. Fantasy, came from his long experience with dyes. He had observed over and over again that certain dyes were specific for certain cell types in the body, so he reasoned that different kinds of cells have different kinds of molecules on their surfaces that react specifically with the dyes. He had already shown that the body can make a specific antitoxin to ricin, or diphtheria, and he knew that different toxins affected different kinds of cells—some toxins damaged cells of the nervous system, some damaged cells of the respiratory system, and some the digestive system. So if cells have molecules that can react specifically with dyes, why should they not have molecules that react specifically with toxins?

But this was counterintuitive; why should different cells have different molecules on their surfaces, and more to the point, why should they have molecules specific for toxins? One obvious reason is because different cell types have different functions and must do different things, but another is that cells must get their food from inside of the body (Bernard's *milieu intérieur*). Perhaps, he reasoned, different cells take up different food molecules from the blood. Because there is no logical reason to think that the body has molecules on its cells for the purpose of reacting with dyes or poisons, perhaps the dyes and poisons by chance have the ability to react with the molecules the cells use for food. A small area of the dye or toxin molecule could be identical to a part of a molecule the cell uses for food. If the small part of the molecule that acts as a flag to identify it to the cell is shared by food and also by the toxin, the cell has no way of telling if the rest of the molecule is its proper foodstuff, a harmless dye, or a dangerous toxin. Ehrlich called these molecules—the ones on the surface of the cells able to identify the unique chemical configuration on the dye, toxin, or food—side chains. (For the biologically sophisticated reader, these are what we today call receptors.)

All well and good so far, but this seems to be a long way from antitoxin in the blood. Well, hadn't he saved Behring's antitoxin therapy by showing him that it was necessary to start with a small dose of toxin to immunize a horse and then slowly build up the amount of toxin in succeeding injections until, after what might be a long wait, the amount of antitoxin in the blood increased to levels where the blood could be used as a therapeutic? This useful but seemingly oddball fact held the clue he needed. In Ehrlich's model of how the body makes specific antitoxins, the first time a cell that has the proper side chain meets the flag (i.e., the specific molecular configuration that tells it that food is at hand) but finds that it has taken up a poison instead of some food, it responds to the trick by making more of the cell surface molecules. Absurd, you say! But his cousin Weigert had proposed the idea of "cellular overcompensation" in response to injury several years before, and Ehrlich built on this idea for his side-chain theory of immunity. The side chain, having reacted with a molecule of toxin rather than a molecule of food, overcompensates for the damage done to it by producing more side chains. On each subsequent confrontation with toxin, more and more side chains are produced, so that soon the number is so great that they are shed from the surface of the cell and begin to circulate in the blood. And what is the primary characteristic of these free-floating side chains? They react specifically with the toxin. And what is the primary characteristic of antitoxins? They react specifically with toxin!

Ehrlich thought that each cell had hundreds, if not thousands, of different kinds of side chains on its surface but that it was only the specific side chains that reacted with the toxin and only these that were overproduced. In one glorious theory he had explained specific defense by bringing together antitoxins and cells; he had merged elements of vaccination and inflammation. Granted, phagocytosis does not enter into the picture, and even though Ehrlich knew Almroth Wright and respected him, it is not clear what he thought of "stimulating the phagocytes."*

---

* This ingenious theory was debated constantly for almost twenty years before it was replaced by a theory of antibody formation that was much less counterintuitive. But strange to say, when the era of modern immunology began circa 1950, immunologists returned to a variant of Ehrlich's side-chain theory that was even more counterintuitive than the original. This theory is still the dominant theory of immunology.

Ehrlich believed that "[W]hat makes Serum-therapy so extraordinarily active is the fact that the protecting substances of the body are products of the body itself, and that they act purely 'parasitotropically' [on the parasite] and not 'organotropically' [on the body]. Here we may speak of '*magic bullets*' which aim exclusively at the dangerous intruding parasites, strangers to the body, but do not touch the body itself and its cells. Serum-therapy is therefore obviously, where it can be carried out, superior to any other mode of action." Here is the new scientific medicine writ large; when he thought about therapy, he had given up completely attempting to treat the body, of balancing the humors; disease has a specific cause and *so the only rational therapy must be aimed at what is causing the disease itself.* But by 1906 the realization had slowly been growing for him that if by the chance occurrence of similar chemical configuration dyes and poisons could react specifically with cells, then why couldn't he create other chemicals that would have similar configurations to molecules on the surface of the bacteria that cause disease, chemicals that would have a therapeutic effect by specifically killing them? It was already clear to him that the promise of therapy by antitoxins, as powerful as it was in cases where it worked, had a rather limited utility. After all, there was no indication that the bacteria that caused tuberculosis or syphilis, two of the great killers, caused disease by producing toxins.

For the rest of his life, Ehrlich's goal was to find chemicals that reacted specifically with the infecting organism and killed it but did not react with the cells of the patient. His idea was to replace specific serum-therapy with specific chemotherapy whenever possible; these chemicals were to be his "magic bullets."

Ehrlich had found security, fame, and respect in Frankfurt, where his institute had gained world renown as a center for immunology research. He was able to convince a wealthy Frankfurt widow, Frau Franziska Speyer, to build a whole new institute, adjacent to the existing Serum Institute, devoted exclusively to work on chemotherapy. Against seemingly insurmountable obstacles, "little Ehrlich," who would never pass his examinations and who signed away a lifetime of financial security on the wild hope of becoming the director of an institute, was now director of two institutes!

His lifelong passion for dyes had led him to this point and now, because of the economic developments in the German dye industry, it led to an alliance with a local chemical company.

With the rapid industrialization of the nineteenth century had come enough wealth for a consumer-oriented middle class to emerge, and these new consumers had an insatiable appetite for dyed fabrics. Dyes had been made from coal tar for years, but in the middle of the century, German chemists had discovered ways of producing synthetic dyes of brilliant shades, leading to the formation of the German chemical industry. By 1876 it became necessary to institute strict patent laws in order to prevent the outright copying of competitors' dyes, and the larger chemical firms instituted the first industrial-research laboratories. By one of those strange accidents of fate, in 1886 two Alsatian doctors ordered a dye called naphthalene, for the treatment of intestinal parasites, from the local pharmacist. It failed to have the expected effect on the parasites, but to the doctors' surprise, it lowered the fever of their patients. The next batch they ordered from the pharmacist had no effect on fever but did work on the intestinal parasites. Rather than leave it at that, the two physicians delved into the question and found that the original material they had been provided with was not naphthalene at all but another chemical, called acetanilid, a coal-tar derivative used in the dye industry. The ability of acetanilid to reduce fever fortunately had not escaped their notice and aspirin was discovered!

This chance discovery changed the character of the German chemical industry, because now dyes were not only of value in producing cloth for the growing number of consumers, they became the forerunner of the modern pharmaceutical industry. So it was only natural that in the early 1900s, the director of the Cassella Works (which would later become part of the vast I. G. Farben company) was very much interested in working with Ehrlich in his quest for chemical magic bullets. A full-time chemist was assigned to synthesizing dyes that Ehrlich tested in his Chemotherapy Institute. This arrangement allowed Ehrlich to work in his own idiosyncratic way, which Ludwig Benda, the chemist assigned to the institute, described in a reminiscence for Ehrlich's sixtieth birthday. "Coming into Ehrlich's laboratory we find to our great surprise that many things generally found in a laboratory are missing. In a medium-sized room stands an immense laboratory bench on which, closely packed together, are hundreds of small, some of them very small, bottles filled with different chemicals. It seems a hopeless chaos, but Ehrlich, having arranged the substances according to a peculiar system of his own, finds everything he looks for. From this ocean of bottles rises a single large Bunsen burner. Close to it there is a small wooden box containing test tubes. These, with some boards and shelves along the walls containing the usual reagents and substances for making solutions, complete the equipment of this laboratory, in which Ehrlich works without any assistance. Here one would look in vain for cylinders and retorts, funnels, beakers and jar, bowls and basins, a refrigerator or thermometer, and all the vessels and accessories which are the normal tools of the chemical worker."

Dyes and their chemical derivatives were being increasingly tested for their potential drug action, and because the major medical problems were still infectious diseases and the fever and inflammation that went with them, these were the targets the drugs were directed against. What separated Ehrlich from the developing pharmaceutical-industrial scientists was his idea of using the potential specificity of chemicals. In 1906 two English physicians had found that an arsenic-containing dye called atoxyl was useful in treating experimental infections with trypanosomes, but the drug could not be used in humans because it was toxic to the optic nerve. The chemical structure of atoxyl was such that the industrial chemists were convinced the molecule could not easily be altered to remove its toxic properties. To the consternation of the industrial chemists who had been assigned to work with him, Ehrlich, working in his own way, so unorthodox and bizarre to chemists, concluded that the original formula worked out in 1863 was wrong. He concluded that in fact atoxyl could be modified to make it toxic for the parasite but not for the patient. The industrial chemists were so appalled at the idea that this idiosyncratic loner was challenging accepted chemistry that several of them resigned. The few who remained followed his instructions and came up with a compound that was less toxic yet still killed trypanosomes. This was compound number 418.

Ehrlich and his chemists continued modifying the basic arsenic compound. One such compound, which was not successful on experimental trypanosome infections, was number 606, which had been patented by the Cassella company and put on the shelf. In the spring of 1909 Kitasato, who had returned to Japan and was the director of an institute in Tokyo, sent a student named Sahachiro Hata to work with Ehrlich. In Tokyo Hata had been working on experimental syphilis infections in rabbits. The bacteria that cause syphilis had been isolated in 1905, but Ehrlich did not have the means of testing any of his compounds on them until Hata arrived, and he now assigned him the laborious task of going through all of the compounds to see if any of them were effective against syphilis. In due course Hata found that compound 606, which had been ineffective against trypanosomes, was remarkably effective against the bacterial spirochete that caused syphilis. Ehrlich's clinical collaborators had been testing the effect of compound 418 on their patients with syphilis, but now he insisted that they try number 606.

The clinical success of compound 606 on syphilis was announced at the Congress for Internal Medicine at Wiesbaden in April 1910. The effect was electrifying, and compound 606, now called Salvarsan, showed the reasonableness of Ehrlich's search for specific chemotherapeutics. Scientific medicine, through specificity, seemed to be truly able to change the world, and today part of the accepted lore of medical science is that Ehrlich opened the path to chemotherapy with his specific magic bullets. As is often the case, the accepted lore has only passing relationship to the facts.

How Magic Was the Magic Bullet?

As soon as Ehrlich made the announcement that compound 606 was effective against syphilis, doctors from all over the world wanted to use it on their patients. He was besieged by hundreds of letters a day, cables from all over the world, and doctors filling the corridors leading to his office. A Chicago physician wrote: "Not since Koch's tuberculin has there been such an onslaught of medical men to Germany." But Ehrlich would only give the drug to trained syphilologists who had adequate clinical and laboratory facilities at their disposal. The *Journal of the American Medical Association* (JAMA) printed a cable it received from him: "Ehrlich says doctors stay home, don't write; 606 market November."

Word of how effective compound 606 was in treating syphilis was spread by word of mouth from the enthusiastic professors who were using it before any studies evaluating just how effective it really was appeared in print, and these claims naturally found their way into the popular press. *The American Journal of Urology* carried an editorial saying, "The daily press in every civilized country has given columns to the discussion of the new treatment, investing the new remedy, after the fashion of journalism, with wonderful properties, even more striking than those actually observed." But it was the doctors themselves who were passing along the word that 606 was effective against things Ehrlich had never made claims for. Scurvy, malaria, psoriasis, pernicious anemia, Sydenham's chorea, leprosy, several skin diseases, even cancer—all were claimed by euphoric doctors to have been treated by this "magic bullet." Salvarsan may have been a triumph of the specificity of scientific medicine, but both practitioners and patients wanted an old-fashioned cure that took care of everything.

Not surprisingly, a backlash developed. The excessive use and misuse showed that 606 was not a magic bullet; it was only a toxic drug that when used in too high a dose had severe ill effects. Ehrlich now spent so much of his time explaining the proper use of 606 that he was accused of being defensive. The editor of JAMA complained that Ehrlich and his followers had exercised "too great ingenuity"; they seemed to be explaining away the claims of adverse reactions to 606 as actual manifestations of syphilis that those who had studied the disease for years had been "too obtuse to recognize." The editor even questioned whether the good that 606 did was worth the harm. Others said it was no better than the horrific treatments with mercury that were then so common, and by 1914 JAMA warned against the hope that 606 was even an adequate substitute for mercury. War sentiment led a French professor to write an article entitled "*Le 606 ou Le poison Allemand*" ("606 or the German Poison"), in which he claimed that 606 had never cured syphilis at all, it had only allowed skin to grow over the syphilitic ulcer without healing it. In the end, doctors found that at proper doses, and interspersed with mercury and, later, bismuth, 606 could be used to treat syphilis, but both the early euphoria and the idea of a magic bullet were gone.

In fact, even though Ehrlich had talked of absolute specificity in both serum therapy and chemotherapy, there were immunologists who were fighting his contention that antitoxins were totally specific, and from the very beginning of his work on chemotherapy, even as he was talking about magic bullets, Ehrlich was devising a measure that is still used today in the evaluation of pharmaceuticals that compares the toxic effect of the drug on the bacteria with the toxic effects on the patient. In his imagination he may have had a vision that total specificity—one disease, one cure—was possible, but in reality he knew that he had not achieved it. Although specificity was the driving force in making medicine scientific, the application of specificity to medicine was far from simple.

On Becoming a Mature Science

In order for the theory of specificity to be converted into the technology of the cure, scientific medicine required a new social structure, a common conceptual ground from which all scientists could operate. This common ground, which serves as a basis for experiments as well as for scientific disagreements, is called a *paradigm*. The notion of the paradigm is of great importance to anyone who wants to try to understand how and why we hold certain scientific views. But it is equally important for observers of science to understand that the way scientists arrive at this common ground is an unspoken, integral part of the daily functioning of scientific life. It is part of what scientists take for granted from their earliest training and pass on to their students.

One of the most influential books of our times about how science is carried out is *The Structure of Scientific Revolutions,* by Thomas Kuhn. The book has been widely read and much discussed among those who study the history, philosophy, and sociology of science. Kuhn, who was trained as a physicist, attempted to write a nonromanticized version of how scientists function at a time (1962) when science was still all too often treated in a highly romantic way. Kuhn's ideas have served as the basis for much of the work that goes on in a new field of study called science studies, and while these historians, sociologists, and philosophers have gone well beyond the original ideas, for our purposes it will be useful to look at unadulterated Kuhn.

The great twentieth-century philosopher Karl Popper began the discourse among philosophers by introducing the notion of *falsification* into the analysis of how science works. His argument is simple: A scientific hypothesis can never be *verified;* it can only be *falsified.* No matter how much evidence you gather to "prove" a point, there is always the chance that some crucial contrary evidence will be discovered. As the Scottish philosopher of the Enlightenment David Hume had pointed out many years before, it is not possible to *prove* that all swans are white. If you tried to do it by sitting on the bank and counting the white swans that go by, no matter how many white swans you count, you can never say for certain that all swans are white, because the next swan that comes around the bend may be black. But when the black (or gray or blue) swan does appear, you can now say with absolute confidence that all swans are *not* white. So you have learned something very concrete about the world by showing what is *not* true. You can falsify the assertion that all swans are white, but you can never prove it. Now, one need not be a trained philosopher to see the logic in this, but it is most certainly not how working scientists function. So how do scientists work, and how does scientific progress occur?

The basis of Kuhn's analysis is that a science becomes a "mature" science when it acquires a *paradigm*. The exact nature of a paradigm has been rather difficult to pin down and it has been pointed out that Kuhn himself used the term in a variety of ways in his book. For our purposes, a *paradigm* is an important assumption that all of the workers in a scientific field agree upon. This is not to say that it is true or that it is inviolate. Quite the opposite: Because progress is an essential element of science, the paradigm will change as science progresses. Major scientific progress is therefore associated with *paradigm shifts*. So paradigms represent the state of the field that all of the practitioners in the field can agree upon. The importance of this agreement is not that it gives science a clubby atmosphere; in fact, it does exactly the opposite. When all of the workers in the field have a common ground to start from, it gives them a common basis from which to argue among themselves. Since science is basically the solving of problems, there must be agreement about the questions to be asked. It has been pointed out that scientists are like children, because they never lose their sense of wonder or their argumentiveness, and the paradigm allows both the sense of wonder and the argumentiveness to go forward in a reasonably orderly manner. For example, all astronomers agree that the sun is the center of the solar system, so it is from this assumption that they make their arguments about the nature of the solar system. All biologists agree that evolution through natural selection is an important mechanism in biology. The arguments are reserved for how biological systems function given the fact that natural selection is an important biological phenomenon. It becomes obvious that without a set of paradigms, a science cannot move forward, because there would be constant debate over the rules of the game (witness the violence of the response by scientists to religious fundamentalists who want to call the biblical version of creation a "science").

Once a paradigm (or a set of paradigms) is established as the fundamental assumptions of a field, the scientists in that field have the rules of their game. They now ask their questions, design their experiments, interpret their results, and carry out their arguments about what the experiments and interpretations mean within boundaries that serve as benchmarks against which progress in the field is measured. Young scientists who are new to the discipline have a clear set of fundamentals to use when they enter the field, and they make their reputations by how clever they are at asking questions within the overarching assumptions of the paradigms. Authority is established, and careers are made or fall by how brilliant one is at solving the problems, the edges of which the paradigm has defined. This is what Kuhn calls "normal science": the relentless forward movement of science that both lay public and scientists take for granted. Normal science must not be mistaken for dull science. In the golden age of bacteriology, the germ theory of disease was the overarching paradigm and the normal science was the exhilarating discovery of the organisms responsible for various diseases.

Another very important element in Kuhn's analysis of how science functions is, of course, the question of how a paradigm changes. If all progress consisted of functioning within the paradigm, there would be no room for a Copernicus, Darwin, or Einstein. So, obviously, paradigms change. But how? Because the paradigms confer stability on the field, they are only changed after great resistance, which means that the price a scientific discipline pays for its stability and continuity is great difficulty in introducing radical changes in its course. Neither Kuhn nor any of the people who have commented on and analyzed his work have a clear idea of how or why a paradigm changes. Probably there is no single answer or set of answers. But what Kuhn is clear about is that when the change does occur, it is not gradual; there is no slow erosion of the paradigm. It occurs as a revolution.

Specificity became the paradigm of scientific medicine, and by this definition it had become a mature science by the early years of the twentieth century. Our other criterion, that the science be clearly seen to be able to do something practical to be taken seriously, was also met; diphtheria antitoxin and Salvarsan certainly fit into the hopes of the ordinary people for technological wonders. The idea that diseases could be specifically cured had become part of the accepted vision of what the new century would bring; if balloon ascensions, steam power, and electrification were wonderful, how could they compare to the world that science told them was just around the corner, a world without disease? Just how science worked was of no more interest to either the scientists or the men and women who were watching their children die and were at risk of disease themselves than how the phonograph, telegraph, or internal combustion engine worked. A mature science without authority was of no interest to anyone, and authority was gained by touching the lives of people. Scientific medicine was now certainly touching the lives of people and, in so doing, raising their hopes for a century in which disease would be abolished.

Chapter

9

The Therapeutic Revolution

To people at the beginning of the twentieth century, the speed with which the microbes responsible for so many diseases were identified showed the power of science, and the success of antitoxin therapy and compound 606 served as dramatic proof that specific cures were not only possible, they were already at hand. This belief in the power of science to bring about social change was reflected in what the social reformer Beatrice Webb called the "time-spirit" of the late Victorian age, which had just ended: "a trust in science and a commitment to mankind." It is now unfashionable to talk about a "time-spirit" or *Zeitgeist*, but these were the terms used by the late Victorians themselves. It may not be possible to isolate for analysis the elements of the "spirit" of a time, but few who live in interesting times would disagree that there is a "spirit," even if they cannot verbalize and analyze it, and one very large part of the spirit of the age in the beginning years of the twentieth century was faith in the power of science.

In art, the Neoimpressionist painter Georges Seurat had developed a whole "scientific" explanation for his method of applying paint in small dabs similar to a printed picture. In retrospect, it seems clear that his references to scientific texts and methods served as a justification for his breaking from the Impressionist movement, and he was probably only using science to lend authority to what he was doing. Even the makers of patent medicines appealed to the authority of science through bacteriology. At the turn of the century, a Texan named William Radam sold a patent medicine, called Microbe Killer, based on the germ theory. So successful was this mixture of water laced with traces of red wine, hydrochloric acid, and sulfuric acid that by 1890 he had seventeen factories producing the elixir. The idea made perfectly good sense to the public; bacteriology (which to the public represented the highest realms of science) had shown that diseases are caused by microbes, so what better inducement than a nostrum that killed the microbes that caused the disease? One historian has noted the irony of the fact that when science could for the first time explain disease, it "was the very age in which patent medicines reached their apogee." Now that medicine was the science of specific causes of disease, who would not expect specific cures for everything?

Until now, healers had done all they could to bring the body to the point of health, and then let divine will take its course. Now, with the new scientific way of looking at the world and our place in it, that had changed. The faith that had been reserved for divine control of the outcome of disease was being transferred to science; the power of science would now prevent suffering and death. We can see what T. H. Huxley meant when he likened the growing authority of science and scientists in the late nineteenth century to the church. He called it the Church Scientific.

But the new therapies that the "Church Scientific" promised were slow in coming. Lewis Thomas, the well-known physician and a scientist who has written eloquently about biology, medicine, and the changes scientific medicine has brought to our lives, gives us an instructive comparison of how little had changed in medical practice and medical education between 1901, when his father was a medical student at the College of Physicians and Surgeons of Columbia University, and 1933, during his own medical education at Harvard.

> By the time my father reached P&S, the principal concern of the faculty of medicine was the teaching of diagnosis. The recognition of specific illnesses, based on what had been learned about the natural history of disease and about the pathological changes in each illness, was the real task of the doctor. If he could make an accurate diagnosis, he could forecast from this information what the likely outcome was

to be for each of his patients' illnesses. . . . [I]t was assumed that he [the physician] would stand by, on call, until it was over. . . . [G]ood medical schools produced doctors who could make an accurate diagnosis and knew enough of the details of the natural history of disease to be able to make a reliable prognosis. This was all there was to science in medicine, and the store of information which made diagnosis and prognosis possible for my father's generation was something quite new in the early part of the twentieth century.

Thirty-two years later, when Lewis himself went to medical school, he recalls, things had not changed all that much:

We were provided with a thin, pocket-size book called *Useful Drugs*, one hundred pages or so, and we carried this around in our white coats when we entered the teaching wards and clinics in the third year, but I cannot recall any of our instructors ever referring to this volume. *Nor do I remember much talk about treating disease at any time in the four years of medical school except by the surgeons* . . . [author's emphasis]. The medicine we were trained to practice was, essentially, Osler's medicine. Our task for the future was to be diagnoses and explanation. Explanation was the real business of medicine. What the ill patient and his family wanted most was to know the name of the illness, and then, if possible, what had caused it, and finally, most important of all, how it was likely to turn out.

Comfort was what the scientific physician could offer as recently as 1933! Comfort would come from the "bedside manner," but most of all from being able to tell the patient the name of his or her illness so that he or she could better cope with what the fates had in store. The growth of the clinical laboratory and the introduction of new tools for diagnosis aided the physician in this role; the description and diagnosis now visibly took on scientific precision. But this was not enough for patients, who, reasonably enough, clamored for delivery on the promise by scientific medicine of more therapies. They were to be gravely disappointed; the therapies were slow in coming.

The Promise of Vaccines

The research that scientists and the public alike had the highest hopes for in the new era of specific therapies was the development of vaccines. Just as Salvarsan raised the hopes that there would be other "magic bullets" to cure bacterial infections, diphtheria antitoxin raised the hopes that there would soon be vaccines to prevent them. Although the general principle for vaccination had been established by Pasteur twenty years before, at the turn of the century its application to the development of new and important vaccines was not going well. As one student of the situation put it:

> As one surveys the vast literature on immunization one is impressed by the effectiveness of vaccination as developed by Pasteur. . . . The basic principles laid down by the pioneers in vaccination were distorted and at times ignored. The selection of appropriate cultures for vaccine production was often superficial, careful evaluation of the administered doses was lacking. . . . This confusion in clinical medicine persisted during the first quarter of the twentieth century.

A representative example of the problem is the attempt to develop a cholera vaccine. Waldemar Haffkine, a former student of Pasteur's, tried to attenuate the bacteria that cause cholera and to carry out trials of a vaccine in India. He used these vaccines "on numerous tea estates, in regiments, gaols, and families. The numbers of inoculated and uninoculated were often unequal; the two sets were unevenly exposed to risk of infection; in some instances the inoculation was performed during the progress of the epidemic; in others the disease did not break out for a year or more after inoculation; and the cases that did occur were too few to afford a correct idea of the comparative immunity of the two groups." One need not be a trained scientist to see that these trials—compared with the elegant field trial at Pouilly le Fort by his teacher—were a fiasco.

It is not that Haffkine was an incompetent. Far from it. This episode points out the incredible difficulty of doing a clinical trial on humans, as compared to one on animals, in an experimental setting. Pasteur could choose the exact numbers of animals to be in the vaccinated and the unvaccinated control groups and could assure that *both* groups received exactly the same challenge of virulent organisms at exactly the same time. The field trial at Pouilly le Fort was such a success because the unvaccinated control animals died before the eyes of the spectators. But how can one do such a study on a vaccine for humans? Is it ethical to have an unvaccinated control group, and if it is, would anyone knowingly want to be in it? And how does the investigator make sure that the vaccinated and unvaccinated groups have equal contact with the disease-causing organism? Pasteur could inject all of the animals with the bacteria; only a barbarian would consider doing this with humans. Haffkine, even if he had been the equal of his teacher, could not have carried out as rigorous a trial as did Pasteur.

Jenner had only been able to show that his smallpox vaccine prevented the eruption usually seen by the relatively harmless inoculation of pus into Joseph Phipps's arm. It would have been unthinkable for him to have subjected the boy to smallpox to prove his point as was done in the royal experiment when the pardoned convict was made to share the bed of the boy with smallpox, because if the original inoculation had not worked, she would have come down with smallpox. Even Behring had a less formidable task of proving the efficacy of the antidiphtheria serum therapy, because children already showing symptoms of the disease were admitted to one of two hospitals and the antiserum therapy was used in one hospital but not in the other as a matter of hospital policy. The 50 percent reduction in case mortality in the hospital where the antiserum was used was clear for all to see. Such clear-cut and definitive conditions for a field trial are rare, so the actual demonstration that a particular vaccine or dose or injection schedule is correct is extremely difficult to prove. The outrage that civilized societies feel at the "science" of the Nazi doctors or the Tuskegee syphilis experiment in the United States shows how deeply ingrained are these basic human values and make clear the difficulty of doing "clean" scientific experiments on people in real settings. And yet there is equal desire to have the fruits of science converted to life-saving therapies. Even at this earliest of stages of the new scientific medicine, people were beginning to see that there are no free lunches; the application of science to medicine may bring benefits, but they come with a cost. These questions and problems are still with us today, when there is talk of an AIDS vaccine by the beginning of the twenty-first century. Given an incubation period of ten years for

HIV and all of the problems we have just mentioned, while it is understandable that people are impatient, our ability to get a technological fix on the situation through a vaccine is clearly limited.

What was perhaps most disappointing in those early years and still remains a problem today is that many of the scientists who were trying to develop vaccines in the face of these terrible difficulties were either claiming that the vaccines were successful or allowing others to say it for them. Indeed, Almroth Wright thought that "the method of vaccination which has proved so effectual in combating cholera epidemics in India [sic!] might, *mutatai mutandis*, be applied to the prophylaxis of typhoid fever." Between 1897 and 1908, Wright himself carried out trials with various forms of typhoid vaccines, always claiming that they were successful. Yet, "[I]n spite of his interest in morbidity and mortality rates, Wright simply could not master vital statistics, so essential in evaluating a vaccine." The results were always controversial. We have already seen that in his inoculation department, Wright was "vaccinating" against acne, pyorrhea, boils, pneumonia, bronchial colds, influenza, gonorrhea, sore throats, intestinal troubles, tuberculosis, and even cancer. In most cases he was using vaccines made from bacteria that did not cause the disease, and it is doubtful he would have been allowed to continue if his therapies had been subjected to the kind of scrutiny by regulatory agencies we have today. But the power of the faith in vaccination made Wright and his colleagues wealthy and gave great hope, if not cures, to his patients. If people wonder why a half century later there is need for governmental regulatory agencies such as the FDA, let them look back at these situations.

As if the difficulties of carrying out studies to test the efficacy of vaccines on humans were not enough, in the early days of vaccine development this task was very often put in the hands of clinicians who were untrained in the methods required to develop and test vaccines. As a result, vaccine development for the next half century would be separated from the "pure" science of immunology, so theory and practice were slowly but surely separating into two separate disciplines. Both the public and scientists were still functioning in the "time-spirit" of the ardent belief that science was certain to continue to provide wonderful practical results, but the energy of the "pure" scientists was directed toward the question of how vaccination worked, while the energy of the "applied" scientists was directed to developing vaccines and diagnosis.

Increasingly, the two groups had less and less to say to each other as the development of vaccines became part of the application of science and was seen to be the responsibility of the pharmaceutical industry. Fortunately, the introduction of the methods of molecular biology into vaccine development has brought basic and applied scientists together to work on vaccines today.

It would not be until 1955 that there was a vaccine trial of as much drama as the one at Pouilly le Fort. On April 12 of that year, the announcement of the successful field trial of Jonas Salk's polio vaccine was made to a nation that breathed a collective sigh of relief. As a chronicler of the event has written, the story of the vaccine ". . . had the drama of life and death, the charm of little children, the awesome spectacle of decades of obscure and difficult research, and the human interest of families and ordinary people involved in a great and selfless effort." Yet even the testing of this vaccine, which has been one of the unquestioned high marks of successes of modern vaccines, was fraught with conflict and scientific disagreement. Should the trial have "observed" controls or "blind" controls? How many children in each group should get the vaccine and how many the placebo? Should there even be a placebo? Polio struck primarily children in the summer months, so the difficulties of proving that a vaccine worked or didn't should have been a walk in the park compared to testing vaccines against cholera or typhoid, which struck only sporadically and unpredictably. The tension was intense between those who wanted to give the possibility of protection to as many children as possible and those who argued that at all costs the trial must be carried out with statistical rigor, so that there could be no question of the efficacy of the vaccine. Fortunately, the results were so dramatically obvious that they were clear even without sophisticated statistical analysis.

Between the Salk and the later Sabin polio vaccines, the children of the world can now be protected from a terribly crippling disease and the polio vaccine has become a standard against which we measure not only other vaccines but the efficacy of all medicine. Is it any wonder that Jonas Salk has become as well known a figure in his time as Louis Pasteur was in his? The only difference is that Pasteur was honored by scientists as well as the public; Jonas Salk has never been elected to the prestigious National Academy of Sciences and has never won a Nobel prize, even though that honor was specifically designated for discoveries that have practical application. Our faith in the power of science to bring about lifesaving drugs is undiminished, but we seem to have ceased giving the professional honors to those who are responsible.

The Era of Antibiotics

The advance in therapy that probably did most to change our expectations about what medicine, drugs, and science could and should do for us was the discovery of penicillin, the drug that opened the era of antibiotics. The credit for penicillin, in the popular mind, goes to Alexander Fleming, a Scottish bacteriologist who had happily spent the bulk of his career under the influence and in the shadow of Almroth Wright. A reticent, humorless, not too ambitious man, Fleming earned a great deal of money by isolating and growing in pure culture the bacteria that were used in Wright's vaccine therapy in the inoculation department at St. Mary's. The romantic story of the discovery of penicillin, perpetuated in no small part through the efforts of Fleming and his wife, is that like Pasteur returning from his summer vacation to find the attenuated cultures of chicken cholera, Fleming returned to his lab to find an area free of bacterial growth on one of his culture plates. In this mythic version, Fleming realized in a flash that whatever was killing the bacteria on the culture plate could be used to kill bacteria in wounds, and at that moment penicillin was discovered! But then, others tried to claim credit for the discovery, until in the end justice triumphed. This is history with Jimmy Stewart in the starring role! The real story is of course quite different.

The genesis of the discovery of penicillin goes back to the First World War, when the inoculation department of St. Mary's, including Fleming, was moved to France to serve as a wound-infection unit in Boulogne. The members of the unit had seen the army surgeons attempting to kill the infecting organisms in wounds, following in the footsteps of Lister, with harsh chemicals. Since more soldiers were lost from infections of wounds than from direct injuries, army surgeons tried to use the best scientific reasoning in their treatments. But Wright believed that these harsh chemicals killed the phagocytes. So rather than cutting down on the loss of life and limb from wound infections, he believed, the harsh treatment actually had the opposite effect. He and his people came away from the war more convinced than ever that the way to control infections was to develop vaccines as a means of "stimulating the phagocytes." So the need of some less draconian treatment of wounds and infections in general had been in Fleming's mind for a long time.

The actual discovery of penicillin, as near as it can be reconstructed, was the simultaneous occurrence of two improbably rare events. Fleming had been asked to write a chapter on the staphylococci (pronounced staff-low-cocks-eye) bacteria for an encyclopedia of bacteriology and set about collecting cultures of as many strains and varieties as he could lay his hands on. His intent was to catalogue the pigment production of these organisms to see if there was a correlation of the pigments with their ability to cause disease. It happens that, like most bacteria that infect humans, staphylococci grow at 37° C (98.7° F, or normal body temperature). Their pigments, however, are only produced at room temperature (around 20° C), after the bacteria have stopped growing. So Fleming did in fact have a large number of plates on his laboratory bench, but it was not because he was too frugal to throw them out or because he had been away and was cleaning up before getting back to work. The plates were there at room temperature so that he could watch the pigments develop. To examine the pigments of the bacteria on the plates, he had to lift the lids occasionally, and on more than one of these occasions, as every bacteriologist knows, a stray mold from the air could have landed on the surface of the plate. This was not a rare occurrence and it would be very surprising if he did not have an occasional plate contaminated by airborne molds. But on one occasion Fleming noticed that on one plate there was a clear area with no bacterial growth for several millimeters around a colony of mold. Unlike Archimedes, who leapt from his bath shouting, "Eureka," Fleming rather calmly noted the event and thought that he was seeing yet another example of the action of a bacterial enzyme called lysozyme.

Lysozyme was Fleming's first thought, because his only important scientific discovery had been its discovery. Lysozyme is an enzyme produced by bacteria and other living systems that causes the lysis, or disruption, of bacteria. At the time of that discovery, both he and Wright had had high hopes that lysozyme might have therapeutic value in treating bacterial infections. To their great disappointment, however, they found that while lysozyme killed bacteria on the petri plate or in the test tube, it had no therapeutic effect in experimental animals. So when Fleming saw that area of lysis in the lawn of bacteria around the mold on his petri plate, it was natural that his first thought should be that he had found yet another source of lysozyme. Since he had spent a very large amount of time testing every conceivable living source for lysozyme and found it present in virtually all of them, this was to him a less than historic moment. Nevertheless, he isolated the mold in pure culture and did the appropriate tests to determine if it was, in fact, making lysozyme. To his surprise, he found that it was not. Therefore, he had discovered some other antibacterial agent. Now his interest was aroused, and he asked the mycologist working on the floor below (the very person who many feel may have been the source of the original contaminating mold) to identify the kind of mold he had isolated. The answer was that it belonged to one of the most common genus of mold, *Penicillium*, the common bread mold. Fleming realized that the *Penicillium* was creating a substance that diffused through the agar in the petri plate and had the ability to kill bacteria. He named the material *penicillin*, a name of which he was very proud, because he alone had given it to the substance, in contrast to lysozyme, which Wright had insisted on naming—to the chagrin of Fleming, who had discovered it.

What made the discovery so improbable? The molds that produce penicillin grow at room temperature (20° C), but the bacteria grow at normal body temperature (37° C). This means that the original stray mold had settled on the culture plate *after* the bacteria had grown at 37° C. That makes sense, but it also means that the penicillin which the mold produced had killed the bacteria *after* they had grown. The strange thing about Fleming's mold was that when he tested its ability to kill a wide variety of bacteria, including other staph, he found that it only killed bacteria *while* they were growing—it wasn't very good at killing any of them when it was added to cultures that were already grown. So the culture of staphylococci on the original plate that had been killed by the material the mold produced must have been a rare mutant that was susceptible to killing by penicillin *after* it had finished growing. Unfortunately, Fleming did not keep the culture of the bacteria so we will never know if this is really the case, and in later years, when people intentionally tried to find such mutants, they turned out to be so rare that they were almost impossible to find.

The second improbable event was that the particular *Penicillium* mold that lit on the plate on which the mutant staph had grown was able to produce enormous amounts of penicillin. When Fleming later tested all of the samples of *Penicillium* molds he could get his hands on, none of them had very much antibacterial activity. So, as bizarre as it seems, the plate with the rare mutant bacteria that were susceptible to lysis when they were not growing had been contaminated by a rare mutant *Penicillium* mold that produced large amounts of penicillin. Even Jimmy Stewart would have had trouble making that story believable!

There is a third improbability here as well. Fleming made a few attempts to test the therapeutic effect of penicillin, but it appears that he quickly gave up on it! After his experience with war wounds, his opposition to harsh chemical treatment, and the failure of lysozyme to be a biological wound disinfectant, one would have thought that he would have been even more single-minded in seeing if this new antibacterial agent could solve the enormous clinical problem of bacterial infections caused by staphylococci and streptococci, to say nothing of the venereal diseases. In the end, the most useful application he saw for penicillin was the killing of staphylococci in mixed cultures of bacteria that were isolated from patients for use in preparing vaccines for the highly profitable inoculation department at St. Mary's! If he could get rid of the staphylococci in a quick manner, he would more easily be able to isolate the other organisms that he wanted to grow in pure culture to use for the vaccines.

In 1932 Fleming referred to the use of penicillin in the treatment of septic wounds by saying it has "been used in a number of indolent septic wounds and has certainly appeared to be superior to dressings containing potent chemicals." Clearly a dig at those using harsh disinfectants but not a clarion call to the new age of antibiotics. He referred to those *same* cases again in 1941 and yet again in 1945, leading one to believe that he had made little if any further attempt to use penicillin as a therapeutic agent. In a 1945 lecture, he said, "We tried it tentatively on a few old sinuses in the hospital, and although the results were favourable, there was nothing miraculous." As a somewhat less than adoring biographer wrote, "These, Fleming's only published references to his early clinical work with penicillin, do not convey any sense of great effort or enthusiasm either on his part or that of the clinicians to whom he offered it. *One cannot avoid the conclusion that neither side had much confidence in penicillin as a therapeutic agent*" (author's emphasis).

P enicillin required the aid of Howard Florey to organize the experiments and arrange for industrial help in its production. Florey was an Australian pathologist who had made a rapid rise in British academic medicine, and as Britain was preparing for the Second World War, his research group at Oxford began to look for means of reducing deaths from wound infections. He commissioned his associate, a German-born biochemist named Ernst Chain, to do a search of the published literature to try and find reports of any biological substances with potential antibacterial activity that might be able to be produced on an industrial scale. Chain found the early and all-but-forgotten reports of Fleming and was even able to obtain a sample of the original mold from someone who had maintained it in a culture collection, a not insignificant point since, as we have said, strains of the mold that produce enough of the antibiotic to make it useful are extremely rare.

In short order, the Oxford group was able to confirm Fleming's original discovery that the culture fluids in which the *Penicillium* mold had grown contained a substance that inhibited the growth of the kinds of bacteria that cause wound infections (staphylococci, streptococci, and a few others). But unlike Fleming, they quickly found that penicillin had extremely promising properties as a therapeutic agent in experimental animals and humans. Almost from the start, the Oxford group realized that it had a drug of potentially monumental importance, and given the wartime pressure, they immediately began to devise methods of extracting the active material.

Since the time of Alexander, armies had suffered more deaths from disease than from direct warfare. In World War I, the death rate from disease for the American army was 14.1 per 1,000 soldiers; in World War II, because of sulfa drugs and then penicillin, the rate had dropped to only 0.6 per 1,000 soldiers. When the public became aware of how effective penicillin was, it indeed became a "miracle drug." Salvarsan and then sulfonamide had shown that it was possible for science to discover substances of some use in curing bacterial infections, but now the powers of science seemed to be limitless. Penicillin worked not only on the kinds of bacteria that are found in war wounds but against syphilis and gonorrhea, bacterial meningitis, and a wide variety of other infections. And it did so with what seemed to be no toxic effects; the dose that did harm to human blood cells in the test tube was 250,000 times more than the dose needed to kill bacteria. Granted, it did not work against dysentery, cholera, tuberculosis, and whooping cough, but could there be any question that science would provide even more miracle drugs?

Penicillin's discovery marked the start of the antibiotic era. With antibiotics, physicians could now treat individual infections as well as control communicable diseases in populations. The pharmaceutical industry was transformed into the industry we know today because of the antibiotic era and became even more closely associated with the therapeutic power of medicine. But many students of the discovery and development of penicillin feel that had it not been for the pressures of the war and the active participation of the United States government in assuming a large part of the development costs, there is little chance that industry would have been willing or even able to pay for the development costs of the drug.

Florey never tried to take the glory for the original observation of the antibiotic action of the mold, but Fleming emerged from his obscurity to claim credit for the discovery of penicillin. The press played up the romantic story of the reticent, eccentric Scot whose lonely, pioneering work was being ignored and whose thunder had been stolen, although nothing could have been further from the truth. He shared the Nobel prize with Florey and Chain in 1945.

In 1944, Selman Waksman and his students at Rutgers began a systematic search for molds that were active against tuberculosis. They were successful, and after a disappointing first clinical trial, streptomycin was added to the list of antibiotics that were "conquering disease." Chloramphenicol, Aureomycin, neomycin, and Terramycin followed. In the minds of the public, the press, scientists, and physicians, the antibiotic era was the visible proof of the promise and the power of scientific medicine because they saw antibiotics as only the first type of drug that would give us a world without disease.

The Changing Pattern of Disease

Recall Edward Kass's presidential lecture. As the fruits of sanitation and improved living conditions took hold, there had been a steady and seemingly inexorable decline in death rates from the common infectious diseases, and as infant and childhood mortality dropped, life expectancy rose. In 1800 around 2 percent of the American population was over sixty-five years of age, and that number had risen to around 4 percent by 1900. But by 1925 the number began to rise, so it is projected that by the year 2000 around 12 percent of Americans will be sixty-five or older and by the year 2050, 20 percent. The mean life expectancy as we enter the twenty-first century is over seventy-five years. As the terror and the toll exacted from infectious diseases subsided, people became more aware of other conditions of ill health that had always been among them. Diabetes, cancer, goiter, cretinism, dwarfism, rheumatism—all had been known since time immemorial, but they were a background to the acute tragedies of assorted fevers and plagues. As the acute infectious diseases were beginning to lose their place on center stage, people became more aware of those *chronic*, noninfectious background maladies. The hope of specific cure that scientific medicine had brought to the acute infectious diseases would now be brought to bear on the chronic noninfectious diseases. The work of Claude Bernard had paved the way for the understanding and treatment of one of these chronic diseases.

We are all familiar with the fact that extracts of plants have always been used by healers, but most of us associate the use of extracts of animals with the witches' brew in *Macbeth:* eye of newt, and toe of frog, wool of bat, and tongue of dog, etc. But the fact is that organs of animals had been widely used in nonsupernatural therapy for countless years. In that long period when healers were attempting to balance the humors, knowing that "each organ of the body gives off emanations which are necessary and useful to the body as a whole," it only made sense that they would use these extracts of animal organs to reestablish the balance of the body. Farmers had long known that castration showed that male characteristics of animals were controlled by the testicles, and it was common knowledge that the ovary and uterus controlled female characteristics (the word *hysterical* derives from the Greek word for "uterus"). So why not treat with extracts of testicle to increase manliness, liver to return color to the wan, or heart to give courage to the meek? When Claude Bernard brought the idea of "internal secretions" into the scientific understanding of how the body worked, it both fit into the newly emerging paradigm of specificity and helped establish it.

Extracts of the endocrine glands, which we now know contain hormones, had long been used in these therapies, and in the process of scientification of medicine their specific roles began to be discovered. As early as 1855 the English physician Thomas Addison showed that pathology of the adrenal gland correlated with symptoms of the patients when they were alive, and described the malady we call Addison's disease. As the systematic correlation between symptoms in life and the pathology found at autopsy progressed, and with the acceptance of the importance of Claude Bernard's internal secretions to the maintenance of the *milieu intérieur*, there seemed to be ample "scientific" justification for the therapeutic use of extracts of animal tissues. The difference was that now a healer could use them not to establish *general* balance but rather to maintain levels of whatever it was inside of these organs that the body needed for its *specific* balance.

Claude Bernard's successor as professor of medicine at the Collège de France, Charles-Edouard Brown-Sequard, followed his illustrious predecessor by carrying out a systematic search for the internal secretions. He electrified his audience at the Society of Biology in Paris in 1889 by reporting that he had shown the remarkable rejuvenating properties of testicular extracts of young, healthy guinea pigs by injecting them into himself. In the next few years he went on to show that other organs from other animals had therapeutic effects, presumably because each was responsible for a different, specific internal secretion. This wonderful use of science was not lost on physicians or the public. It is estimated that by 1890, twelve thousand physicians were giving testicular extracts to their patients (and no doubt many, emulating Brown-Sequard, to themselves as well). In fairness, Brown-Sequard was alarmed and upset by the indiscriminate use of animal extracts; because "bacterial products taught us how active the chemical compounds created by the infinitely small were: the living cell, of each tissue that belongs to the organism, must, by analogy, secrete some products, of which the efficacy is no less," he was genuinely interested in how the knowledge of the functions of the body could be used for rational, scientific therapy.

While there have always been opportunists, the physicians who jumped on the healing powers of extracts of animals before any real therapeutic value had been shown were probably for the most part honest people who wanted the best for their patients. No doubt also, the patients read exaggerated stories about the wondrous properties of extracts of testicles and other organs in the press and demanded the most modern, "scientific" treatment. If the idea of specificity was growing rapidly in the scientific and medical professions, it was probably also beginning to get through to the people to whom it really mattered, the average patients. Understandably, they wanted cures and not explanations, but unfortunately the indiscriminate use of extracts did not bring about the cures that were promised.

The first dramatic therapeutic dividend of this new scientific era to come from the use of extracts of animal tissues was insulin. Diabetes was one of those diseases that came into the public awareness as nations became richer, people became better nourished, and the death rate from infectious diseases began to decline. Diabetes is not an infectious disease—it is a disease of metabolism, an alteration of the *milieu intérieur*. Chemistry had shown that in diabetes there was a malfunction of the normal body mechanism involved in the breaking down of sugar. Today we know that the symptoms of the disease all come from the resulting high level of sugar in the blood (hyperglycemia). When we think of diabetics, we think of people who must take regular injections of insulin, a key molecule the body uses to break down sugar but one that their bodies do not produce. In fact, around only 10 percent of people with diabetes fall into this category; insulin is usually not required for the vast majority of the 2 to 4 percent of the population in the United States and Europe that have the disease. But for those who have the insulin-dependent form of diabetes, the symptoms are severe and a diagnosis of the disease before the introduction of insulin was a virtual death sentence. For these people, most of whom were children, the discovery of insulin and the control of the disease was a success story of the scientific application of medicine, a case in which the "miracle" was truly what the press proclaimed it to be.

The functions of the ductless glands (the pituitary, thyroid, and adrenals, for example) were discovered at the turn of the century and were perhaps the most dramatic proof of Claude Bernard's *milieu intérieur.* With the advent of scientific medicine, it came to be realized that since these glands produce hormones that act on distant parts of the body in incredibly small amounts to control their function or development, a disturbance of one of these glands can result in a specific disease at a distant part of the body. The total amount of the hormone thyroxine, secreted by the thyroid gland in the normal human body, is only about 0.004 ounces in the course of a whole year, but "this pinch of material spells all the difference between complete imbecility and normal health." Insulin, the hormone that is lacking in diabetes, is produced by specialized cells in the pancreas, and the effects of high concentrations of sugar that result from its absence can cause blindness, impotence, or the degeneration of tissues in the limbs, leading to the need for amputation.

By 1920 the science of endocrinology had advanced to the point that several workers around the world were on the trail of the secretion of the pancreas to use for specific therapy, but the credit for the isolation and therapeutic testing of insulin has gone to Frederick Banting. The story of the discovery of insulin is one of great human emotion, because its clinical effect was almost beyond belief. Since a defect in insulin production results in an inability to metabolize carbohydrates, prior to the discovery and use of insulin, the only specific therapy for diabetes was to reduce carbohydrate intake to an absolute minimum. This meant that the only therapy was starvation! As a consequence, insulin patients were pathetic creatures whose only reason for living was the hope that a cure for their disease would someday be found.

I n 1920 Fred Banting was a small-town surgeon in Ontario with a rapidly failing practice. He had been an undistinguished medical student at the University of Toronto and now it seemed he was destined to be an even less distinguished physician who would have to supplement the meager income from his almost nonexistent practice by giving lectures on physiology at the local university. The mythology that developed around the discovery of insulin was that one night, while preparing one of those lectures, it occurred to Banting that it would be possible to obtain the hormone secreted by the cells of the pancreas by using the simple surgical method of tying off the duct of the organ. He entered the following in his notebook on October 31, 1920:

> *Diabetus* [sic]
> *Ligate pancreatic ducts of dog. keep dogs alive till acini degenerate leaving Islets.*
> *Try to isolate the internal secretion of these to relieve glycosurea.*

In later years, Banting perpetuated the drama of the moment to establish himself as a lone, embattled genius who not only fought the disease but also had to fight established academic greed for power. In fact, as historians have looked into the events around the discovery of insulin, the consensus seems to be that Banting's original idea was only partly correct and that he was an eager but less than adept experimenter who had neither the training nor the experience to carry out the difficult experiments to test the idea and follow through with the isolation of a lifesaving molecule and convert it into a drug.

Banting did, however, realize that his idea had enough merit to pursue and he requested a meeting with J.J.R. Macleod, the professor of physiology at the University of Toronto, to discuss his idea and the possibility of spending some months testing it in Toronto. On November 8, 1920, they held a meeting in Macleod's office, which in later years each would remember quite differently. Banting remembered that "[Macleod] was tolerant at first, but apparently my subject was not well presented for he commenced to read the letters on his desk." Macleod remembered that "I found that Dr. Banting had only a superficial text-book knowledge of the work that had been done on the effects of pancreatic extracts in diabetes, and that he had very little practical familiarity with the methods by which such a problem could be investigated in the laboratory." But inexplicably, Macleod gave the inexperienced and inarticulate young Toronto graduate the use of some small laboratory space and several dogs on which to test his idea. He also assigned a young graduate student, Charles Best, to work with him. As inconceivable as it seems, these two neophytes in the laboratory set out to isolate the secretion of the pancreas that would relieve the symptoms of diabetes!

Their lack of experience in the laboratory showed, and Macleod urged, cajoled, and eventually forced them to do more rigorous experiments. When he finally became convinced that it might indeed be possible to isolate a secretion from the pancreas (but not by the method initially jotted down in Banting's notebook), Macleod brought in a highly qualified chemist named James Collip to solve the formidable problems of chemical isolation of the material. Collip succeeded, and the University of Toronto attempted to produce enough insulin of high enough purity to test it in diabetic patients but soon found the difficulties to be insurmountable. The difference between producing small quantities of a material in the laboratory and large enough quantities of sufficient purity for clinical testing and commercial distribution can be daunting. Fortunately, George Clowes, an English chemist who had recently become the research director at Eli Lilly, the pharmaceutical manufacturer in Indiana, heard of the Toronto work and offered the manufacturing services of the company. Lilly had been active in isolating other glandular products. Furthermore, the company not only was in a position to work out methods of isolation and purification of insulin, but it offered to share any improvements it made in the manufacturing process with the University of Toronto. Most important, Lilly would supply all of the insulin for clinical trials at cost. In return, the company wanted a license to manufacture insulin on the same terms that the university would license other manufacturers when the experimental period was over.

This turned out to be the event that made the Eli Lilly company a leading pharmaceutical giant and exemplifies the close association the developing pharmaceutical industry had with the academy in the development of modern therapeutics. Few fundamental discoveries were made at these companies, but they provided manufacturing expertise, facilities, and the ability to marshall cadres of "industrial scientists," who could solve the practical problems so important in getting drugs from the concept in the laboratory to the patient. It is rather unfortunate that in later years the pharmaceutical houses, now some of the most profitable corporations in the world, would claim full credit for the discovery of important drugs when in reality they were essential and equal partners.

The first use of insulin in patients was almost miraculous, the promise of science fulfilled. Banting and Macleod shared the Nobel prize in 1923. In a dramatic gesture, Banting announced that he would share the award money equally with Best, and Macleod countered by sharing his money with Clowes.

Rheumatic conditions had always been thought of as one of the uncomfortable consequences of having escaped an early death, but as the number of older people began to grow and as life became less harsh for more and more people, they came to be seen as serious diseases. Rheumatic conditions, like many chronic diseases, are the result of chronic inflammation. Recall that inflammation is one of the major defenses of the body, so many chronic diseases are the result of some alteration inside the body that triggers the inflammatory response. Current thinking is that whatever it is that acts as the trigger does not go away and the body continually reacts to the physiological "insult." The accumulation of cells, fluid, and other products of inflammation ultimately results in the destruction of tissues. The discovery that secretion of steroid hormones from the cortex of the adrenal gland can act as *anti*-inflammatory drugs meant that the symptoms of many forms of debilitating arthritis could be controlled.

People had always suffered from allergies, which are immune responses against seemingly harmless substances such as pollen and house dust. Many of the symptoms of allergy are the result of the liberation of histamine from cells of the body. But compared to the other health problems people faced before the middle of the twentieth century, the sneezing, itching, and skin eruptions had for the most part been looked at as a nuisance. In the modern world, however, they became serious impediments to living a full life, and the discovery that a whole class of compounds called antihistamines could control the symptoms of allergy meant that allergic individuals could lead close to normal lives. The same story can be told for high blood pressure, depression, and a large number of chronic conditions.

We had entered an era in which the medical arts were replaced by the medical sciences. Science had given us the ability to understand how the body functions and as a result we were able to devise specific therapies for the new medical problems. But as valuable as these therapies were—insulin, cortisone, and the antihistamines relieved the symptoms of the chronic diseases for which they were used—they did not prevent or cure those diseases as vaccination and antibiotics had done for infectious diseases. There was another, very important difference: Infectious diseases had single, identifiable causes, so the strategy was clearly to prevent or eliminate the cause to cure the patient. Science could describe the nature of the problem in *le milieu intérieur* responsible for the chronic diseases, but it could not yet identify what had caused the problem. It is one thing to say that diabetes is the result of insufficient secretion of insulin by the pancreas or that rheumatoid arthritis is the result of chronic inflammation in the joint; it is quite another thing to be able to say what caused the pancreas to malfunction or the joint to be chronically inflamed. Because we had lived so long with infectious diseases and were so relieved that they had been brought under control, *we set the goal of scientific medicine to identify and eliminate the causes of the chronic diseases.* We had entered an era in which the medical arts were fully replaced by the medical sciences, and we were certain of the fact that science would give us the specific causes and the specific cures for the chronic diseases. The revolution in genetics now seemed to be able to fulfill that certainty.

The Genetic Revolution

Breeders of plants and animals had known from time immemorial that traits are passed from parents to offspring. The description of the rules of inheritance that represents our modern view was published in the middle of the nineteenth century, but it was not until 1900 that the "laws" of Gregor Mendel (1822–84), an Austrian monk who conducted experiments on the transmission of characteristics of garden peas at the Augustinian monastery in Brno, were brought to light. In 1866 Mendel had published the results of his work in an obscure local scientific journal, where they remained, for all practical purposes, unread until they were discovered by three separate investigators in 1900. In very short order whatever was responsible for the transmission of heritable traits were named genes, and a science to study the whole process, called genetics, became established.

By 1900, the scientific world was ready for Mendel's laws about how traits are inherited as units. We have seen the importance of studying the functions of cells, the basic units of life, in the development of medicine during the time when Mendel's paper went unread. Darwin had prepared the minds of scientists and educated laypersons for the importance of the origin of species (and hence the mutability of biological properties). The scientific *Zeitgeist* made it seem only natural that there were scientific rules of inheritance, and so genetic studies were carried out in earnest. Only two years after the papers were discovered, an English physician named Archibald Garrod showed that Mendel's rules of inheritance worked in humans by tracing a trait in which the subject's urine turns "terrifyingly but harmlessly black" through several generations in several families. Since classical times it had been realized that some very serious human diseases ran in families, so this study on a harmless medical curiosity was important because it showed that there was great medical utility in the study of genetics.

But for knowledge of genetic mechanisms to be gained it was necessary to have an easily manipulated experimental subject. Fruit flies turned out to be an ideal subject of genetic research; they breed rapidly, their breeding can be experimentally controlled, and the traits they transmit can be easily monitored. Humans also have traits that can be easily monitored, but because they "reproduce slowly, independently, and privately, [they] are not good subjects for research." The application of genetics to humans was apparent from the earliest days of the birth of genetics, either as a means of studying genetically transmitted disorders so that they could be treated or, more ominously, as a means of "improving the race" for eugenic reasons. The transmission of coat color genes in small mammals like the mouse, biochemical traits in the common mold *Neurospora*, and eye color and body shape in fruit flies were the models that had to be used to discover the rules governing the transmission of traits through the genes before serious attention could be turned to humans. As useful as fruit flies, mice, and bread molds were for genetics experiments, probably the most useful experimental tool turned out to be bacteria. The common bacteria that reside in the gut (called *E. coli*, for short) double in number every twenty minutes when grown in the laboratory, and they do it without need of privacy. Bacteriologists soon learned that even though the mode of reproduction of the bacteria was asexual, they still had genetic traits (and therefore, they had genes) that were passed on from generation to generation. Not only that, but bacteria can be infected by viruses, and even these bacterial viruses have genes and genetic traits that can be studied.

By 1941 studies with these model systems had convincingly shown that the function of a gene is to control the production of a protein; one gene, one protein became the rule that defined the subject of genetics. The scope of study was now reduced to manageable size, and genetics shifted from the examination of patterns of inheritance to the study of the ultimate of specificity, how individual genes encode specific proteins.

By the end of the Second World War, genetics was firmly established as a science, and its importance in medicine was beyond question. It was important for everything from typing of blood for transfusions to identifying genetic disorders with the hope of doing genetic counseling with people who were potential transmitters of these disorders to their children. But the promise of the power of science was in understanding the mechanisms by which genes functioned; the goal became to discover the nature of the gene and the material of which it was made.

The story of the discovery of DNA and the birth of modern molecular genetics has been told often and well. Max Delbrück was a pivotal figure in the conversion of genetics into the most elite of scientific subjects in the years immediately after the Second World War. Delbrück was already a well-known physicist when he emigrated from Germany to the United States in 1937. In a 1949 article called "A Physicist Looks at Biology," he predicted that biology was going to be the new frontier of physics.

Delbrück and Salvatore Luria organized what would become a famous summer course on bacterial genetics at the Cold Spring Harbor Laboratory on Long Island Sound. Here the physicists and chemists, many of whom had worked on the atomic bomb and who were attracted to the new vision of scientific work for the understanding and improving of life, could literally learn the tools of their new trade. This privately funded research laboratory would become the summer home and intellectual center for the group around Delbrück, with winter headquarters at Caltech. Caltech and Cold Spring Harbor became the breeding places of most of those who shaped the revolution in molecular genetics. James Watson, the codiscoverer of the double-helix nature of DNA, began as a graduate student of Luria's and was in the first generation of graduates of this group of scientific elite.

This wasn't the genetics of plant breeding or familial inheritance of urine that turned black in the air. This was the genetics of bacteria and their viruses, and it was led by people who thought in the quantitative, reductionist, abstract terms of physicists. The physical-chemical, reductionist mode of analysis that exemplified the group would grow into the glamorous field of molecular genetics and give rise to biotechnology. A new breed of biologists emerged who would transform biology and make it possible to transform medicine. Little did the physicists who founded the new discipline realize that their heirs would face some of the same moral and ethical issues they had faced when they gave us the atom bomb.

T he double helix, the structure of DNA, has become the icon of molecular genetics, but the understanding of the composition and function of the genes contained in that double helix is what the new genetic revolution is all about. The culmination of the research program in modern genetics came in the 1980s, when it became possible to chemically "read" the genetic code in DNA and to isolate genes and clone, or duplicate, them. The technology used to understand how genes function and what they are composed of became the basis for the biotechnology industry, which is based on taking the idea of specificity to its ultimate limit. Diseases and conditions caused by the absence of a specific gene product or a defective one could now be treated by isolating the gene that encodes the protein and using it to produce large quantities of the desired protein. Insulin, which had been made since the days of Banting by extracting the molecule from the pancreases of pigs, could now be generated by the new methods of biotechnology in the spotlessly clean industrial setting of pharmaceutical companies. Human growth hormone, a protein that is very scarce because it must be isolated from the minute pituitary gland, would now be available for all of those suffering from dwarfism, its deficiency. It did not take much imagination to realize that a technology that allows the scientist to know the sequence of a gene and to have unlimited copies of it on hand would be the prelude to rapid testing for carriers of genetic traits, as well as the ability to correct them by replacing a "bad" gene with a good one. And this is exactly the future of scientific medicine that scientists, entrepreneurs, and some physicians have put forward as the high-tech future that patients should anticipate. In this vision of our medical future, we would move from "laboratory medicine" to the new era of high-tech "genetic medicine."

The first "big science" project in biology, the Human Genome Project,* came into being in the early 1990s. Its goal was nothing less than to clone and sequence all of the human genes. The Genome Project has become the major driving force to encourage large-scale genetic testing for inherited diseases and to move scientific medicine to an era of gene transplantation as a means of curing them. Science, medicine, and industry have come together in a powerful alliance to provide the technology that will move medicine into the twenty-first century. After two millennia of framing health and disease in general terms, the paradigm change initiated by Pasteur, Bernard, and Virchow is so complete that we leave the long twentieth century with the prospect of the ultimate in specific medicine, the manipulation of our genes!

In 150 years, we have gone from life coexisting with the constant presence of death to a time when we have the ability to manipulate our own genes, the stuff of life itself. We have gone from a time of faith in the goodwill of the healer to the necessity of confronting the social, moral, ethical, and financial issues of what we really want science and medicine to do for us. And we have come to a time when science must once again reframe our conceptions of disease and therapies. But this time the goals and limits of medicine will be changed by the outcome of the new reframing. And this time we are all aware of what the choices and consequences might be. Knowing what we know, there is no reason for future patients to be passive about the future of medicine.

---

* The *genome* is the collection of all of the genes in an individual.

Part
III

Framing the
Future

Reshaping the Goals of Medicine in the Era of Chronic Diseases

Genes and Disease

The argument that specificity of disease is the basis of scientific medicine is a central theme of this book. Because genes are the ultimate of specificity and the era of infectious diseases was an era of extreme specificity, the majority of biological and biomedical scientists have placed great faith in the power of genes to explain the causes of chronic diseases and in the idea that the study of the genes will point the direction to specific cures. But there is a growing divergence of opinion among scientists about where we are in the process and whether the solutions to either cause or cure are really to be found in our genes.

The lines of the reframing began to be drawn as early as 1981, with Stephen Jay Gould's widely read book *The Mismeasure of Man*, which was a strong indictment of biological determinism, the idea that "biology is destiny." Gould took on the idea of racial differences in IQ testing and showed that bad social policy can result from misunderstood and misapplied science. This was followed in 1984 by *Not in Our Genes*, written by the respected and controversial Harvard evolutionary biologist Richard Lewontin and two colleagues, a neurobiologist and a psychologist. The authors, who have always been forthright about their political positions, began by voicing their concern about "the rising tide of biological determinist writing, with its increasingly grandiose claims" for the genetic basis of IQ, and the "inequalities of status, wealth, and power between classes, genders, and races in Western society." But the true importance of *Not in Our Genes* was that it raised very serious questions about the assumptions biologists bring to their work. The title conveyed the authors' thesis that genes not only do not determine our behavior; except for a few very specific cases, they said, it is very difficult to predict the role of genes in *any* complex biological function. Ultimately, their book was an argument against a strict reductionist kind of science, one that "attempts to derive the properties of wholes from intrinsic properties of parts." But reductionism has been the foundation of modern biology from Pasteur, Bernard, and Virchow to Watson and Crick, so the book was not only an attack on the role of genes and the misuse of genetic information in society, it was a critique of how science itself is done and raised questions about what we can expect from biology.

Ten years later a book by Ruth Hubbard, yet another Harvard biologist, has picked up these arguments against biological determinism, reductionist science, and the role of genes. In the intervening decade the idea that the gene is the ultimate of specificity has become the dominant paradigm of biology, and the public is now constantly being told of new "breakthroughs" in the cloning of various genes. Each news report of a "breakthrough" is of course accompanied by a description of the practical significance of the discovery, and a casual glance at the newspaper or local evening news broadcast shows that scientists are convinced that the era of the gene will lead to the era of ultimate specific therapy for chronic diseases. Furthermore, the Human Genome Project is being hailed as the locus from which all of the benefits will flow. The director of the part of the Genome Project controlled by the U.S. National Institutes of Health calls the project "the most important and the most significant project that humankind has ever mounted."

The title of Hubbard's book, *Exploding the Gene Myth: How Genetic Information is Produced and Manipulated by Scientists, Physicians, Employers, Insurance Companies, Educators, and Law Enforcers*, makes it very clear that she disagrees with this assessment. Hubbard's message is that our genes act in the context of the whole body and the environment, and therefore it is an error to use the reductionist approach and think that by understanding everything about a single gene, we will be able to predict what that gene does in the context of all of the other factors affecting the normal and pathological functioning of the body.

The reductionist view is clearly and forcefully represented in a book called *The Code of Codes: Scientific and Social Issues in the Human Genome Project*, edited by historian Daniel Kevles and geneticist Leroy Hood. In the preface of their book, published in 1992, the editors quote the Nobel Prize–winning geneticist Walter Gilbert, who says that the human genome is "the very key to what makes us human, what defines our possibilities and limits as members of the species *Homo sapiens.*"

The promise of the power of genetics is more modestly and realistically laid out by Hood in a chapter titled "Biology and Medicine in the Twenty-First Century." Here he discusses the great advances in technology and fundamental understanding of how genes are organized:

> This technology will figure in the diagnosis of genetic diseases whose single-gene defects have been identified; in determining the presence of dominant or recessive oncogenes that may predispose an individual to cancer; in the identification of infectious agents, such as the AIDS virus; and in forensics . . . perhaps the most important area of DNA diagnostics will be the identification of genes that predispose individuals to disease. However, many such diseases—cardiovascular, neurological, autoimmune—are polygenic. . . . *Human genetic mapping will permit the identification of specific predisposing genes and DNA diagnostics will facilitate their analysis in many different individuals* [author's emphasis].

It is in this last statement that the differences in the viewpoints of the two sides are clearly seen. By now the fact that intelligent and well-meaning people are found on the polar extremes should come as no surprise to the reader, and the outcome of the debate is as important as the debates in which Pasteur engaged with the German chemists or the French physicians. *Nothing less is at stake than the way we frame health and disease, the therapies we develop, and the goals of medicine in the twenty-first century.*

Given the importance of the debate, how is the nonscientist reader to balance the claims of those scientists who are certain that the reductionist approach to understanding our genes will provide the understanding of normal functions and the cures for chronic diseases with those scientists who argue that this is a futile enterprise because the functions of genes are too complex to be understood using traditional reductionist approaches? As is almost always the case when polar positions are taken, the truth will probably end up somewhere near the middle, but over the last two years I have become convinced that the nonreductionist side has more going for it than the reductionists in this case. Reductionism is still a very powerful tool, and absolutely essential most of the time, but the data from new laboratory experiments and from what we are learning about how genes function have begun to convince me that we must find a way of studying not only the functions of our genes but the causes and cures of most chronic diseases in a new, more integrative way.

Cystic fibrosis, the most common genetic disease, is a case study from which we can take a closer look at the problem. It will also give the non-scientist reader a glimpse of how scientists approach problems and a chance to see how our often unexamined assumptions drive these approaches.

As early as the seventeenth century, there were scattered reports of peculiar cases of children who died young and "tasted salty." In that time of such high infant mortality rates, these children were merely interesting anomalies to be noted and discussed, but three hundred years later, when infant and childhood mortality rates had decreased so dramatically, the strange cases appeared often enough that they clearly represented a specific disease affecting the lungs and the pancreas. After the Second World War, when basic biomedical research began to burgeon, it was found that the same mechanism accounted for both the elevated levels of salt in the skin (thus the salty taste) and the dire symptoms in the lungs and pancreas that resulted in debilitation and, often, in early death. At that time the nature of the movement of water and salt across cellular membranes was a "hot" topic of investigation by physiologists, and children with cystic fibrosis were found to have a defect in this mechanism. The result is not only an accumulation of salt in the skin but, most important, a clogging of the lungs with mucus, which in the normal lung is diluted and flushed away by water.

By the 1930s it was already known that the disease was genetically transmitted; the children who developed cystic fibrosis had the misfortune of inheriting from their parents the genes responsible for the disease. But the parents themselves, who did not have the disease, were passing on a "defective" or mutated form of the gene (for cystic fibrosis) to some, but not all, of their children. Each of the parents may be a carrier—that is, they each may carry one mutated form of the gene—but they do not have the disease themselves, because it requires two mutated genes for cystic fibrosis to develop. If both parents are carriers of a mutated gene, then there is a fifty-fifty chance that each will pass on that gene to a child, which means that on average, one quarter of their offspring will have two mutated genes. It is these children who will have the disease.

So both physiologists and geneticists had an interest in the mechanism and, of course, the treatment of cystic fibrosis. The nature of the malfunction had been determined by physiologists to be the transport of chloride across cellular membranes, and since there was already a precedent for developing drugs that have an effect on the transport of calcium across membranes (the calcium channel blockers used in heart disease), a promising avenue for therapy existed. But by the 1980s all of biomedical science was caught in the thrall of genetics and the attention of the public, much funding of science, and the hopes of those who suffer from the disease was focused on the cloning of the "cystic fibrosis gene." The very important point here is that this view was the natural one for scientists to take because the history of scientific medicine had been pointing toward the ultimate specificity of the genes. By 1985 geneticists had identified the chromosome on which the cystic fibrosis gene was located, and then, using the technology of molecular biology, the gene itself was isolated and cloned in 1989, with much fanfare in the press. As predicted, the normal form of the gene encoded one of the channels in membranes that are used to transport chloride. The promise was that now it would not take long to identify how the defective gene differed from the normal.

It is at this point that the complications of the kind that made me change my view on the subject began to appear. It has been very surprising to find there are an enormous number of different mutations in the genes from patients with cystic fibrosis; so far mutations at over 350 different places in the gene have been found. Considering that it requires two mutated forms of the gene to have the disease—one from each parent—this means that the number of possible combinations is astronomical. It is now becoming clear that different combinations of the mutations result in very different effects. For example, some combinations may cause crippling cystic fibrosis and some may cause a very mild form of the disease; some may result not in cystic fibrosis at all but in asthma or chronic bronchitis or infertility, because of the absence of the vas deferens, the tube that carries sperm from the testes to the penis. Some may result in no symptoms at all. But perhaps the most surprising finding has been that some combinations of mutations that result in cystic fibrosis in some people result in no signs of any disease in others. These kinds of results have led to the idea that genes other than the one that has been called the "cystic fibrosis gene" are important in the expression of the mutated forms of the gene.

A similar kind of complication has also arisen in Huntington's disease, the rare neurological disorder that is also transmitted genetically. The disease was first called to wide public attention when it became known that the folk singer Woody Guthrie was afflicted with it. Because of the unique symptoms of the disease, neurologists have believed that only certain cells of the brain are affected, but it has now been discovered that the mutated gene is found in virtually all cells of the brain. The reason why the same gene can be present in many different kinds of cells but only some are affected is not known, but the explanation of another gene or genes interacting in some way with the "Huntington gene" is reasonable.

Much of the promise of identifying the genes involved in disease is the idea that the "defective" gene can be replaced by a normal one through gene-replacement therapy. Even with the complications discussed above, it is still true that cystic fibrosis is caused by a "defective" gene, and the idea of replacing it with a normal one is logical. But gene-replacement therapy is still in its early experimental phase, and given all the other surprises that have greeted us in the revolution that biology has been undergoing in the last ten years, we should be girding our intellectual loins for more surprises to come. Meanwhile, the effort spent on the genetic approach has taken attention and perhaps funding away from less newsworthy approaches that could possibly lead to drugs that would not cure cystic fibrosis but would alleviate its symptoms as efficiently as insulin controls the symptoms of diabetes. We all want specific and absolute cures for this and other diseases, but it seems to me that the genetic approach is much more complex than scientists had anticipated, and certainly more difficult than most newspaper stories would lead the lay reader to expect. The possible payoff of gene-replacement therapy as a routine and affordable mode of treatment for cystic fibrosis is decades away, and this is a disease in which we already know the major gene that is responsible.

The greater problem on the horizon is that most diseases for which there is a genetic component are already known to involve multiple genes. Schizophrenia, atherosclerosis, and manic depressive disease, to name only a few, are conditions in which the genetic component will most probably turn out to play an important role, but because we know there will be many genes involved, we are decades away from knowing which genes are important and how they interact with each other and with other components in the body and the environment. Unraveling this great complexity, I am convinced, will be the great challenge of biology in the twenty-first century. We are already beginning to see the shape of the complexities of the biological landscape in some of the most fascinating experiments ever carried out, in which the function of a gene can be tested by creating genetically engineered mice that lack a specific gene.

Decades of experiments have culminated in the identification, cloning, and sequencing of hundreds of genes in every experimental system used by biologists from yeast and fruit flies to mice and humans. Reductionist experiments, many of them quite brilliant, have identified the function of these genes, but missing was a way to intentionally make a gene *mal*function in an experimental animal so that experimenters could be sure that the reductionist experiments had given the correct description of what goes on in the complexity of the living system.

Well-meaning people worry about the possible abuse and frivolous use of laboratory animals. I know of no scientist who is in favor of inflicting gratuitous pain and suffering on animals, and any who do should be prevented from ever carrying out experiments on animals again. But anyone who argues that computers can tell us everything we need to know and that there is no need to use the living animal is just wrong! Protesters certainly have the right to say that they are not interested in gaining scientific understanding at the expense of laboratory animals, but they are not correct in saying that the kind of information we are getting can be obtained without them, as will be clear from the case of the "gene-knockout" mice.

A few years ago it became possible to test the validity of information of gene function obtained from test tube experiments. A method was developed in which a defect could be introduced into a cloned gene so that it is impossible for the gene to carry out its normal function. When this unusable gene is introduced into mice, they become *carriers*, so that when two carriers are mated, one quarter of their offspring have two copies of the nonfunctional gene. The first reports of these "gene-knock-out" mice—so named because the function of the gene has literally been knocked out—were electrifying because now the formal proof of all the reductionist experiments would be at hand. The reductionist experiments had shown us that a given gene encoded a given protein, which is necessary for a certain function. Theoretically, the gene-knockout mice should not have that function and we should not only be able to test the correctness of the reductionist experiments, we should also be able to see what other roles the gene product plays in the intact animal.

The gene-knockout mice have been a continuing source of surprises, but taken together with what we are seeing in the analysis of the genes in cystic fibrosis and other human diseases, they are giving us a glimpse into the glorious complexity of the body. It was assumed that when the genes were inactivated in the knockout mice, the animals would either stop developing at an early embryonic stage if the knocked-out gene acted in early development or would lack the single gene function the gene was thought to control in the adult. While some gene-knockout mice do meet our expectations, the majority do not. In some cases the animals seem perfectly normal; in others the expected effect is there but is so small it can hardly be seen; and in the most interesting cases a defect occurs that has no relationship to the expected function of the gene.

In a recent description of some experiments in which the prediction of the function of the gene was fulfilled, a molecular biologist wrote facetiously that "a sigh of relief went up from the [muscle research] community when it became clear that engineering mice to lack [a gene thought to be crucial in muscle development] does indeed have a drastic effect on their skeletal muscle." The reason for the relief was that the year before when a gene called *myf-5* was knocked out, the prediction had been that the animals would die early in embryonic development because of poor muscle development. The animals did die in early development, but they had normal muscles; they had severely malformed ribs! The reason for the feigned "sigh of relief" from the research community was because the new experiments showed that when another gene, one that encodes a molecule called *myogenin*, is knocked out, muscle development is impaired. These two experiments have allowed researchers in the field to gain a clearer view of the complexities of muscle development because they now can begin to analyze the relationship between the functions of the two genes.

In another surprise, researchers knocked out the gene encoding a molecule called TGFα that is known to be important in both normal development of embryos and in the normal function of cells in adults. In other words, the scientists had predicted that the mice would either not develop normally or, if they did, they would have severely impaired cellular functions as adults. But the knockout mice do develop normally, and the only malfunction in the adults seems to be that they had wavy hair and curly whiskers! In this case, it is known that TGFα shares a receptor with another molecule that is important in both development and adult function. Does the result of the knockout mean that the other molecule took over the function of TGFα? Further experiments will show if this is the case, but once again we are getting a glimpse at the rich complexity of the body.

This kind of result prompted one molecular developmental biologist to ask his colleagues, "Don't you just love experiments that raise more questions than they answer?" This is a question every scientist understands and a sentiment we all agree with, but it is one that is often disquieting to laypersons, who have been led to believe that scientific discoveries lead us down an unbroken path to truth and straight to a technological fix.

In my own opinion, the complexity of genetic diseases in humans and the results from the gene-knockout mice have opened the door to the biology of the twenty-first century, and we should walk through that door to make the scientific discoveries we need to reexamine the therapeutic goals we seek of scientific medicine. The surprises should be lessons that make us realize that much of the talk in the media by scientists and biotech entrepreneurs about our having entered the era of genetic medicine is too often glib. Few would disagree that in time, one of the *options* we will have for therapy is the replacement of "defective" forms of genes in those cases where there is a clear one-to-one relationship between the gene and the disease. But to take us down a path of expecting the *therapeutic* mode to be replacement of genes because in the *experimental* mode we studied the gene to discover the nature of the disease is the kind of decision making about the goals of medicine and the applications of scientific knowledge that the public must begin to understand and to discuss.

The Limits of Medicine

I want to emphasize here what I said at the very start of this book: A world without vaccination, penicillin, safe surgery, and insulin is unthinkable. Scientific medicine may have been given too much credit for the steady elimination of infectious disease, but which of us has not had our life or the life of a loved one saved because of it? The fact that most physicians have now become specialists who rely on the laboratory and high technology has meant that we have received the benefits of scientific medicine in a social framework that is very different from that in which healing was carried out through history, but hardly anyone would give up its real benefits. Yet what is it we really want from scientific medicine in a century when science has been elevated to the level of religion and the scientific healer has become the custodian of knowledge about our most personal and intimate selves? After all, as patients we have all been more or less willing participants in this change and so we can alter what we have done if we are dissatisfied.

The problem is that we have come to expect that by using the technology derived from science, the modern physician would make all parts of our lives free from the suffering that was the lot of our ancestors. Yet strangely, even though we in the industrialized nations should consider ourselves demonstrably healthier than people have ever been, there is growing unrest and even fear about technology and medicine as we prepare to enter the twenty-first century. We fear the dire consequences to our health from atomic power plants and voltage transformers in our neighborhoods, the stress of urban living and traces of insecticides on our apples, often even the consequences of some of the therapies themselves. As a backlash to the effect of being asked to turn over the responsibility of what we think and feel about health to the practitioners of scientific medicine, many are beginning to question its very healing power. In 1990 one American in three tried relaxation therapy, herbal medicines, acupuncture, chiropractic, spiritual healing, and other "alternative" medical approaches in addition to "standard" medicine. An estimated 425 million visits were made to "alternative" practitioners, in contrast to the 388 million visits made to family doctors and other primary-care physicians. In terms of money, $13.7 billion was spent on these unconventional therapies, of which $10.3 billion was out of pocket (not covered by insurance). When this amount of time, money, and hope is spent on "alternative" approaches to therapy, it is clear that scientific medicine is not giving a significant number of people everything they want. But what do we want, and is there a way for us to articulate it and get the message to what Arnold Relman, the former editor of *The New England Journal of Medicine*, called the "medical-industrial complex"? A very telling statistic is that of these people who sought "alternative" therapy, the majority did so in addition to consulting a physician. I think this fact tells us that they had not completely given up on scientific medicine, rather that they craved something more from it.

The problem is that the goals and the *limits* of science and medicine have continued to go unexamined. After the Second World War, the promise of specific therapies became a dramatic reality with antibiotics and immunizations—exemplified in the mind of the public by penicillin and the Salk vaccine. In the prevailing wartime mentality, science began to grow and an all-out "attack" on disease was made. Remember, before the acceptance of the germ theory, healing was not a battle against some defined "enemy," but with the realization that disease is specific, it became a foe we could deal with as we do any other foe. And just as we had marshalled science to give us the technology to win the real war (World War II has been called the first war won by science) and were building our science establishment to use it as the engine that would drive the technology to wage the Cold War, so too would we marshal science to give us the technology to defeat disease, suffering, and even death. The military metaphor helped ensure that money would flow to medical science, and with the launching of Sputnik, the general increase in spending on science as part of our "national security" meant that research in medical science was a ship that rose on the rising tide. Since then we have waged a "war" on cancer, activists are now demanding that we wage a "war" on AIDS, and through all of this a multibillion-dollar health industry was being put into place. Without very much reflection, *curing* replaced *caring* as the dominant ideology of this new technology-driven medicine. We are slowly realizing that most people want both.

And in fairness, while this was happening, what was there to reflect upon? Was it not the common perception that science and medicine had removed the constant presence of death? Who would be so churlish to suggest that the forces of the technology spawned by science, combined with the growing technical specialization of physicians and the pharmaceutical industry, all united with the full force of capitalism, which the Cold War had made synonymous with democracy, would not give us health and even youth eternal? But the uncontrolled costs of medical care in the United States and the obvious searching for an alternative to scientific medicine tell us that we no longer have the luxury of allowing the goals and the limits of the system to go unexamined or be set by groups with their own agendas. Because it is technology-driven, it is important that we know what we want from medicine before we introduce new technologies. Since science does not translate directly into technology, someone has to decide what kind of technology gets developed. Why not those who pay for it?

The overwhelming majority of the scientific knowledge that is available for conversion into the technology of modern medicine has come from science paid for by taxpayers with the understanding that it will be used for our well-being. Unfortunately, there is little mechanism for the public to participate in the process of deciding what kinds of technology gets developed and, therefore, of what kind of medicine will be practiced, yet we must begin to decide what we want from medicine. Only a scientifically aware population can do that, but being scientifically aware is not to be merely bombarded with announcements of "breakthroughs" and "miracles." It is understanding how science functions, what it can provide and, even more important, what it cannot.

One thing is clear: If the people who pay for the science don't make the decisions about how it is used, others will. Just as we found that we could not trust the goals of our national defense to the military-industrial complex, we are beginning to learn that we cannot trust the goals of scientific medicine to the medical-industrial complex. The medical-industrial complex is not an evil cabal; it is for the most part composed of people who are convinced that they are doing what is right for society, and of course, much of what is done does work toward the public good. But there is little place for alternative viewpoints (I find that I must constantly stress to my friends and colleagues in science and the biotech industry that I am not an enemy), and the force this collection of con-

216

stituencies exerts is powerful. The collective weight of the professional scientists and physicians; the pharmaceutical and biotechnology industries; the large research universities; the groups of patients organized into politically potent fund-raising groups; the sentimentality, sensationalism, and gullibility of too much of the media; the religious beliefs of different groups—all are forces at work. Out of all of this, as a society we must somehow decide what we want.

Saying we should be able to control the technology science can give to medicine is fine, but to do it we must ask ourselves some hard questions. As a society do we want scientific medicine to prevent death indefinitely, to relieve all suffering, to take the responsibility for health and disease out of our hands altogether, or some more modest middle ground? A strong case can be made that the normal human life span is only slightly more than the biblical three score and ten (seventy years). Has scientific medicine received a signal from society to roll back death indefinitely? As we have seen, in the twentieth century death has become associated with old age for the first time in recorded history; is death at any age now to be seen as a defeat of science? A profile in the financial pages of *The New York Times* with the title "Laying Pipe for the Fountain of Youth" told of an entrepreneur who made his fortune by designing a better toothbrush and has now decided to invest vast amounts of money in a company that will refine technology for organ and tissue transplantation, with the goal of keeping people alive for two hundred years. One wonders how much thought he has given to where all of these people he hopes to be putting spare parts into will spend their extra 130 years, what they will do to occupy themselves, or if he is also contemplating brain transplantation to prevent declining mental function? Should we assume that an entrepreneur who can use modern technology to design a better toothbrush can be trusted with the idea that technology can be used to more than double the life span—especially when he expects the company he has formed to have annual sales of a billion dollars?

Is this how the public wants the decisions made about how science is turned into technology? An entrepreneur has every right to spend his money and the money of investors in any legal way he chooses, but what are the counterforces? In a free-market economy, the forces that shape the market are among the most powerful in determining what technology will be derived from scientific discoveries. But we must remember that in the industrialized world it is the taxpayers who pay for the vast majority of the research on which the technology is based, and it is carried out in academic and nonprofit organizations. No reasonable person wants to reinvent the Soviet economic system, but since the public's money paid for the research, does not the public have some say in the development of technology? There seems to be little enthusiasm for removing the development of medical technology from the free market, yet there must be some way to ensure that the public interest is being looked after.

I f the goal of scientific medicine is not to extend life indefinitely, is it to focus on the heartbreak of the rare disorder that takes a life too soon? Does society want high-tech individualized therapies for individual tragedies? Now that our genes are being identified and cloned, the technology is already in place to tell us if we carry a gene that will lead to such diseases as cystic fibrosis, Tay-Sachs, sickle-cell anemia, or any of a myriad of diseases caused not by infectious agents or by our parts wearing out but by a gene that does not function "properly." As we have seen, there is already a concerted effort of public funding and private capital in the development of therapies for some of these diseases that involve replacing the "defective" gene with one that functions properly. While the costs of this kind of therapy in the short term will be colossal, the hope is that in time it will become routine and less expensive. But in the industrialized nations there are children who do not yet receive immunizations that can prevent them from getting measles or polio; adults who have such poor nutrition that they develop heart and kidney problems so debilitating that they have impaired function and shortened life spans; people who are so poorly educated that they do not follow through on the simple medications when they or their children develop tuberculosis. Eric Cassel has written that the "obligation of physicians to relieve human suffering stretches back into antiquity," but how do we define *whose* suffering we will turn our knowledge and technology toward? Should the technology that comes from science be applied to finding inexpensive ways of delivering basic medical care to relieve the suffering of those who cannot afford or do not avail themselves of what scientific medicine has even today? Or are these political problems that society must take care of while moving to an even higher-tech medicine of the twenty-first century, because there is little doubt that science *can* provide us with the basis for very high-tech, very expensive technology. There is also little doubt that it can provide us with less glitzy, less costly technology.

Daniel Callahan says that "health itself, we sometimes need reminding, is a means and not an end," and that "a goal of extension of life combined with an insatiable desire for improvement in health . . . is a recipe for monomania and bottomless spending." He sees a more reasonable "goal of medicine that stresses the avoidance of premature death and the relief of suffering." If this sage counsel is heeded, then neither the scientist, the all-knowing physician, nor the entrepreneur will carry the day. But how can we begin to come to some consensus about what the goals are and what we want transferred from science to become medical technology?

We certainly have to ask how much technology we want in the scientific medicine of the twenty-first century. Considering that we have an infectious-disease mentality, with the expectations of the same effectiveness from all drugs that we get from penicillin and Salk vaccine in a time when we will be confronting chronic illnesses, one goal of medicine will have to be to educate the patients to the new realities. Consider this from Stanley Reiser, editor of *The Journal of Technology Assessment in Health Care:* "[I]t is unlikely (though certainly desirable) that illness will be treated by quick fixes stemming from basic causal knowledge about disease processes and simple remedies that follow from it. It is unlikely that the prime example of such a fix—treating bacterial illness with penicillin—will be replicated in the near future to deal with the spectrum of chronic illnesses and the degenerative changes of an aging population. A more likely prospect for the immediate future is the use of an increasingly complex and generally more expensive technology for a growing array of health problems." Reiser is not advocating more expensive technology for the growing array of health problems, he is warning us that unless we do something, this is where we are headed.

So what can be done?

Reshaping Our Search for the Cure

I f the infectious-disease mode of thinking is inappropriate for the era of chronic diseases, what should we expect from medicine and what can science do to further the goals? I think there are three things we can do—two short-term and one long-term:

- *We can quickly begin to stop relying so heavily on the promise of high-tech solutions to problems for which low-tech solutions already exsist.*

I t has been very painful to watch the kaleidoscopic changes among scientists, people infected with HIV, the public, and the press over the past decade. The story of the appearance of AIDS in our midst, the intense homophobia in the initial responses, the despair and then newfound militancy of the gay community have been told often. But through all of this there runs the cadre of scientists who became media figures, quoted daily, it seemed, in the press and on television. These scientists had a message that everyone wanted to hear: Given the money, science will deliver the cure. A vaccine before the end of the century was all but guaranteed and new drugs based on the scientific knowledge gained from studying the virus would soon be available. Any scientific paper appearing in virtually any scientific journal became the subject of an article in which one of the new media-wise scientists was quoted.

The tragic consequence was that although we knew the causative agent of AIDS (the HIV virus), the manner in which the disease is spread (unprotected sex and contaminated needles), and who were the people most at risk, we chose to put our faith in technology. Remember Edward Kass's presidential address: Tuberculosis and most other diseases were brought under control not by immunization or antibiotics but by public health. As a society, however, we chose not to arouse people who are offended by the very fact of homosexuality, let alone that it is an integral part of our society, or people who out of religious conviction don't want to inform teenagers who engage in unprotected sex about condoms. It was easier for us to not ask why so many in our population have turned to drugs, as we would have had to if we instituted needle-exchange programs. And we could turn away from these questions because science was going to save us the discomfort; it was going to give us a high-tech cure.

As we all know, there has been growing gloom and despair over a vaccine. The problems faced in developing a vaccine for cholera at the turn of the century or the polio vaccine after the Second World War were enormous—but they are greater for an AIDS vaccine. With the virus's incubation period of over ten years, even if we had the perfect candidate vaccine in hand today, we would not know for sure that it works for years and years. But we don't have the candidate vaccine in hand. In fact, the greed of the medical-industrial complex, the difficulty of marshalling large but still limited resources, and the painful question of the inclusion of controls all have made it so that we cannot say when, or even if, we will have a vaccine. And then there is the reality that most vaccines are not as effective as those against smallpox, polio, and measles. Will we be content with a vaccine that is 60 percent effective?

Meanwhile, behavioral changes in the middle-class gay male population have brought a reduction in the number of those who become infected with the virus and who will develop AIDS. Public health measures and education work! But what about the urban poor, who transmit the disease through contaminated needles? Who will change their habits? Will it take an even greater rise in tuberculosis among them for us to realize that we must face the low-tech solutions to poverty, despair, and homelessness that fuel the spread of the disease in that world?

- *We can begin to replace the "penicillin mode" of expectations from therapies with the "insulin mode."*

By this I mean that we have become accustomed to the dramatic eradication of the cause of infectious diseases by antibiotics, the "penicillin mode" of thinking. But because of the complexity of their causes, it is likely that we will realistically only be able to treat the symptoms and not eliminate the causes of most chronic disease. I am calling this the "insulin mode" because insulin does not cure diabetes, but it gives diabetic people a large portion of normalcy in their lives and may have to become the mode of therapy we live with. This is not to say that science should not and will not go on looking for outright cures where they are feasible and affordable, but we must not rely solely on the promise of their coming with the next generation of technology and must devote energy and money to seeking therapies that eliminate pain and allow a semblance of normal life to go on.

The double-helix structure of DNA has become the icon of modern medicine, simultaneously representing both the power of scientific research to discover the deepest mysteries of life and the promise of research to deliver relief from pain and suffering. The similarity between the twined snakes of the caduceus, the symbol of the medical profession, and the structure of our genetic material is becoming deeply ingrained in our expectation from science and medicine. The promise of eliminating disease and suffering through engineered genes, replaced parts, and synthetic molecules has replaced the thrill people felt when insulin was introduced in the 1920s and cortisone in the 1940s. Those condemned to an early death by diabetes or to middle and later years of incapacitation due to rheumatoid arthritis or hypertension have known that through the application of science, medicine can give them lives that approach normal without curing their disease.

The new biology of complexity that genetics is revealing is beginning to strike a cautionary note in the planning of many scientists. If the wondrous complexity that is being revealed continues—and I know of no one who doubts that it will—we are going to be in for more and more surprises. The very good news is that as we begin to understand the complexity, whole new avenues of creative therapies should become opened to us, but we must begin to make it clear that we aren't waiting for miracles but want a steady stream of improvements in therapies to give each of us the optimal amount of health during our lifetime.

- *We must begin the slow and difficult process of changing our views of aging and death.*

When life expectancy was only thirty years, death usually came suddenly and was the universal enemy. Now that life expectancy approaches eighty, we have time to contemplate the approach of death and to become accustomed to our aging bodies and minds. How we deal with these questions will determine the quality of our extended life spans.

Through all of the two thousand years when death came early and healers could only attempt to balance the humors, the holding back of death was the noblest goal of the healer and the inability of the healer to prevent death was the main limit of medicine. Now the role of the healer has changed: We all must die, and death must not be seen as a defeat of the healer or a weakness of the patient. What do we mean when we say that someone "lost his battle with cancer?" Was it a sign of weakness or a character flaw? None of us knows how we will face the end when it comes, and one can argue in the abstract that it is wasteful of limited resources to turn the full force of modern high-tech medicine onto someone who has lived eighty-eight years. My mother has lived that long, and how will she react when the time comes to face heroic measures—and just as important for me, how will I react? One's own mother is not an abstraction.

That is why I said that two of the solutions were relatively short-term, but one was long-term. Even though scientific medicine has been with us a relatively short time, 150 years compared to the two thousand years of Galenic medicine, we have no memory of the earlier times and know only how to look at aging and death as we learn it from our parents and grandparents. Technology can change our expectations quickly, but how we look at aging and death is a question of spirituality. Slowly over the next generations we must develop a new spiritual sense of how we value ourselves as well as others as we grow old, and we must learn to make a comfortable place for death at the end of our lives. The goal and the limit of medicine must be to maximize health, to hold back premature death and, according to Daniel Callahan, "remove the unpleasant, distressing *causes* of death, thus transmuting it from a condition to be feared to one that can be managed and tolerated."

Finale: Changing the Metaphor

By all objective standards, people in the industrialized nations are healthier than they ever have been, yet there is growing dissatisfaction with health care and growing evidence that people perceive themselves as less healthy. Costs have become uncontrollable; there are too few primary-care physicians, endless waits, and impersonal treatment—the list goes on and on. An aging population worries about spending its waning days without dignity and in pain, and vast amounts of money and resources are spent on high-technology solutions that benefit only a few or keep people alive a few painful months longer. Harsh therapies with little effect are administered at the same rate as those that give great benefit. It is a system seen to be out of control, with every segment of society blaming the other. The sad facts are that if there is an essential element of truth in this litany, it is that we all are to blame because we have all been willing partners in making promises about and expecting miracles from scientific medicine. Scientists have promised wondrous cures as a result of basic research, physicians have promised to roll back death and eliminate pain through specialization and high-tech medicine, the pharmaceutical industry warns that if profits are curtailed they will stop developing innovative lifesaving drugs, the press breathlessly reports yet another medical miracle, and patients urge all of them on by wanting desperately to believe each of them.

But when we look at the history of how we got to where we are, it begins to look as if all is not lost. In this book we have seen that our present situation has not been developing inexorably through the long corridors of history. Scientific medicine as we know it is a product of the *long twentieth century* and the worst of its aspects have been with us for only the last fifty years. The old people who worry about financial ruin caused by spending their last days on expensive machinery are the first generation to have lived through the modern era. Someone who will be eighty years old in the year 2000 was born when insulin was developed. People who were teenagers when penicillin became commonly available and the Salk vaccine was developed are still in their productive years. Almost all of our parents or grandparents lived a significant part of their lives without much of what we have come to take for granted as "modern" medicine. Given the fact that the problem of unreasonable expectation is a relatively recent one, the situation can be brought into a proper alignment. It is not too late to educate a Pulitzer Prize–winning playwright who declared that "now is the time to end the AIDS crisis— we can with enough money, and will, and President Clinton, we are watching you" that all the money and will in the world are wasted without realistic promises and expectations.

But a society whose individuals refuse to take responsibility for their actions, one in which growing numbers of people see themselves as victims of the actions of others, will have a very difficult time placing the present into a historical context that allows its citizens to make judgments and decisions about the allocation of its limited resources and results that are more in line with chronic diseases. Our crisis in health care is really a crisis in facing the problems of our modern world in the twenty-first century. I have argued in this book that at the center of the difficulty is our misunderstanding of how we got to where we are and how long we have been here. It comes in part from making science a secular religion and then expecting miracles from it, and from not having developed a context in which to understand and handle physical suffering and death in a scientific world. There are no easy solutions, and I have urged caution in relying on experts for advice about what to do rather than on getting the information we need to decide for ourselves.

Perhaps one way we can begin to change our expectations is to change our metaphor. It is no coincidence that our high hopes and goals for modern scientific medicine were formed during the period of great expansion of scientific research that followed the Second World War. We have come to accept as an inviolate truth that just as science brought victory over totalitarianism, so too will it bring victory over disease and death. The metaphor fit into our thinking during the Cold War years, when we learned that price was no object for victory, and it bordered on the treasonable to question technology because it was technology that would secure our safety. In this half century we have learned to think about disease and dying as unnatural, as enemies to be fought and vanquished. We don't talk about people dying from cancer or other chronic diseases, we talk about their losing the battle; scientists do not work to find causes and cures, they battle deadly killers; physicians do not treat their patients, they do battle with disease and death. Infectious diseases lent themselves to the imagery—microbes *do* invade, and the body does respond—but the metaphor has failed us with chronic, degenerative, and genetic diseases.

No society wants to see its freedom and land lost to an enemy, and no person wants to give an inch to the enemies of disease; but are internal alterations in metabolism or in our genes or the decline of our powers with age really the enemy? The description of the complexities we are beginning to see in the forms of disease caused by the various "defective" forms of the cystic-fibrosis gene, or the surprises that the gene-knockout mice are giving us, should be the alarm bell telling us that the functions of the body are more complex than we had become accustomed to thinking about in our infectious-disease mentality. I think that we are beginning to see the biology of the twenty-first century, and it is a *biology of complexity*. I predict that, ironically, this complexity will cause us to return to understanding that health really is a form of internal balance. Of course it will not be a balance based on mystical ideas or on the humors of the Greeks; it will be the balance of cells, molecules, and gene expression, an understanding of which has come from modern physiology and cell biology. I have come to believe, as a result of writing this book, that in the twenty-first century we will rediscover Claude Bernard and elevate him to the level of reverence in which we hold Louis Pasteur, because the idea of balance as *milieu intérieur* fits the chronic diseases. In the twenty-first century we will be learning to live and die with this more realistic view of ourselves rather than with the idea of rigorous specificity we inherited from the era of microbe hunting. And when we do that, we will begin to change our metaphor.

We return to Susan Sontag: "The body is not a battlefield. The ill are neither unavoidable casualties nor the enemy. . . . About that metaphor, the military one, I would say, if I may paraphrase Lucretius: Give it back to the war-makers." But just returning the metaphor will not be enough. Giving up the military metaphor means giving up the idea that experts will carry out the job for us; it means that as patients, physicians, and scientists, we must begin to develop a vision of what we want from science and medicine. The limits of medicine are not technological, they are conceptual, and all of us together must define the concept.

Readings and Notes

This is not a scholarly work, and I have made no attempt to document every statement made in the book. Instead, I have listed some of the significant works used in the research for each chapter and identified the quotes in the text. I hope this will allow readers who want to pursue any of the topics a way of getting started.

Introduction

Callahan, Daniel. *Setting Limits: Medical Goals in an Aging Society.* Simon & Schuster, 1987.

Chorover, Stephan. *From Genesis to Genocide: The Meaning of Human Nature and the Power of Behavior Control.* MIT Press, 1979.

Cummings, E. E. *Six Nonlectures.* Harvard University Press, 1965.

Delaporte, François. *Disease and Civilization: The Cholera in Paris, 1832.* MIT Press, 1986.

Duster, Troy. "Genetics, Race, and Crime: Recurring Seduction to a False Precision," in *DNA on Trial: Genetic Identification and Criminal Justice.* Cold Spring Harbor Laboratory Press, 1992.

Kass, Edward. "Infectious Diseases and Social Change." *Journal of Infectious Diseases* 123 (1971) 110.

Rosenberg, Charles. "Framing Disease: Illness, Society, and History," in Rosenberg, *Explaining Epidemics and Other Studies in the History of Medicine.* Cambridge University Press, 1992.

p. 3. "all that we have asked" Kass, p. 111.

p. 5. "Let me simply put my own view" Delaporte, p. 6.

p. 5. "In some ways disease does not exist" Rosenberg, p. 305.

p. 5. "while you and i have lips . . . " cummings, p. 47.

p. 6. a "disease" called *drapetomania* . . . Chorover, p. 149.

p. 6. The potential rascist implications . . . see Duster.

p. 6. "I want Clinton to save my life," *The New York Times,* 17 June 93.

p. 8. "[w]e owe science our understanding" Arthur Kornberg, *Science,* 14 Aug 92.

1. The Constant Presence of Death

Amelang, James S. *A Journal of the Plague Year: The Diary of the Barcelona Tanner Miquel Parets 1651*. Oxford University Press, 1991.

Aries, Philippe. *Western Attitudes Toward Death: From the Middle Ages to the Present*. Johns Hopkins University Press, 1974.

Barroll, Leeds. *Politics, Plague, and Shakespeare's Theater: The Stuart Years*. Cornell University Press, 1991.

Braudel, Fernand. *The Structures of Everyday Life: The Limits of the Possible—Civilization and Capitalism 15th–18th Century*. Harper & Row, 1979.

Cipolla, Carlo M. *Faith, Reason, and the Plague in Seventeenth-Century Tuscany*. W. W. Norton, 1979.

Cipolla, Carlo M. *Fighting the Plague in Seventeenth-Century Italy*. University of Wisconsin Press, 1981.

Corbin, Alain. *The Foul and the Fragrant: Odor and the French Social Imagination*. Harvard University Press, 1986.

Delaporte, François. *Disease and Civilization: The Cholera in Paris, 1832*. MIT Press, 1986.

Douglas, Mary. *Purity and Danger: An Analysis of Concepts of Pollution and Taboo*. Praeger, 1969.

Fitzgerald, Frances. *Cities On a Hill: A Journey Through Contemporary American Cultures*. Simon & Schuster, 1986.

Grmek, Mirko. *Diseases in the Ancient Greek World*. Johns Hopkins University Press, 1983.

Hopkins, Donald. *Princes and Peasants: Smallpox in History*. University of Chicago Press, 1983.

Lederberg, J., R. E. Shope, and S. C. Oaks, Jr., eds. *Emerging Infections: Microbial Threats to Health in the United States*. Institute of Medicine, National Academy Press, 1992.

McKeown, Thomas. *The Origins of Human Disease*. Blackwell, 1988.

McNeill, William, H. *Plagues and Peoples*. Doubleday, 1977.

Nathan, Carl F. *Plague Prevention and Politics in Manchuria 1910–1931*. pub. The East Asian Research Center, Harvard University; distrib. Harvard University Press, 1967.

Powell, J. H. *Bring Out Your Dead: The Great Yellow Fever in Philadelphia in 1793*. The University of Pennsylvania Press, 1949.

Reid, Donald. *Paris Sewers and Sewermen: Realities and Representations*. Harvard University Press, 1991.

Riley, James. *Sickness, Recovery and Death: A History and Forecast of Ill Health*. University of Iowa Press, 1989.

Stone, Lawrence. *The Family, Sex and Marriage in England 1500–1800*. Harper & Row, 1977.

Temkin, Owsei. "An Historical Analysis of the Concept of Infection," in Temkin, *The Double Face of Janus and Other Essays in the History of Medicine*. Johns Hopkins University Press, 1977.

Thucydides. *The Peloponnesian War.* Penguin Classics, 1954.

Vigarelly, Georges. *Concepts of Cleanliness. Changing Attitudes in France since the Middle Ages*. Cambridge University Press, 1988.

Whitehead, Barbara. "Dan Quayle Was Right." *The Atlantic Monthly*, April 1993, p. 47.

Winslow, C.-E. A. *The Conquest of Epidemic Disease: A Chapter in the History of Ideas*. Princeton University Press, 1944.

———. *Man and Epidemics*. Princeton University Press, 1952.

Ziegler, Philip. *The Black Death*. Harper & Row, 1971 (first published in 1969).

p. 14. "It is easy to imagine being transported" Braudel p. 27.

p. 15. "The strong smell of excrement pervaded" Corbin p. 27.

p. 15. Livestock defecated in the great gallery . . . Corbin, p. 27.

p. 15. Statistics help us understand . . . Fitzgerald, p. 205.

p. 16. *"the constant presence of death"* Stone, p. 66.

p. 16. "here, even in the dead of winter" Areis, p. 24.

p. 16. orphanages filled the literature and thinking . . . Whitehead, p. 47.

p. 17. Philadelphia was a low, level town . . . Powell, p. vi.

p. 17. Domestic garbage and filth . . . Winslow, p. 12.

p. 18. living nearby in a kind of cosmic revenge . . . Lederberg, *Emerging Diseases*.

p. 18. The diseases caused by most parasites probably . . . MacNeill, p. 16.

p. 19. "we owe the origin of most serious infectious diseases" McKeown, p. 51.

p. 20. "If humanity succeeded fairly quickly in gaining mastery" Grmek, p. 85.

p. 22. "That year, as is generally admitted, was particularly" Thucydides, p. 124.

p. 23. "Words indeed fail one" Thucydides, p. 125.

p. 23. "a Malthusian check to the over-exuberance" Ziegler, p. 33.

p. 23. To understand the conditions . . . Reid, p. 10.

p. 24. The utter enormity of death due to the visitations of disease . . . Zeigler, p. 230.

p. 24. "As a rough and ready rule-of-thumb" Ziegler, p. 230.

p. 26. *"an infection is basically a pollution"* Temkin, p. 457, emphasis added.

p. 26. A Brahmin should not be in the same part of his cattle shed . . . Mary Douglas, quoting Professor Harper, Douglas, p. XXX.

p. 27. "The more deeply we go into this and similar rules" Douglas, p. 34.

p. 27. The rules were . . . a vestige of the means used by the priestly caste . . . Joseph Mazer, personal communication to the author.

p. 28. the establishment of special *Magistracies* . . . Cipolla, *Faith, Reason*, p. 4.

p. 28. The first death was attributed to garments . . . Winslow, *Conquest*, p. 121.

p. 29. It has been claimed by one scholar that a London preacher . . . Barroll, p. 96.

p. 29. For details of the closing of the theater, see Barroll.

2. *La Longue durée*

Ackerknecht, Edwin H. *Therapeutics: From the Primitives to the Twentieth Century.* Hafner Press, 1973.

Baldwin, Martha. "Toads and Plague: Amulet Therapy in Seventeenth-Century Medicine." *Bulletin of the History of Medicine* 67 (1993) 227.

Brooke, John Hedley. *Science and Religion: Some Historical Perspectives.* Cambridge University Press, 1991.

Bury, J. B. *The Idea of Progress: An Inquiry into its Origin and Growth.* Macmillan, 1932.

Butterfield, Herbert. *The Origins of Modern Science, 1300–1800.* Bell, 1949.

Dobell, Clifford. *Antony van Leeuwenhoek and His "Little Animals."* Russell & Russell, 1958.

Febvre, Lucien. *Life in Renaissance France.* Harvard University Press, 1977.

Forster, Robert, and Orest Ranum, eds. *Medicine and Society in France: Selections from the Annales, Economies, Sociétés, Civilisations.* Johns Hopkins University Press, 1980.

Foucault, Michel. *The Birth of the Clinic: An Archaeology of Medical Perception.* Vintage Books, 1975.

Grmek, Mirko D. *Diseases in the Ancient Greek World.* Johns Hopkins University Press, 1989.

Gundert, Beate. "Parts and Their Roles in Hippocratic Medicine." *Isis* 83 (1992) 453.

Hale, J. R. *Renaissance Europe: Individual and Society, 1480–1520.* Harper & Row, 1971.

Hall, Marie Boas, *Promoting Experimental Learning: Experiment and the Royal Society 1660–1727.* Cambridge University Press, 1991.

Hamburger, Jean. *The Diary of William Harvey: The Imaginary Journal of the Physician Who Revolutionized Medicine.* Rutgers University Press, 1992.

Hunter, Michael. *Establishing the New Science: The Experience of the Early Royal Society.* The Boydell Press, 1989.

Knight, David. *The Age of Science: The Scientific World-View in the Nineteenth Century*. Blackwell, 1986.

Laqueur, Thomas. *Making Sex: Body and Gender from the Greeks to Freud*. Harvard University Press, 1990.

Lindberg, David C., and Robert S. Westman, eds. *Reappraisals of the Scientific Revolution*. Cambridge University Press, 1990.

McKnight, Stephen A. *Sacralizing the Secular: The Renaissance Origins of Modernity*. Louisiana State University Press, 1989.

Merton, Robert K. *Science, Technology and Society in Seventeenth-Century England*. Fertig, 1970.

Nicolson, Marjorie. *Pepys' Diary and the New Science*. University of Virginia Press, 1956.

Nutton, Vivian. "Healers in the Medical Market Place: Towards a Social History of Graeco-Roman Medicine," in Andrew Wear, *Medicine in Society: Historical Essays*. Cambridge University Press, 1992, pp. 15–58.

Porter, Dorothy, and Roy Porter. *Patient's Progress: Doctors and Doctoring in Eighteenth-Century England*. Stanford University Press, 1989.

Porter, Roy, ed. *Patients and Practitioners: Lay Perceptions in Medicine in Pre-Industrial Society*. Cambridge University Press, 1985.

Rabelais, François. *The Histories of Gargantua and Pantagruel*. Penguin Books, 1965.

Rosenberg, Charles. *Explaining Epidemics and Other Studies in the History of Medicine*. Cambridge University Press, 1992.

Rossi, Paolo. *Francis Bacon: From Magic to Science*. Routledge & Kegan Paul, 1957.
———. *Philosophy, Technology, and the Arts in the Early Modern Era*. Harper & Row, 1962.

Sarton, George. *Galen of Pergamon*. University of Kansas Press, 1954.

Schmitt, Charles, and Quentin Skinner. *The Cambridge History of Renaissance Philosophy*. Cambridge University Press, 1988.

Shapin, Steven, and Simon Schaffer. *Leviathan and the Air-Pump: Hobbes, Boyle, and the Experimental Life*. Princeton University Press, 1985.

Siraisi, Nancy. *Medieval and Early Renaissance Medicine: An Introduction to Knowledge and Practice*. University of Chicago Press, 1990.

Smith, Wesley D. *The Hippocratic Tradition*. Cornell University Press, 1979.

Solomon, Julie R. "Mortality as Matter: Towards a Politics of Problems in *All's Well That Ends Well*." *English Literary Renaissance* 23 (1993) 134.

Stewart, Larry. *The Rise of Public Science: Rhetoric, Technology, and Natural Philosophy in Newtonian Britain, 1660–1750*. Cambridge University Press, 1992.

Temkin, Owsei. *Galenism. Rise and Decline of a Medical Philosophy*. Cornell University Press, 1973.

Wear, Andrew, ed. *Medicine in Society: Historical Essays*. Cambridge University Press, 1992.

p. 32. The reader can get a good feel for the concepts and practice of Greek medicine in Grmek, Sarton, Smith, and Owsei.

p. 33. "an era from which we have not yet emerged" Foucault, preface.

p. 34. "health is maintained by equal rights" Alcmaeon of Croton in 500 B.C., quoted by Grmek, p. 40.

p. 34. "health is a mixture of the qualities in proper proportion" Grmek, p. 40.

p. 34. "One consumptive is born from another" Grmek, p. 190.

p. 35. "In the wife of Polycrates" Grmek, p. 191.

p. 37. "showed his teeth when laughing" Temkin, p. 68.

p. 38. even the gods are bound by matter; Temkin, p. 24.

p. 38. By the end of the fourth century . . . see chapter 1 of Siraisi for discussion.

p. 39. "I fully realize that you live in an unhealthy region" Siraisi, p. 14.

p. 40. The ailments of Peter the Venerable are discussed in Siraisi, pp. 115–118.

p. 41. Regarding the origins of science with the poet Petrarch, see McKnight, p. 6.

p. 41. "stone and marble monuments stood" McKnight, p. 10.

p. 42. In this rebirth they turned with renewed purpose . . . Hale, p. 276.

p. 42. "All men's actions from birth to death" Febvre, p. 74.

p. 43. Interestingly, it is the plague ravaging Boccaccio's world . . . McKnight, p. 26.

p. 43. In two hundred years we see the movement . . . McKnight, pp. 32–37.

p. 43. The Renaissance humanists were fascinated with . . . Rossi, *Bacon*, chapter 1.

p. 44. "the English intellectual was more than half medieval" Rossi, *Bacon*, intro.

p. 46. Bacon wrote that Aristotle had "corrupted natural philosophy," quoted in Lindberg and Westman, p. 4.

p. 46. "changed the character of men's habitual mental operations" Butterfield, preface.

p. 46. "the promoting of experimentall [sic] philosophy" quoted in Hall, p. 9.

p. 47. . . . the protection and encouragement of the newly reestablished monarch. . . . Shapin and Schaffer, p. 110.

p. 48. And medicine was one of the things that fascinated the *virtuosi* the most. See Nicholson, especially about early attempts at blood transfusion.

p. 48. "learne thy philosophy exactlie" quoted in Cook, p. 406.

p. 49. One scholar has argued that Shakespeare's *All's Well* . . . Solomon.

p. 49. "the vagina really is a penis" Laqueur, p. 79.

p. 50. During the middle of the seventeenth century, amulets were a valued cure . . . Baldwin, p. 228.

p. 50. "pulverized toads and specified quantities of the first menstrual blood" Baldwin, p. 231.

p. 51. "a toads pisse is so hot" Baldwin, p. 240.

p. 52. "divers times examined the same matter [human semen]" Dobell, p. 104.

p. 53. "When people fell sick in 1660" Roy Porter, in Wear, p. 92.

p. 54. "I am sorry that you have been plagu'd" Roy Porter, in Wear, p. 102.

p. 56. "the advocacy of a specific drug" Rosenberg, p. 14.

p. 56. "every part of the body was related" Rosenberg, p. 12.

p. 56. "by belching, breaking wind" Corbin, p. 11.

p. 56. "The child seemed perfectly well" Rosenberg, p. 18.

3. The Seeds of Change

Abelove, H. "Some Speculations on the History of Sexual Intercourse During the Long Eighteenth Century in England." *Genders* 6 (1989) 125.

Ackerknecht, Edwin. "Anticontagionism Between 1821 and 1867." *Bulletin of the History of Medicine* 22 (1948) 562.

———. *Medicine at the Paris Hospital. 1794–1848.* Johns Hopkins University Press, 1967.

———. "Elisha Bartlett and the Philosophy of the Paris Clinical School." *Bulletin of the History of Medicine* 24 (1950) 43.

Burnet, F. M., and D. White. *Natural History of Infectious Diseases.* Cambridge University Press, 1972.

Coleman, William. *Death Is a Social Disease: Public Health and Political Economy in Early Industrial France.* University of Wisconsin Press, 1982.

Crouzet, François, *The Victorian Economy.* Methuen, 1982.

Edsall, Nicolas C. *The Anti–Poor Law Movement 1834–44.* Manchester University Press, 1971.

Evans, Richard J. *Death in Hamburg: Society and Politics in the Cholera Years 1830–1910.* Penguin Books, 1987.

Foucault, Michel. *The Birth of the Clinic: An Archaeology of Medical Perception.* Vintage Books, 1973.

Gay, Peter. *The Enlightenment: An Interpretation—The Science of Freedom.* Knopf, 1969.

Gelfand, Toby. *Professionalizing Modern Medicine.* Greenwood Press, 1980.

Hankins, Thomas L. *Science and the Enlightenment.* Cambridge University Press, 1985.

Hobsbawm, E. J. *Industry and Empire.* Penguin Books, 1968.

Holloway, S. W. F. "Medical Education in England, 1830–1858: A Sociological Analysis." *History* 49 (1964) 301.

Jewison, N. D. "Medical Knowledge and the Patronage System in 18th-Century England." *Sociology* 8 (1974) 369.

———. "The Disappearance of the Sick-Man from Medical Cosmology, 1770–1870." *Sociology* 10 (1976) 225.

Lewis, R. A. *Edwin Chadwick and the Public Health Movement 1832–1854.* Longmans, Green & Co., 1952.

Maulitz, Russel. *Morbid Appearances: The Anatomy of Pathology in the Early Nineteenth Century.* Cambridge University Press, 1987.

McKeown, Thomas. *The Origins of Human Disease.* Blackwell, 1988.

Pelling, M. *Cholera, Fever and English Medicine, 1825–1865.* Oxford University Press, 1978.

Porter, Roy. *The Enlightenment.* Humanities Press International, 1990.

Risse, Guenter B. "Medicine in the Age of Enlightenment," in Andrew Wear, *Medicine in Society: Historical Essays.* Cambridge University Press, 1992, p. 149.

Rose, Michael, R. *The Relief of Poverty, 1834–1914.* Macmillan, 1972.

Schama, Simon. *Citizens: A Chronicle of the French Revolution.* Knopf, 1989.

Smith, F. B. *The People's Health, 1830–1910.* Weidenfeld and Nicolson, 1990 (first published in 1979).

Taylor, James S. *Poverty, Migration, and Settlement in the Industrial Revolution: Sojourners' Narratives.* Society for the Promotion of Science and Scholarship, 1989.

Thomson, David. *England in the Nineteenth Century.* Pelican History of England, Penguin Books, 1950.

Thompson, John, and Grace Goldin. *The Hospital: A Social and Architectural History.* Yale University Press, 1975.

Waddington, I. "The Role of the Hospital in the Development of Modern Medicine: A Sociological Analysis." *Sociology* 7 (1973) 211.

Wrigley, E. A. "The Growth of Population in Eighteenth-Century England: A Conundrum Resolved." *Past and Present* 98 (1983) 121.

p. 59. "No, we are living in an age of enlightenment" Hankins, p. 2.

p. 59. "Everything must be shaken up" Gay, p. 142.

p. 59. "hand it down to those who follow us" quoted in Rosen, p. 133.

p. 60. "the misery of the human condition" Gay, pp. 102–104.

p. 60. "certainly helped to create a situation in which ideological" Porter, p. 60.

p. 61. Hospitals have a long tradition in human civilization. . . . see Thompson and Goldin.

p. 62. But slowly the characteristics we know in our modern hospitals . . . Risse in Wear, and Porter, p. 180.

p. 62. "The general policy of the Hôtel-Dieu" 1788 report, quoted in Ackerknecht, *Medicine at the Paris Hospital,* p. 16.

p. 63. "While banks of roses perfumed" Schama, p. 836.

p. 63. "was thrust onto the plank" Schama, p. 846.

p. 64. It was really a system of patronage . . . Holloway, p. 303.

p. 64. "always required to conduct themselves" Waddington, p. 213.

p. 65. The second crucial change . . . see Ackerknecht, *Paris Hospital.*

p. 66. The well-born private patient . . . Jewison, "Medical Knowledge."

p. 66. The proximity of the deathbed . . . For a discussion of the growth of morbid anatomy and changing practice, see Maulitz.

p. 67. This rise in population was not due to . . . Wrigley, p. 121.

p. 67. One fascinating theory . . . Abelove.

p. 68. population of the entire world began to rise . . . Braudel, p. 39; McKeown, p. 65.

p. 68. "Crowded together in such filthy" Burnet and White, p. 13.

p. 69. "death is a social disease" Coleman.

p. 69. "the middle and upper classes lived in such splendid squalor" Lewis, p. 41.

p. 69. "their bedroom, their kitchen" Chadwick report on internment in towns, quoted in Lewis, p. 69.

p. 70. "a really outstanding specimen" Lewis, p. 3.

p. 70. "to protect factory children" quoted in Lewis, p. 9.

p. 73. a city where "we observe hundreds of" Hobsbawm, p. 56.

p. 73. "measures are urgently called for" quoted in Rosen, p. 213.

p. 74. while they may have been shocked by the facts . . . Lewis, p. 163.

p. 74. What specific things could be done? Lewis, p. 159.

p. 75. "Lack of cleanliness makes the population" quoted by Evans, p. 119.

p. 76. "by favoring instruction, work" Benoiston de Châteauneuf, quoted in Coleman, p. 298.

4. "Pasteur" and the Authority of Science

Brock, Thomas D. *Robert Koch: A Life in Medicine and Bacteriology.* Science Tech Publishers, 1988.

Brooke, John Hedley. *Science and Religion: Some Historical Perspectives.* Cambridge University Press, 1991.

Darton, Robert. *Mesmerism and the End of the Enlightenment in France.* Harvard University Press, 1968.

Dubos, René. *Louis Pasteur: Free Lance of Science.* Scribners, 1960.

Hankins, Thomas L. *Science and the Enlightenment*. Cambridge University Press, 1985.

Latour, Bruno, *The Pasteurization of France*. Harvard University Press, 1988.

Rosen, George. *A History of Public Health*. MD Publications, 1958.

Vallery-Radot, René. *The Life of Pasteur*. Garden City Publishing Co., 1926.

Wellman, Kathleen. *La Mettrie: Medicine, Philosophy, and Enlightenment*. Duke University Press, 1992.

p. 78. "Medicine is philosophy at work" Gay, quoted in Wellman, p. 9.

p. 78. an obstructed spleen was all that was necessary . . . Brooke, p. 172.

p. 79. All around them, Parisians saw . . . Darton, p. 10.

p. 79. "because I only like poems when" Darton, p. 28.

p. 79. "[T]he women in tears, the common people" January 1784 account of a balloon ascent, quoted by Darton, p. 20.

p. 80. Newton, gave serious consideration . . . Rosen, p. 104.

p. 82. Mesmerism may have captivated the minds . . . Darton, p. 162.

p. 82. "the Republic is in no need of chemists." Dubos, p. 7.

p. 86. only his interest in portrait painting . . . Dubos, p. 26.

p. 88. "a child who would explain the rapidity of the Rhine" quoted in Dubos, p. 122.

p. 88. "I would be much pained if M. Pasteur" Dubos, p. 208.

p. 90. Robert Koch was a modest man . . . Brock, p. 23.

p. 92. "[n]ever, surely, could a man have found himself . . ." Brock, p. 27.

p. 93. "before I publish my work" Brock, p. 44.

p. 93. "He has done everything himself" Brock, p. 47.

p. 93. "there is little which is new" Brock, p. 169.

5. Rewriting History: The Triumph of Science

Ackerknecht, E. H. "Anticontagionism between 1821 and 1867." *Bulletin of the History of Medicine* 22 (1948) 562.

Delaporte, François. *Disease and Civilization: The Cholera in Paris, 1832*. MIT Press, 1986.

Evans, Richard J. *Death in Hamburg: Society and Politics in the Cholera Years 1830–1910*. Penguin Books, 1987.

Fee, Elizabeth, and Dorothy Porter. "Public Health, Preventive Medicine and Professionalization: England and America in the Nineteenth Century," in Andrew Wear, ed. *Medicine in Society: Historical Essays*. Cambridge University Press, 1992, p. 249.

Hamlin, Christopher. *A Science of Impurity: Water Analysis in Nineteenth-Century Britain.* University of California Press, 1990.

Morris, R. J. *Cholera 1832: The Social Response to an Epidemic.* Croom Helm, 1976.

Pelling, M. *Cholera, Fever and English Medicine, 1825–1865.* Oxford University Press, 1978.

Riley, James C. *Sickness, Recovery and Death: A History and Forecast of Ill Health.* University of Iowa Press, 1989.

———. *The Eighteenth-Century Campaign to Avoid Disease.* St. Martins Press, 1989.

Rogers, Naomi. *Dirt and Disease: Polio Before FDR.* Rutgers University Press, 1990.

Rosen, George. *A History of Public Health.* MD Publications, 1958.

Rosenberg, Charles E. "Cholera in Nineteenth-Century Europe: A Tool for Social and Economic Analysis," in Rosenberg, *Explaining Epidemics and Other Studies in the History of Medicine.* Cambridge University Press, 1992.

Rosenkrantz, Barbara G. *Public Health and the State: Changing Views in Massachusetts, 1842–1936.* Harvard University Press, 1972.

Snow, John. *Snow on Cholera.* Hafner Publishing Co., 1965.

Thomson, David. *England in the Nineteenth Century.* Pelican History of England, Penguin Books, 1950.

Vandenbroucke, J. P., H. M. Eelmlkan Rooda, and H. Beukers. "Who Made John Snow a Hero?" *American Journal of Epidemiology* 133 (1991) 967.

Wilson, Charles-Edward A. *The Conquest of Epidemic Disease: A Chapter in the History of Ideas.* Princeton University Press, 1944.

p. 96. "fetid, marshy areas" . . . "civilization . . ." etc. . . . Delaporte, Introduction.

p. 97. In the next ten years virtually all the physicians . . . Ackerknecht, chapter 3.

p. 97. One German authority . . . Evans, p. 235.

p. 98. *"but it has never appeared except"* Snow, p. 2.

p. 98. "[T]he communicable diseases of which we have a correct knowledge . . ." Snow p. 10.

p. 99. "In consequence of this intermixing of the water" Snow, p. 68.

p. 100. "to take a list" Snow, p. 39.

p. 102. "The attack had so far diminished" Snow, p. 51.

p. 103. "Who made John Snow a hero?" Vandenbroucke, p. 970.

p. 104. "I have disposed, once and for all" Evans, p. 238.

p. 107. As two modern authorities of the subject . . . Fee and Porter, p. 265.

p. 107. "Before 1880 we knew nothing" Fee and Porter, p. 267.
p. 107. "only passing notice to housing" Fee and Porter, p. 268.
p. 107. "preventing disease, prolonging life" Winslow, quoted in Fee and Porter, p. 269.
p. 107. "unlike garbage and overflowing sewers" Rogers, p. 18.
p. 108. Between June and December in New York City . . . Rogers, p. 10.

6. "Never to Die of a Disease in the Future"

Brock, Thomas D. *Milestones in Microbiology.* Prentice-Hall, 1961.

———. *Robert Koch: A Life in Medicine and Bacteriology.* Science Tech Publishers, 1988.

Chase, Allan. *Magic Shots: A Human and Scientific Account of the Long and Continuing Struggle to Eradicate Infectious Diseases by Vaccination.* Morrow, 1982.

Creighton, Charles. *Jenner and Vaccination: A Strange Chapter of Medical History.* Swan Sonnenschein, 1889.

DeLacy, Margaret. "The Conceptualization of Influenza in Eighteenth-Century Britain: Specificity and Contagion." *Bulletin of the History of Medicine* 67 (1993) 74.

Dubos, René, *Louis Pasteur: Free Lance of Science.* Scribners, 1960.

Duclaus, Emile. *Pasteur: The History of a Mind.* W. B. Saunders, 1920.

Frank, Robert, and Denise Wrotnowska. *Correspondence of Pasteur and Thuillier Concerning Anthrax and Swine Fever Vaccinations.* University of Alabama Press, 1968.

Hopkins, Donald. *Princes and Peasants: Smallpox in History.* University of Chicago Press, 1983.

Parish, H. J. *Victory with Vaccines: The Story of Immunization.* Livingstone, 1968.

Silverstein, Arthur M. *A History of Immunology.* Academic Press, 1989.

Vallery-Radot, René. *The Life of Pasteur.* Garden City Publishing Co., 1926.

p. 113. "Yet still the ones who felt most pity" Thucyides, *The Peloponnesian War;* p. 126. emphasis added.
p. 114. "The smallpox was always present" Macaulay, quoted in Dubos, p. 317.
p. 115. "I am going to tell you a thing" and all material through p. 115 from Silverstein, pp. 26–29.
p. 119. "the cowpox protects the human constitution" Dubos, p. 321.
p. 121. "chance favors only the prepared mind" Dubos, p. 101.
p. 124. "Microbiolatry is the fashion" Dubos, p. 337.

p. 126. "Well, then! Men of little faith!" Dubos, footnote, p. 339.

p. 128. "my experiments with these substances" Brock, p. 196.

p. 129. "compared the action of Koch's fluid" Brock, p. 206.

7. Reframing the Internal World

Ackerknecht, Edwin H. *Rudolf Virchow: Doctor, Statesman, Anthropologist.* University of Wisconsin Press, 1953.

Brock, Thomas D. *Robert Koch: A Life in Medicine and Bacteriology.* Science Tech Publishers, 1988.

Knight, David. *The Age of Science: The Scientific World-View in the Nineteenth Century.* Blackwell, 1986.

Mazumdar, P.M.H. "Immunity in 1890." *Journal of the History of Medicine and Applied Science* 27 (1972) 312.

Metchnikoff, Elie. *Immunity in Infective Diseases.* Johnson Reprint Corporation, 1968. See Introduction, by Gert Brieger.

Metchnikoff, Olga. *Life of Elie Metchnikoff: 1845–1916.* Houghton Mifflin Company, 1921.

Olmsted, J.M.D., and E. Harris Olmsted. *Claude Bernard and the Experimental Method in Medicine.* Henry Schuman, 1952.

Rosenberg, Charles E., and Janet Golden, eds. *Framing Disease: Studies in Cultural History.* Rutgers University Press, 1992.

Silverstein, Arthur M. *A History of Immunology.* Academic Press, 1989.

Stilwell, Craig R. *The Wisdom of Cells: The Integrity of Elie Metchnikoff's Ideas in Biology and Pathology.* PhD. thesis; University of Notre Dame, 1991.

Tauber, Alfred I., and Leon Chernyak. *Metchnikoff and the Origins of Immunology: From Metaphor to Theory.* Oxford University Press, 1991.

Tauber, Alfred I. "The Birth of Immunology: III. The Fate of the Phagocytosis Theory." *Cellular Immunology* 139 (1992) 505.

———. "The Immunological Self: A Centenary Retrospective." *Perspectives in Biology and Medicine* 35 (1991) 74.

p. 135. *milieu intérieur* . . . Olmsted, p. 224.

p. 137. "It is true that you do not bleed your patients" Olmsted, p. 30.

p. 137. "I have heard thee spoken of" Olmsted, p. 31.

p. 139. "M. Claude Bernard" Olmsted, p. 18.

p. 139. "The blood contains all the elements necessary" Olmsted, p. 107.

p. 142. . . . German "medical science had reached an all-time low" Ackerknecht, p. 6.

p. 143. "this somewhat [sic!] overwhelming complete confidence" Ackerknecht, p. 10.

p. 144. "Germany dead; France dead; Italy dead" Ackerknecht, p. 20.

p. 146. As a recent biography makes clear . . . see Tauber and Chernyak

p. 147. "I was resting from the upheaval" quoted in Olga Metchnikoff.

p. 148. "regard the pus corpuscles as gendarmes" Tauber and Chernyak, p. 127.

p. 149. "You know, I am not a specialist in microscopical" Brock, p. 301.

8. Magic Bullets and the New Paradigm of Medicine

Beer, John. "Coal Tar Dye Manufacture and the Origins of the Modern Industrial Research Laboratory." *Isis* 49 (1958) 123.

Colebrook, Leonard. *Almroth Wright: Provocative Doctor and Thinker.* William Heinemann Medical Books, 1954.

Dowling, Harry. *Fighting Infection: Conquests of the Twentieth Century.* Cambridge University Press, 1977.

Ehrlich, Paul. "On Immunity with Special Reference to Cell Life." Croonian Lecture, in F. Himmelweit, ed. *The Collected Papers of Paul Ehrlich.* Pergamon Press, 1957.

Hounshell, David A., and John Kenly Smith, Jr. *Science and Corporate Strategy: DuPont R&D, 1902–1980.* Cambridge University Press, 1988.

Knight, David. *The Age of Science: The Scientific World-View in the Nineteenth Century.* Blackwell, 1986.

Kuhn, Thomas. *The Structure of Scientific Revolutions.* University of Chicago Press, 2nd ed., 1970.

Lakatos, Imre, and Alan Musgrave. *Criticism and the Growth of Knowledge.* Cambridge University Press, 1970.

Mann, Charles C., and Mark L. Plummer. *The Aspirin Wars: Money, Medicine, and 100 Years of Rampant Competition.* Knopf, 1991.

Marks, Harry. "Notes from the Underground: The Social Organization of Therapeutic Research," in R. Maulitz and D. E. Long, eds. *Grand Rounds: One Hundred Years of Internal Medicine.* University of Pennsylvania Press, 1988.

Marquardt, Martha. *Paul Ehrlich.* William Heinemann Medical Books, 1949.

Parascandola, J., and R. Jasensky. "Origins of the Receptor Theory of Drug Action. *Bulletin of the History of Medicine* 48 (1974) 199.

Silverstein, Arthur. *A History of Immunology.* Academic Press, 1989.

Starr, Paul. *The Social Transformation of American Medicine.* Basic Books, 1982.

p. 161. "a man of keen judgement" Marquardt, p. 2.

p. 162. "with Ehrlich's method of staining" Marquardt, p. 27.

p. 162. "as a highly strung racehorse" Marquardt, p. 28.

p. 163. "[A]ll sources seem to agree" Brock, p. 227.

p. 164. "I always get wild whenever I think" Brock, p. 229.

p. 165. "When we began working together" Marquardt, p. 36.

p. 169. "Coming into Ehrlich's laboratory" Marquardt, p. 134.

p. 171. "Ehrlich says doctors stay home" *JAMA* 55 (1910) 151.

p. 172. "The daily press in every civilized country" Dowling, p. 244.

9. The Therapeutic Revolution

Baldry, Peter. *The Battle Against Bacteria.* Cambridge University Press, 1965.

Bliss, Michael. *The Discovery of Insulin.* University of Chicago, 1982.

Cairns, John, Gunther S. Stent, and James D. Watson. *Phage and the Origins of Molecular Biology.* Cold Spring Harbor Laboratory of Quantitative Biology, 1966.

Chase, Allan. *Magic Shots: A Human and Scientific Account of the Long and Continuing Struggle to Eradicate Infectious Diseases by Vaccination.* Morrow, 1982.

Colebrook, Leonard, *Almroth Wright, Provocative Doctor and Thinker.* William Heinemann Medical Books, 1954.

Corbin, Alain. *The Foul and the Fragrant: Odor and the French Social Imagination.* Harvard University Press, 1986.

Hare, Ronald. *The Birth of Penicillin and the Disarming of Microbes.* George Allen and Unwin, 1970.

Himmelfarb, Gertrude. *Poverty and Compassion: The Moral Imagination of the Late Victorians.* Knopf, 1991.

Judson, Horace F. *The Eighth Day of Creation: Makers of the Revolution in Biology.* Simon & Schuster, 1979.

Kevles, Daniel. "Out of Eugenics," in Kevles and Leroy Hood, eds. *The Code of Codes: Scientific and Social Issues in the Human Genome Project.* Harvard University Press, 1992, p. 3.

———. *In the Name of Eugenics: Genetics and the Uses of Human Heredity.* Knopf, 1985.

Krause, Richard M. *The Restless Tide: The Persistent Challenge of the Microbial World.* National Foundation for Infectious Diseases, 1981.

Lechevalier, Hubert A., and Morris Solotorovsky. *Three Centuries of Microbiology.* McGraw-Hill, 1965.

Maclean, Ian. *The Renaissance Notion of Woman: A Study in the Fortunes of Scholasticism and Medical Science in European Intellectual Life.* Cambridge University Press, 1980.

Macfarlane, Gwyn. *Alexander Fleming: The Man and the Myth.* Chatto & Windus, 1984.

Marks, Harry M. "Cortisone, 1949: A Year in the Political Life of a Drug." *Bulletin of the History of Medicine* 66 (1992) 419.

Parish, H. J. *Victory with Vaccines: The Story of Immunization.* Livingstone, 1968.

Rosenberg, Charles E. *Explaining Epidemics and Other Studies in the History of Medicine.* Cambridge University Press, 1992.

Shryock, Richard. *The Development of Modern Medicine: An Interpretation of the Social and Scientific Factors.* Knopf, 1947.

Smith, Jane S. *Patenting the Sun: Polio and the Salk Vaccine.* William Morrow, 1990.

Spink, Wesley. *Infectious Diseases: Prevention and Treatment in the Nineteenth and Twentieth Centuries.* University of Minnesota Press, 1978.

Starr, Paul. *The Social Transformation of American Medicine.* Basic Books, 1982.

Swazey, Judith, P., and Karen Reeds. *Today's Medicine, Tomorrow's Science: Essays on Paths of Discovery in the Biomedical Sciences.* DHEW Publication No. (NIH) 78–244, U.S. Department of Health, Education, and Welfare, 1978.

Thomas, Lewis. *The Youngest Science, Notes of a Medicine-Watcher.* Viking, 1983.

Wilson, G. S., and A. A. Miles. *Topley and Wilson's Principles of Bacteriology and Immunity.* 4th ed., Williams and Wilkins, 1957.

p. 177. "a trust in science and a commitment to mankind" Himmelfarb, p. 182.

p. 178. "the very age in which patent medicines" Starr, p. 128.

p. 178. "By the time my father reached P&S" Thomas, p. 20.

p. 179. "We were provided with a thin, pocket-sized book" Thomas, p. 28 (author's emphasis).

p. 180. "As one surveys the vast literature" Spink, p. 63.

p. 180. "on numerous tea estates, in regiments" *Topley and Wilson*, p. 1625.

p. 182. "the method of vaccination which has proved" Spink, p. 62.

p. 183. "had the drama of life and death" Smith, p. 207.

p. 188. "*One cannot avoid the conclusion*" Macfarlane, p. 139 (author's emphasis).

p. 190. "each organ of the body gives off emanations" quoted in Swazey and Reeds, p. 54.

p. 191. the word *hysterical* derives from . . . Maclean, p. 74.

p. 191. "bacterial products taught us" Swazey and Reeds, p. 57.

p. 192. Diabetes was one of those diseases . . . Bliss, p. 21.

p. 193. "this pinch of material" G. Hoskins, quoted in Shryock, p. 309.

p. 194. *"Diabetus* [sic]" Bliss, p. 50.

p. 194. "[Macleod] was tolerant at first" Bliss, p. 52.

p. 195. Most important, Lilly would . . . Bliss, p. 139.

p. 198. "terrifyingly but harmlessly black" Horace Judson in Hood and Kevles, p. 42.

p. 198. "slowly, independently, and privately" Kevles in Hood and Kevles, p. 3.

p. 199. The story of the discovery of DNA . . . Judson, *Eighth Day of Creation.*

10. Reshaping the Goals of Medicine in the Era of Chronic Diseases

Callahan, Daniel. *Setting Limits: Medical Goals in an Aging Society.* Simon & Schuster, 1987.

———. *The Troubled Dream of Life: Living with Mortality.* Simon & Schuster, 1993.

Hubbard, Ruth, and Elisah Wald. *Exploding the Gene Myth: How Genetic Information Is Produced and Manipulated by Scientists, Physicians, Employers, Insurance Companies, Educators, and Law Enforcers.* Beacon Press, 1993.

Kevles, Daniel J., and Leroy Hood, eds. *The Code of Codes: Scientific and Social Issues in the Human Genome Project.* Harvard University Press, 1992.

Lewontin, R. C., Steven Rose, and Leon J. Kamin. *Not in Our Genes: Biology, Ideology, and Human Nature.* Pantheon Books, 1984.

Reiser, Stanley J. *Medicine and the Reign of Technology.* Cambridge University Press, 1978.

———. "The Machine at the Bedside: Technological Transformations of Practices and Values," in Reiser and M. Anbar. *The Machine at the Bedside: Strategies for Using Technology in Patient Care.* Cambridge University Press, 1984.

Wills, Christopher. *Exons, Introns, and Talking Genes: The Science Behind the Human Genome Project.* Basic Books, 1991.

p. 205. "the rising tide of biological determinist writing" Lewontin, Preface.

p. 206. "attempts to derive the properties" Lewontin, p. 5.

p. 207. "This technology will figure" Kevles and Hood, p. 155.

p. 208. the complications of the kind that made me change my view. Gina Kolata, "Cystic fibrosis Surprise: Genetic Screening Falters." *New York Times,* 16 Nov. 93; see also Natalie Angier, "Action of Gene in Huntington's Is Proving a Tough Puzzle." *New York Times,* 2 Nov. 93.

p. 211. The greater problem on the horizon . . . see Natalie Angier, "Gene for Mental Illness Proves Elusive." *New York Times,* 13 Jan. 93.

p. 211. "gene-knockout" mice . . . see Natalie Angier, "When a Vital Gene Is Missing, Understudies Fill In." *New York Times*, 7 Sept. 93.

p. 212. "a sigh of relief went up" Margaret Buckingham, "Which Myogenic Factors Make Muscle?" *Current Biology, 4* (1994) 61.

p. 213. In another surprise . . . Pierre Vassalli, "Knocked-out but Not Knocked Out." *Current Biology, 3* (1993) 607.

p. 213. "Don't you just love experiments" *Nature*, 359 (1992) 270.

p. 214. In 1990 one American in three tried . . . see Natalie Angier, "Unusual Therapy Gains Popularity." *New York Times*, 28 Jan. 93.

p. 217. A profile in the financial pages . . . Gina Kolata, "Laying Pipe for the Fountain of Youth." *New York Times*, 1 Nov 92.

p. 219. "health itself, we sometimes need reminding" Callahan, *Setting Limits*, p. 81.

p. 219. "[I]t is unlikely (though certainly desirable)" Reiser, *The Machine at the Bedside*, p. 16.

p. 223. "remove the unpleasant, distressing *causes*" Callahan, *The Troubled Dream of Life*, p. 32.

Acknowledgments

This book has been a labor of love and discovery. Since I started out to write a history of immunology and ended up putting all of biomedical research into a new context, I needed all of the help and encouragement I could get. My scientific colleagues have been of enormous help—even the few who thought that I was being "antiscientific." I hope that when they read the whole book they will see that my ideas have not changed: I still think science is one of the greatest inventions of the human mind and that basic research is more necessary now than ever. For the majority of colleagues who came to agree with my premise, I hope that I have not disappointed them in either the clarity or force of the presentation. For commenting on early drafts and/or helpful discussions I thank my scientific colleagues Joel Buxbaum, Dick Dutton, Paul Edelson, Doug Green, Howie Grey, Lee Hood, Av Mitchison, Stan Nathenson, Ken Paigen, Jonas Salk, Eli Sercarz, Liz Simpson, Fred Tauber, David Weatherall, and Maurizio Zanetti. Special thanks go to Art Silverstein who saved me from some very serious errors. Horace and Penny Judson gave invaluable advice; everyone who knew Penny will miss her and share in Horace's grief.

I have been especially pleased by the willingness of so many historians to take my attempts to learn a little of their craft seriously. I found that doing history is much, much harder than doing science, and while I will never be able to do original historical research, I hope that there are no traces of Whiggishness in this text. Ed Morman arranged for me to discuss the work at an early stage at the Institute for the History of Medicine at Johns Hopkins, where he, Harry Marks and Liz Fee joined in with Art Silverstein to put me on a more solid course. Charles Rosenberg was most gracious with his time after I foisted myself on him. I feel that he and Roy Porter—with whom I almost had lunch in London— were my history mentors even though they didn't know it. Dick Olsen opened up whole new worlds to me, for which I will always be grateful, and Dan Kevles saved me from a serious wrong turn early in the development of the ideas. Bettyann Kevles shared her absolutely brilliant insight that we don't necessarily have to use the technology we used to make discoveries as therapies. Dan Callahan was a great influence on my thinking about the goals of medicine and the nature of health, and his comments on the manuscript gave me great encouragement. If after all of this there are historiographical errors, I apologize.

Very special thanks go to Margaret Wertheim, who read drafts, made comments, shared her great good sense, and also brought me to my wonderful agent, Beth Vesel. Beth saw where the book was going before I did, encouraged it (and me), and brought me to my marvelous editor, Betsy Rapoport. I never understood why Maxwell Perkins was so important to the old Scribner's authors until I began working with Betsy.

Closer to home, my son Mark talked me through various versions of the book and actually got me to take Foucault seriously; my son Jon gave invaluable close critical analysis of arguments; and my mother said I was wonderful. Most of all, my wife, Constance Jordan, taught me history, showed me how to write in nonscientific prose, listened with enormous patience to unformed ideas as they tumbled into the air, and continued to love me in spite of it all.

Solana Beach, California
March 1994

Index

EDWARD S. GOLUB is president of E. S. Golub Associates, consultants in concept-based science education. The author of a widely used textbook in immunology, *Immunology: A Synthesis,* he was professor of biology at Purdue University for twenty years and a director of research in the pharmaceutical industry for five years. He is the founder of the Pacific Center for Ethics and Applied Biology, a nonprofit organization that explores the relationship between basic and applied biology. Golub lives in Solana Beach, California, with his wife, Constance Jordan, a literary historian.